What would Adam Smith Make of Modern Australia?

Praise for *What would Adam Smith Make of Modern Australia?*

"Joseph Healy is the rare combination of public intellectual and successful businessman. He analyses the ills of modern society, with particular reference to Australia, and illustrates how we have been sleepwalking into a society that has become sick on so many levels. The mental health crisis that is engulfing us is merely one aspect. He reveals that the ideas of the original architect of capitalism way back in the Scottish Enlightenment, Adam Smith, rooted in moral philosophy and a genuine concern for others in society, have been hijacked and distorted. Joseph Healy's tour de force blends heart and head to offer logical solutions which are achievable but will require a paradigm shift and inspired leadership."

Professor Patrick McGorry AO

"Joseph Healy's book is an outstanding and must-read. Capitalism is under threat and Joseph Healy's application of Adam Smith's principles to current economic conditions is very timely. These old insights will aid the search in finding a solution to some of the so-called failures of capitalism and a free society."

John Dahlsen, Chairman, Dahlsen

"In this thought-provoking and entertaining book, Joseph Healy shows that Adam Smith's writings, far from being those of 'some defunct economist' (John Maynard Keynes), have enormous relevance to the challenges facing contemporary Australia. Healy brings Smith to life, highlighting in multiple ways the emphasis the 'founder of economics' placed on the inter-dependence between a 'good economy' and a 'good society'. He draws on Smith's insights to offer sound suggestions for a stronger Australian economy and a better, fairer Australian society. This is a book that deserves to be read by policymakers and citizens alike."

Saul Eslake, Independent Economist and Vice-Chancellor's Fellow at the University of Tasmania

"Healy bridges Adam Smith's principles with today's business reality – proving that what's good for society is ultimately good for business, investors, and the economy as a whole."

Ahmed Fahour AO

"Joseph brings Adam Smith to the Australia of 2025 and the diagnosis is clear: we have more than an economic crisis emerging, we have a moral crisis. We must focus on the fundamentals, be it the tax system or the primary school curriculum. All is not lost, but we are not on the right path. And those that rise to positions of leadership in our society must, above all else, be people of character."

Warren Hogan, Managing Director, EQ Economics and Economic Advisor, Judo Bank

"This remarkable book is a powerful reminder of Adam Smith's 300-year legacy. Healy masterfully re-imagines a flourishing Australian society based on Smith's belief that economics is deeply intertwined with moral philosophy, ethics and humanity. In a world of turmoil, this timely book not only challenges our current economic systems, it clearly articulates a renewed Smithian vision to enhance the well-being of our country."

Dr Leanne Rowe AM, Clinical Professor

"Joseph Healy's book looks at the economy through the prism of Adam Smith's *The Wealth of Nations*. Smith was first and foremost a moral philosopher and Healy's approach and recommendations take such a position as a modern economist. Healy is an experienced and practical economist and his book is well worth reading."

Professor R.R. Officer AM

"Healy brings together the most significant events of the last century and aligns the thoughts of the most influential economists of the era to eloquently interpret the state of the nation today. All thinking people should read this book."

Dr John Wilson AM

"This is an insightful and robust read. Healy draws on the philosophical framework of Adam Smith, and combines it with extensive observations on a wide range of recent and current Australian and international economic and social experiences. The shortcomings – and suggested remedies – cover the full gamut of business practices, moral imperatives, education and, importantly, mental health. The book reflects Healy's hands-on and innovative record as a business leader both in the big end of town and in creating a start-up bank. All in all, an entertaining and very overdue contribution."

John Fraser, Former Secretary to the Treasury

What would Adam Smith Make of Modern Australia?

How lessons from the past provide answers for a better future

Joseph Healy

MAJOR STREET

We shall not cease from exploration
And the end of all our exploring
Will be to arrive where we started
And know the place for the first time

TS Eliot, *Four Quartets*

In memory of my parents, Charlie and Kathleen.
From all that I have learnt about mental health,
I now know that a safe and loving family environment
is one of the greatest gifts parents can give their children.
It can be life-defining. I was lucky to receive such a gift
and am forever grateful.

About the Author

Joseph Healy is an international banker and mental health entrepreneur. He held senior executive positions at two of Australia's major banks and three international banks, working with businesses large and small for 40 years. He was a co-founder and CEO of Judo Bank (2016–2024), a bank created to serve the needs of the SME economy – the baker, the butcher and the brewer. He is also a co-founder and CEO of Malu Health Group (2025–), which specialises in mental health care. Joseph holds six advanced degrees: in Financial Economics, Business Studies, Banking and Finance, Chinese International Management, Contemporary Chinese studies, and the Psychology and Neuroscience of Mental Health. This is his fifth book.

Acknowledgements

Writing a serious book that links contemporary themes of the economy, society, business and politics through the prism of one of the great intellectuals who wrote almost 300 years ago is not a casual undertaking. In conveying Smith's ideas in a relevant way to the contemporary reader, there is much complexity and many traps in trying to project one time onto another.

The complexity problem is mitigated by the quality of the literature on Smith, both in the numerous biographies written about him and the scholarly literature he has attracted. I took a lot of comfort in knowing that I am not alone in arguing that Adam Smith's ideas have enormous relevance to our modern world.

Over the 18-month gestation of this book, many people contributed to my thinking. Reading someone else's manuscript is not something that is taken for granted. It is a significant undertaking, and it can be one of the most cherished forms of friendship. The care with which many people provided comments and challenges on what I had written is something for which I am eternally grateful. For their interest in what I have written, I want to send a heartfelt thanks to John Dahlsen, Saul Eslake, John McFarlane OBE, Murray Gleeson AC, The

Honourable Dr Andrew Leigh, Warren Hogan, Paul Healy, Will Roberts, Ralph Shale, Helen Shale, Professor Bob Officer AM, Dr Leanne Rowe AM, John Fraser, Ahmed Fahour AO, Richard Morgan, Professor Patrick McGorry AO and Dr John Wilson AM.

Whilst they were all kind enough to review my writing, not all of them agreed with aspects of what I had to say or the recommendations I had made. Indeed, in some cases, there was a substantial challenge due to differing perspectives and interpretations of Smith's work and the current problems, as well as how they might be addressed. So, I must emphasise that the framing of the views expressed in this book should not be read as necessarily those of the people whom I am acknowledging.

Writing a serious book is a long and sometimes lonely journey, requiring planning, discipline, and the support and understanding of others, particularly my family. Every time I assure my family that this is my last book or major project, they have become accustomed to knowing that it is not a commitment I will necessarily keep, even though my intentions were always honourable at the time!

Finally, a big thanks to the team at Major Street Publishing. Lesley Williams and Will Allen proved, yet again, to be an absolute pleasure to work with.

Also by Joseph Healy

Corporate Governance & Shareholder Wealth Creation (2003)

Chinese Firms Going Global: Can They Succeed? (2018)

Breaking the Banks: What Went Wrong with Australian Banking? (2019)

Black Belt: A Masterclass for Start-ups and Entrepreneurs (co-authored with David Hornery; 2023)

MAJOR STREET

First published in 2025 by Major Street Publishing Pty Ltd
info@majorstreet.com.au | majorstreet.com.au

A catalogue record for this book is available from the National Library of Australia

Printed book ISBN: 978-1-923186-33-0
Ebook ISBN: 978-1-923186-34-7

Cover design by Typography Studio
Internal design by Production Works

10 9 8 7 6 5 4 3 2 1

Contents

Introduction

This book was triggered by the coalescing of three events in late 2023. The first was a visit to Kirkcaldy, Scotland, the birthplace of Adam Smith. Located on the picturesque Fife coast, just a short drive north of Edinburgh, Kirkcaldy boasts a rich history, fascinating heritage and stunning waterfront views of the Firth of Forth. It is well known for its welcoming and friendly atmosphere. It was the year of the tercentenary of Smith's birth and, as I was planning on being in Scotland at that time, a visit to Smith's hometown seemed a worthy pilgrimage to honour someone who had been a figure of my admiration for close to 40 years.

The second event was a lecture I enjoyed at Gleneagles (home to the golf course that President Donald Trump tried but thankfully failed to buy in the early 2000s) in December 2023 by Professor Sir John Kay, entitled 'What Adam Smith Would Make of the World?' The lecture was followed by reflections from former British prime minister Gordon Brown – a proud son of Kirkcaldy – and then a panel discussion chaired by the prominent Princetown University Nobel laureate economist Professor Sir Angus Deaton, with Gordon Brown and the then Vice-Chancellor of the University of Glasgow, Professor Sir Anton Muscatelli.

On return to the warmer shores of Australia, the third event was the receipt of a just-published excellent paper from The Centre for Independent Studies, written by Professor Paul Oslington and Dr David M Hart, entitled 'Adam Smith and Why He Matters Today'.

As a result of these three events, I wondered, *What would Adam Smith make of modern Australia?* Hence, this book.

Australia today has never been more prosperous by many traditional economic measures such as gross domestic product (GDP) and GDP per capita – though declining in recent times as the population grows, huge demographic shifts became a new and daunting reality, and productivity stagnates – yet getting progressively poorer by many other measures of what would constitute a vibrant, healthy and good society. And the direction of travel is concerning. As I discuss throughout this book, the scale of inequality, for example, results from economic policy mismanagement, even when measures such as GDP growth might suggest progress as a nation. Our economic pie (GDP) might be growing, but too many people are getting smaller and smaller pieces, and a handful of people are getting far more than they can possibly eat. Australia is a rich country, yet close to one in seven people live in poverty, while one in six children do so. (This figure rises to one in three for our First Nations peoples.[1])

Significantly, as I explore in this book, our economic progress seems inversely correlated to a decline in important

1 Community Affairs References Committee, *The extent and nature of poverty in Australia: interim report*, ch. 2, Australian Government, May 2023.

measures of societal well-being, such as the very concerning increase in family dysfunctionality and domestic violence, the scale and scope of mental health-associated problems, a persistently deteriorating trend in baseline education, a deeply flawed taxation system, and growing and apparently entrenched inequality in income and wealth. In many ways, we are becoming a divided society, and this is a serious trajectory if not addressed and corrected.

As we will discuss in detail, one of Adam Smith's core beliefs is that it is impossible to think about and separate the economy from society. Yet, that is exactly what has happened in Australia and other rich countries.

Smith was perhaps the first to argue that economic development could lead to sustainably rising living standards and a richer sense of societal well-being. Still, he would be horrified, for example, at the level of inequality today and the costs that are borne by the less well-off. He would also be horrified by the size of government in our economy and what could be described as a combination of anti-competitive key industry structures that dominate our economic landscape, a tax system that almost codifies inequality and weak productivity, an education system that further cements social divisions, and the corrupting influence of political lobbyists, including trade unions and crony capitalism, all of which are widespread in Australia as they are elsewhere.

Smith saw the economy as much more than the creator of wealth, though that is important – he saw it as part of a broader society, and problems arise when the two become disconnected or divorced. This is the story of Australia, and an important theme explored in this book. While this book emphasises Australia, the trends and problems that I discuss are common to other Western nations, particularly the United States (US) and the United Kingdom (UK). Big economic and social trends are increasingly part of global themes, but important national variations must always be understood and respected. Global themes need not necessarily dictate a path-dependent course for Australia, but they may – and perhaps will – if not addressed. Indeed, as I argue in this book, Australia is at risk of the classic 'boiled frog' syndrome of not reacting to the slow but gradual changes in societal temperature until it is too late. (The boiled frog analogy is that of a frog sitting in a pot of cold water on the stove with the temperature slowly increasing and the frog not noticing this until it is too late to jump out. The analogy conveys the simple reality that we often don't notice big changes if they happen gradually, and we then look back with regret that we allowed these changes to happen in plain sight.)

My association with Adam Smith dates back to my early education. I was introduced to Smith's work in the late 1970s at high school in Edinburgh by my Economics teacher, Mr Donnelly, who declared that Smith was the 'Father of Modern Economics and the greatest economist of all time!' Thanks to Mr Donnelly's enthusiasm, I read and studied Adam Smith's work and contribution to the world. This book's bibliography and the fact that I have extensively referenced his work in two of my earlier books (see Healy, 2003 and 2019) provide some evidence of my enduring interest in Smith.

I set out three goals for writing this book.

First, I hope to highlight how far Australia has drifted from the core principles espoused by Smith. We have become a society that, despite being ostensibly more prosperous than ever in our history, can be criticised for allowing a weakening of the moral and ethical standards in how many things are done. This is particularly evident in the business sector, the conduct of trade unions and in politics.

Second, I want to show how quality of life has deteriorated for many, raise awareness of the inequality prevalent in society, and show how society's 'health' has deteriorated in many ways.

Third, I hope this book highlights the need for all of us to either introduce or reintroduce ourselves to what Smith had to say on these matters and, in doing so, find the foundations for answers to complex contemporary problems. It is not too late. This is not a question of re-creating the past but of shaping a better future. It is time for the range of issues discussed in this book to enter the mainstream of our discussion on economic policy and the kind of society we want and deserve.

I have always believed Adam Smith's legacy should be taught and celebrated more widely. I am confident this book will appeal to students at our universities and those responsible for crafting and administering public policy. A return to fundamentals is a good place to start when considering Australia's many public policy issues.

I must state at the outset, however, that this book is not intended for academics in search of scholarly rigour, though many in academia will find it an interesting read, particularly as I weave together a broad range of disciplines reflective of Smith's polymathic qualities. The target market for this book is the general, intellectually curious reader interested in how business, government and society function in Australia compared to what Smith had to say three centuries ago. The language used in this book reinforces this objective, with jargon kept to a minimum. Where it is used, I hope I've done enough to explain what it means and why it is relevant.

To bring the book to life and give it meaning (and purpose), I use numerous contemporary examples from business and politics – particularly in the second part of the book – and contrast them to the virtues espoused by Smith. This will hopefully make the book contemporary, interesting and meaningful to many readers.

This book is purposely more of a sketch of how Adam Smith saw things, and it simply cannot do justice to the breadth and depth of what he had to say on a broad range of themes. (Fortunately, many scholars have documented his work in detail, as the bibliography to this book demonstrates.) I do hope, however, that for readers with curious minds, this book may whet their appetite to learn more about Adam Smith's importance and the remarkable legacy that he has gifted to humanity.

In attempting to blend the insights from Smith with what we see in the real world, I focus on three overriding themes, or big questions, consistent with the earlier stated goals of this book:

1. What are the promises and problems of our market economy in Australia?
2. Why does our market economy create so much inequality in society?
3. What can be done to address these problems?

As this book will explore, there are many problems in the way business operates in Australia, such as the rhetoric on stakeholder value, corporate social responsibility (CSR), diversity, equity and inclusion (DEI), and environmental, social and governance (ESG); the tacit approach to shareholder value; and the lobbying by many large businesses and industry groups of politicians to advance policy outcomes that benefit the few at the expense of the many. In addition, there is much evidence that corporate governance in many companies is overly process- and compliance-orientated and weak in substance. It often turns a tin ear to societal concerns on topics such as CEO remuneration and how it is aligned to performance – or is it simply no more than a share of economic rents earned by capital due to weak competition or state-granted privileges? – and the growing gap between it and the wages paid to the average employee.

Many of the issues I highlight in this book are not new, but how I weave them together and the tapestry it portrays provide, I believe, a fresh perspective and a more complete picture than has been presented before.

The reader will note the emphasis I give to mental health as one of the concerning indicators of a deteriorating society. The state of mental ill-health in Australia is nearing a crisis point and is arguably a national scandal. *The Mental State of the World in 2023* report ranks the state of mental well-being amongst 71 nations and places Australia 65th (sixth from the bottom). This analysis provides interesting evidence supporting the thesis that all is not well despite strong traditional quantitative economic measures. The causes of this disappointing mental well-being outcome are a major focus of this book, with good reason – including a conservatively estimated cost to the economy of $220 billion a year.[2] It may surprise (and hopefully concern) many readers that one in seven Australians were on

2 Productivity Commission, *Mental health: inquiry report*, Australian Government, November 2020. https://www.pc.gov.au/inquiries/completed/mental-health/report

antidepressant medication in 2023 – one of the highest rates in the world.[3]

The link between inequality and mental ill-health will not surprise the thoughtful reader. One study, for example, highlighted how one in four of the poorest Australians experiences high levels of psychological distress compared to one in 20 of the wealthiest Australians.[4] Many less-well-off Australians are unable to access professional care for treatment, and this may, in part, explain the unacceptably high use of antidepressants.

Readers will find numerous references to the US throughout this book. This is not because I see the Australian economy or society as like the US, but more to highlight the risks of our path-dependent course and what the future might hold if, as the US has done, we sleepwalk and nothing is done to correct the current trend. To highlight further the 'boiled frog' risk, there is an argument that the UK painfully illustrates how a once-vibrant society can find itself in a malaise with ever-growing societal division and economic decline, a path the country has been on since long before Brexit. Again, Australia is not the UK, but it would be foolish to ignore the warning signs and the lessons from a once-great nation that is, in my opinion, in serious decline.

Throughout this book, the reader will note that I have peppered references to the work of others in academic, political and business literature. I have attributed sources as comprehensively as possible; hopefully, there are no omissions.

---

3 Jureidini, J, 'Why are so many Australians taking antidepressants?' *The Conversation*, 9 February 2024. https://theconversation.com/why-are-so-many-australians-taking-antidepressants-221857

4 Isaacs, AN et al., 'Lower income levels in Australia are strongly associated with elevated psychological distress: implications for healthcare and other policy areas', Frontiers in Psychiatry, vol. 9, no. 536, 26 October 2018.

I sincerely apologise for any errors that do appear. Readers will also note that in several cases, in referencing extracts from Smith's work, I do so through the work of others as this makes the task of reading and contextualising what Smith had to say easier on the reader, given the somewhat turgid nature of the prose at that time. Also, the audience that Smith sought to address in the 18th century was more of the intellectual reader, and he was, in essence, competing against other intellectuals to convince his audience of the merits of his ideas. Smith had a habit of writing in rather long sentences and, to the modern reader, archaic words, in keeping with the standards of the time. Reading Adam Smith's work requires the brain to decipher the language and prose of that time. Some of his spelling – for example, 'public' he spells 'publick' – also seems foreign but was no doubt convention at the time.

Before answering the question of book's title, 'What would Adam Smith make of Modern Australia?', we must first understand the man and his legacy. Chapter 1, 'Who Was Adam Smith?', thoroughly explores Smith the man and Smith the thinker.

Chapter 2 discusses why Smith's thinking and philosophy matter, even though he lived almost 300 years ago in a time that is so different from today.

Chapter 3 is focused on the crisis of capitalism and why we know modern capitalism is not what Adam Smith would recognise or condone. This is relevant as Smith is seen by many as the founding father of capitalism. In this chapter, I draw links to what we see in our economic system, particularly the growing role of government and the threats to a vibrant business or private sector. I also, perhaps controversially in the eyes of some, draw parallels to Milton Friedman, another prominent economist greatly influenced by Smith. Like Smith, Friedman's views have also been oversimplified, distorted and greatly misunderstood. Friedman and other great 20th-century economists, such as Friedrich Hayek and Ronald Coase, are closely associated with Adam Smith within the economic fraternity.

Chapter 4 discusses Smith's views on ethical capitalism and presents the current challenges in modern Australia preventing us from building a fairer and more equitable economic environment.

Chapter 5 focuses on education, given the pivotal role that Smith saw of education and his emphasis on education in a broad sense, not narrowly defined as tertiary credentials. I argue that Smith would have strongly advocated public investment in education as central to economic prosperity and social harmony. He would have much to say on how the education system in modern Australia works against social harmony and is a factor enforcing the growing levels of inequality in society.

Chapter 6 is a discussion on why we must rediscover the philosophy of Adam Smith, given the strong evidence that we have a country in which economic and societal well-being have become disconnected, and the consequences of damaging trends already set on what economists call a path-dependent course – that the future is a continuation of the current trajectory. This is not in anyone's long-term interest, and we can look to countries like the UK and the US to see the consequences of societies not being alert to the 'boiled frog' syndrome and being allowed to drift aimlessly and become dysfunctional in so many concerning ways. Australia deserves better.

Chapter 7 takes a bold course and outlines a Smithian vision for Australia, prioritising five areas that I argue should be prioritised in addressing the core issues we face and the economic and societal rewards that may be heralded by the political leadership willing to face issues that others have shied away from addressing.

I passionately believe that our society needs renewal. Smith's writings provide many answers and an important reminder that economic life and economic outcomes do not exist in a vacuum and never have. Economic analysis lacks critical context without understanding law, politics, sociology and psychology. It is not sufficient to assume context is understood, as inevitably, what is assumed or implied is often given inadequate weighting in our understanding. This is particularly true in our all too often 'fake news' world of soundbite headlines and shallow analysis.

I hope you enjoy reading this book as much as I have enjoyed writing it! I also hope that by the end of this book, you will at least reflect on my belief, and that of some others, that the teachings of Adam Smith are very relevant to the world we live in.

1

Who Was Adam Smith?

Adam Smith has earned a reputation as the 'father of economics' and the 'father of capitalism'. He could be equally described as the 'father of sociology' or 'moral philosophy' and, with his instinctive understanding of human behaviour, a 'founding father of psychology'. We need to start from the beginning to piece together which of these epithets best fits Smith.

He was born in Kirkcaldy, a small seaport town on the Firth of Forth some 18 km from Edinburgh, in 1723. (The precise month and day are unknown, though a clue is provided by the records that show he was baptised on 5 June 1723.) The population of Kirkcaldy today is approximately 50,000; the population back in Smith's time would have been less than 20,000. (Census records began in 1801, when Scotland had a population under 2.5 million, half its current level.) Smith died on 17 July 1790 at the age of 67 – remarkable, as the average life expectancy in 18th-century Britain was between 25 and

40 years – and was buried in the grounds of Edinburgh's Canongate Kirkyard.

Smith's birth followed not long after Scotland became part of the UK in 1707, a seminal development in the society he grew up in. Being born in a seaside town was also pivotal. As the son of a customs officer, he saw ships entering and leaving the local port, bringing in and exporting goods to benefit producers and customers. In what at first seems to contradict his core belief in free trade, Smith also became a customs officer for a period later in life. The seeming contradiction, as will become obvious later, is that as a customs officer, Smith's duties included the collection of taxes on international trade and charging tax evaders and smugglers.

Smith grew up in a time of significant social change. The Industrial Revolution was very much in its infancy. Scotland, at that time, was an agrarian economy, and most people worked in agriculture. Limited liability companies were rare, and most business forms were individuals, family businesses, or partnerships. Demonstrating his prophetic powers, Smith became deeply suspicious of limited liability businesses, and of managers' and directors' roles in managing other people's – shareholders' – money, an age-old and topical problem that economists call the 'principal–agent problem'. I come back to this important corporate governance theme in Chapter 4.

He was brought up as an only child in a Christian family home by his mother, Margaret – his father, also named Adam, had died two months before Smith was born. Smith had a half-brother, Hugh, who was fourteen years older, from his father's previous marriage; Adam Smith senior's first wife died, and then he married Margaret. Dedicated to his work, Smith never married and was very close to his mother, with whom he lived for most of his life.[5]

Smith entered the world in relatively prosperous surroundings where there was a strong emphasis on education and the church (or the kirk, as it was known in Scotland). He believed that Christianity was based on two core beliefs: the love of God and the love of neighbour as we love ourselves.[6] Smith argued, however, that 'we love ourselves for our own sakes, not because we are commanded to do so'.[7] In this way, Smith demonstrates that he was not a slave to religious doctrine in the literal sense but critically thought about how it should be interpreted, how this interpretation can comfortably coincide with the literal word, and how religion shapes morality. He was an ardent believer in the importance of compassion. Smith was to question the power of religion progressively, and while not a confirmed atheist – as his best friend, fellow countryman and intellectual companion, the philosopher David Hume, was believed to be – he was not hostage to the literal views of the Presbyterian Church.[8] This posture of expressing qualified views on religion and the Church's role had, at the time, the potential to be controversial. Evidencing the influence and power of the Church, Hume, given the perception that he was an atheist, failed in his endeavour to be appointed Provost (Chancellor) at the Universities of Glasgow and Edinburgh despite his clear credentials, which included his seminal work *A Treatise of*

---

5 Hanley, RP (2023). 'Religion and philosophy', in Mullins, R, Smith, C & Mochrie, R (eds.). *Adam Smith: The Kirkcaldy papers*. Adam Smith Global Foundation, pp32-37.

6 Ibid.

7 Smith, A (2000; originally published 1776). *The Wealth of Nations*. Random House, p171.

8 Norman, J (2018). *Adam Smith: Father of economics*. Basic Books, p6.

Human Nature (1739). Smith was more careful in expressing his views to avoid offending the Church. The Church had a strong control over society and, in many ways, threatened individual liberty and a free society. Religious discrimination was a significant part of life in 18th- and 19th-century Scotland, particularly for those of the Catholic branch of Christianity and non-believers.

Smith the academic

Smith, a private and reserved individual, often rather austere, was a gifted student. His first education experience was at the Kirkcaldy Burgh School, where he studied Latin, maths, writing, history and some Greek.[9] From there, he directly entered the second year at the University of Glasgow at the age of fourteen – not an unusually young age in those days – to study physics and mathematics.

At the University of Glasgow, Smith debated his ideas with Joseph Black, the chemist who discovered carbon dioxide and latent heat; with the 'father of modern geology', James Hutton;[10] and with his aforementioned close friend David Hume. However, it was Professor Francis Hutcheson, an Ulster Presbyterian under whom Smith studied, who had the most significant influence on him, profoundly influencing the values that he developed. Hutcheson impressed upon Smith that human happiness had to be centred on personal liberty and the freedom to live as one saw fit without harming others, and that human motivation and achievement were not derived from the

9 Muscatelli, A (2023), 'Adam Smith & Education'. Mullins, R, Smith, C & Mochrie, R (eds.). *Adam Smith: The Kirkcaldy papers.* Adam Smith Global Foundation.

10 Smith, C (2023), 'From Kirkcaldy to Glasgow'. Mullins, R, Smith, C & Mochrie, R (eds.). *Adam Smith: The Kirkcaldy papers.* Adam Smith Global Foundation.

state, sovereign powers or God but were unique to everyone, intrinsic to human nature, and worthy of study.[11] The influence of Hutcheson was defining for Smith and convinced him that a university education should no longer be confined to those destined for academia, the law, or the Church. With earlier English philosopher Thomas Hobbes, best known for his 1651 book *Leviathan*, Hume is arguably the greatest philosopher to have written in English. His central thesis, which Smith accepted, was that all humans were primarily motivated by self-interest but also by their passions and not always by logical reasoning, a distinction that is fundamentally different to modern economics' emphasis on the 'rational man'.

Smith's academic prowess earned him a scholarship at 17 years old that funded six years of study (1740 to 1746) at Balliol College, Oxford. Smith was more critical of the teaching here than he had experienced in Scotland. He described Oxford as 'a sanctuary in which exploded systems and obsolete prejudices find shelter and protection after they have been hunted out of every other corner of the world'.[12] After six years at Oxford, Smith lectured at the University of Edinburgh and was appointed Professor of Logic at 27. Then, a year later, he became Professor of Moral Philosophy at the University of Glasgow. In this capacity, most of his teaching was in ethics, politics and jurisprudence. In many ways, Smith was an accidental economist; his dominant field was philosophy. Economics as a discipline only really emerged in the 19th century, long after Smith had left this world. However, there is no dispute that, more than anyone else, he shaped what we

---

11 Herman, A (2002). *The Scottish Enlightenment: The Scots' invention of the modern world.* Fourth Estate, pp71-73.

12 Ibid.

now know as economics. If he had lived to see it, he would no doubt be critical of how economics, in establishing its scientific credentials, has become detached from important contexts defined by sociology, psychology, cultural norms and politics. More on this later.

From 1764 to 1766, Smith took a detour in his academic career, becoming the private tutor to the third Duke of Buccleuch, an appointment that saw him accompany the young duke on European tours. These travels, particularly in Paris, allowed Smith to expand his network of influential thinkers beyond Scotland to include the great French philosopher Voltaire, the influential French thinker on politics François Quesnay, and – hugely significantly, as I discuss later – a founding father of America, Benjamin Franklin. (It also eventually earned him a generous pension that would sustain him in later years.) François Quesnay warrants special mention. Smith met Quesnay in Versailles while the Frenchman was the physician to Louis XV, and his admiration for Quesnay was strong. Quesnay died in 1774, before the publication of *The Wealth of Nations*, the second of Smith's two classic works. Had he lived to see that publication, he would have seen the many similarities with his own earlier work *Reflections on the Formation and Distribution of Wealth* (*Reflexions sur la formation et al distribution des richesses*; 1769).[13]

Smith the enlightened intellectual

Smith became part of what came to be known as the 'Scottish Enlightenment', a movement of intellectuals at the end of the

13 Conlin, J (ed.; 2019). *Great Economic Thinkers: An introduction – from Adam Smith to Amartya Sen*. Reaktion Books, p26.

18th and beginning of the 19th century to create a modern society focused on science and rationality. (The term 'enlightenment' was defined by the Prussian philosopher Immanuel Kant in 1784 to mean 'man's emergence from self-imposed immaturity: self-determination replaces reliance on the guidance of priests, rulers or rules and formulas'.) The Scottish Enlightenment, known as 'men of genius and learning', was a roll call of the good and great of Scotland (most of whom we encountered earlier in the chapter): David Hume, the philosopher; James Hutton, the geologist; Joseph Black, the chemist; Adam Ferguson, the sociologist; and many others. Smith and Hume's ideas were central to the intellectual horsepower of the Scottish Enlightenment.[14] Through its lasting contribution to the modern world, the Scottish Enlightenment can arguably be credited with introducing the social sciences: anthropology, ethnography, sociology, psychology, history, and, of course, through Smith, economics.[15]

Smith also befriended James Watt, whose work on the steam engine in 1776 was fundamental to the Industrial Revolution and today's world. Indeed, Adam Smith might claim a more than casual link to the steam engine and the Industrial Revolution. Consistent with his philosophy of economic freedom, Smith was critical of restraints on membership by what were known as 'trade guilds' (broader in nature than trade unions but with some common underpinnings). He took sympathy on a young James Watt, who had been denied membership of a guild and was, therefore, unable to pursue his career. Smith arranged for

14 Rasmussen, DC (2017). *The Infidel and the Professor: David Hume, Adam Smith, and the friendship that shaped modern thought.* Princeton University Press, pp45-48.

15 Herman, A (2002), p133.

Watt's employment in the equipment maintenance department at the University of Glasgow with the freedom to continue his experiments with steam engines. Today, a statue of James Watt stands alongside the kings and queens in Westminster Abbey.[16]

Members of the Scottish Enlightenment were all unionists and progressives, committed to creating a new golden age.[17] The historian Hugh Trevor-Roper, speaking at an annual event at the Edinburgh Sir Walter Scott Club in 1971, said:

> *The new science of political economy, particularly philosophy and sociology, were being taught to the whole world from Edinburgh and Glasgow, and Thomas Jefferson, the greatest scholar-statesman of the New World, could declare that the universities of Edinburgh and Glasgow were the two new eyes of the Old.*[18]

The origins of the Scottish Enlightenment movement may have reflected a sense of frustration with capitulation on the part of the Scottish establishment in succumbing to union with England in 1707. If so, there may be parallels to other defining catalysts throughout history, such as the creation of The May Fourth Movement in China following the disappointment of broken promises in the Treaty of Versailles in 1919, which proved to be the catalyst for, and the origins of, the Chinese Communist Party, established in 1921 under the leadership of Mao Zedong.[19] The Scots, of course, were not to follow such a

---

16 Morgan, R, 'Adam Smith 'Adam Smith Virtue Economics and His Real-World Economics'. An address to the Australian Adam Smith Club, Melbourne, July 11, 2017.

17 Magnusson, M (2001). *Scotland: The story of a nation.* HarperCollins, p642.

18 Ibid.

19 Mitter, R (2004). *A Bitter Revolution: China's struggle with the modern world.* Oxford University Press, p44.

drastic course, though the movement for Scottish independence from Westminster remains a live issue in 21st-century British affairs. Smith's views were clear regarding the economic merits of the union with England: 'the Union was a measure from which infinite Good has been derived to this country'.[20]

The influence of the Scottish Enlightenment propelled Edinburgh as an intellectual centre to the same status as London and Paris at that time. Yet, Edinburgh did not benefit from the state institutions and social hierarchy that defined London and Paris. It was a centre where self-directed intellectuals debated big ideas and, to quote prominent 19th-century MP and social reformer Lord Shaftesbury, a place where there was a 'sort of freedom which is taken amongst Gentlemen and Friends, who know each other well'.[21] At the time of the Enlightenment, the best universities in Europe were widely viewed to be in Scotland – St Andrews, Glasgow, Aberdeen and Edinburgh.[22] The Enlightenment was also important in promoting science and human reason and, in doing so, weakening the grip that the Church and traditional religious beliefs had on society.

Remarkably, there is also much evidence that Smith and the Scottish Enlightenment helped frame the US Constitution: 'Except for their tolerance of slavery, they [the framers of the American Constitution] applied the most relevant and sophisticated social theory available to the Constitution they created. Much of this theory was provided by the Scottish

---

20 Smith, A (1776). *The Wealth of Nations*, p28.
21 Herman, A (2002), p128.
22 Goodhart, D (2020). *Head, Hand, Heart: The struggle for dignity and status in the 21st century*. Allen Lane, p42.

Enlightenment.'[23] A comprehensive and widely read book by Garry Wills (1978) documents the role of Scottish thinking on how the founding fathers had thought about the Constitution and the Declaration of Independence. *The Wealth of Nations* was published in 1776, the same year that the American colonies declared their independence, and many of those who sought to break from Great Britain were influenced by Smith's writings.[24]

Beyond moral philosophy and political economy, Smith's work was enjoyed by the famous Scottish poet Robbie Burns and later indirectly influenced Charles Darwin, a leading thinker on evolutionary biology and author of *The Origin of Species*. Darwin, who attended medical school at the University of Edinburgh between 1825 and 1827, on his return to the University of Cambridge complained that his studies in Edinburgh 'consisted of Adam Smith and John Locke'.[25] Smith's shadow was already growing and drifting beyond his domain expertise.

Adam Smith was reported to have accumulated a library of 3,000 books covering a broad range of topics reflecting his interests. An analysis of his library showed an equal number of books in the following categories:

- literature and art
- classical (Latin and Greek)
- law, politics and geography

---

23 Howe, DW (1989). 'Why the Scottish Enlightenment was useful to the framers of the American Constitution'. *Comparative Studies in Society and History*, vol. 31, no. 3, pp572-587.

24 Phillips-Fein, K (2023). 'The betrayal of Adam Smith'. New Republic. https://newrepublic.com/article/170242/betrayal-adam-smith

25 Norman, J (2018). *Adam Smith: Father of economics*, p65.

- political economy and history
- science and philosophy.[26]

Smith the writer

As much of our understanding of Adam Smith comes from his writing, we can't leave our discussion on 'Who is Adam Smith?' without introducing his two classic texts.

The Wealth of Nations (1776), comprising five volumes and 1,000-plus pages, took a decade to write. It is often cited as the origin of economics as a complete system and serious academic discipline. In Smith's view, it was a system that argued for limited state, free trade and the development of competitive free markets.

It was, however, *The Theory of Moral Sentiments* (1759) which he regarded as the better of his two classics, in which he argues the importance of moral values derived from human empathy, the limitations of human reason, the emptiness of excessive materialism and the dark side of fame and power. In *The Theory of Moral Sentiments*, which the great economist and the recipient of the Nobel Prize in Economic Sciences, Professor Ronald Coase, argues is a study of human psychology,[27] Smith seamlessly blends history, ethics and what we know today as psychology and political philosophy into a cohesive volume of 1,000 pages.

While some have argued that these two classics were contradictory – such as the Chicago academic Jacob Viner, who described the perceived inconsistencies as the 'Adam Smith

26 Morgan, R (2017).
27 Coase, RH (1994). 'Adam Smith's view of man.' *Essays on Economics and Economists*. University of Chicago Press, p28.

problem'[28] – there is no conflict between the central arguments.[29] This important point was underlined by Gordon Brown, who declared in a speech, 'Coming from Kirkcaldy as Adam Smith did, I have come to understand that his *Wealth of Nations* was underpinned by his *Theory of Moral Sentiments*, his invisible hand dependent upon the existence of a helping hand'.[30] Coase reinforced this sentiment when he wrote, 'I can find no essential difference between the views on human nature in *The Theory of Moral Sentiments* and those expressed in *The Wealth of Nations*'.[31] Similar sentiment is reflected in a review of the words of University of Sydney Economics Professor Tony Aspromourgos: 'Smith's conceptualization of economic analysis is shown to constitute a unified intellectual piece for understanding economic society and its dynamics.'[32]

While many economists focus on the latter of Smith's works and sometimes ignore the former, I argue, as others have, that this convenient approach diminishes the understanding of how his significant contribution to economics should be understood. In many ways, these books laid the foundation for what was to follow and received wide praise from intellectual giants such as Immanuel Kant and Voltaire, who wrote, 'We have nothing to compare with him, and I am embarrassed for my dear compatriots.'[33]

---

28 Conlin, J (ed.; 2019), p23.

29 Boettke, PJ (2024). 'Why read Adam Smith today?'. *GMU Working Paper in Economics No. 24-15*. https://papers.ssrn.com/sol3/papers.cfm?abstract_id=4741993#

30 Norman, J (2018). *Adam Smith: Father of economics*, pxi.

31 Coase, RH (1994), pp25 & 28.

32 Aspromourgos, T (2008). *The Science of Wealth: Adam Smith and the framing of political economy*. Routledge.

33 Herman, A (2002), p46.

Many expert commentators believe that Smith's two classics are amongst the most intellectually significant books ever written and that the ideas that they frame continue to influence the world today.[34] In the views of some scholars, *The Theory of Moral Sentiments* is one of the most important books of the Age of Enlightenment. It provides the moral meaning of Adam Smith's merits of markets.[35] The importance of reading Smith's two classics and seeing them as complementary was brilliantly summarised by the University of Oxford Professor Colin Mayer CBE, who wrote in answer to the question 'Where did capitalism go wrong?':

> *The capitalist equivalent of the Messiah came to Earth in the guise of Adam Smith. He delivered us our capitalist learnings. But we only read half of them. It was as if we forgot to turn over the tablet of stone and failed to read what was on the other side … We have avidly consumed his second book,* The Wealth of Nations, *while conveniently forgetting its predecessor,* The Theory of Moral Sentiments.[36]

*

We've been introduced to Adam Smith's early life and education and his contribution to the intellectual landscape of his time, the legacy of which has lasted for three centuries. We now consider Smith's thinking on various subjects that challenge modern-day Australia's politicians and leaders. First, further background reflects the complex legacy that Adam Smith

34 Norman, J (2018). *Adam Smith: Father of economics*, p156.
35 Mayer, C (2024). *Capitalism and Crises: How to fix them.* Oxford University Press, p14.
36 Ibid., pxvii.

leaves with us and how his works and thinking have been (mis) interpreted to suit different agendas.

The lessons from Adam Smith, while having a strong emphasis on individual liberty, market forces, international trade and small government, also have much to say on fairness, social equity, the importance of community over individualism, the criticality of education, the corrupting nature of cronyism and the absence of moral values. Smith's writings strongly suggest that he cared about people and society. He would most certainly have been appalled by former British prime minister Margaret Thatcher – an ardent believer in free markets – when she allegedly proclaimed in 1987, 'Who is society? There is no such thing!'[37] Margaret Thatcher is also on record as saying that poverty is a 'personality defect'.[38]

The irony is that Thatcher is said to have carried a copy of *The Wealth of Nations* in her handbag.[39] (She also apparently carried a copy of Friedrich Hayek's *The Constitution of Liberty* in her handbag.) To highlight the enigma that Smith has become, it is also true that the principal architect of communism, Karl Marx, was influenced by Smith's work, as were the founding fathers of the US.

Former British prime minister Gordon Brown notes that Adam Smith believed strongly in the importance of morals and ethics. Smith argued that the market economy had to be based on ethical values, on the hand of compassion just as much as the 'invisible hand' of the market. Yet, there is little

---

37 Stiglitz, JE (2024). *The Road to Freedom: Economics and the good society.* W.W. Norton & Company, p277.

38 Bregman, R, 'Poverty isn't a lack of character; it's a lack of cash', TED, 14 June 2017, https://www.youtube.com/watch?v=ydKcaIE6O1k.

39 *The Economist*, 'An enlightened life: rescuing Adam Smith from myth and misrepresentation', 27 July 2018.

to demonstrate that these values – ethics and compassion – are evident in the way markets work today, a problem clearly illustrated, for example, by the events that led to the global financial crisis (GFC) in 2008. Ironically, Brown, then UK chancellor (treasurer), initially played an unhelpful role by supporting the conditions leading to the GFC, only to later be the chief political architect, working closely with then Australian prime minister Kevin Rudd and other world leaders and central bankers, in developing plans to stabilise the global economy during the fallout from the GFC.

Many economists, business leaders and politicians still view Adam Smith as the godfather or personification of free-market economics, capitalism and the greed-is-good philosophy; he has become a stereotype and pin-up poster hero for those of this ideology. Others, particularly those in academia who have studied his work, argue that such an interpretation of Smith is to misread and misunderstand what he had to say and is thus a disservice to his legacy. This is the strong view that I hold; I intend to show that the legacy of Smith cannot be held prisoner to any right-leaning ideology. The University of Chicago's Professor George Stigler, when giving a lecture in honour of Smith in Scotland, is alleged to have said that Adam Smith was 'alive and well and living in Chicago', only to hear a member of the audience call out, 'You mean held a prisoner in Chicago,' as Smith would not have endorsed the framing of free-market, laissez-faire economic philosophy that is widely associated with that excellent institution. I will argue in Chapter 3 that much of what is associated with the 'Chicago school' is often misinterpreted and devoid of the important context in which their views should be understood, as is the case with Adam Smith.

Many who reference Adam Smith do a disservice to him by condensing the full complexity of his thinking to the catchphrase 'the invisible hand', particularly as this phrase appears only three times in the entire corpus of *The Wealth of Nations.*

It is to do a further disservice to Smith – and perhaps to slander him – to lazily view him as a champion of the political right, as many are prone to do. It has become common parlance for neoliberals – champions of unfettered capitalism, according to Nobel Prize winner in Economic Sciences Joseph Stiglitz – to invoke the good name of Adam Smith in their arguments for a reduction in the frontiers of the state and to promote the unconstrained animal spirits of the market to roam free. Indeed, the leading UK-based think tank The Adam Smith Institute is positioned as right-wing. Its historical links to the British Conservative Party are well known, as is its influence on the policy of Prime Minister Margaret Thatcher's government in the 1980s. The Adam Smith Institute's corporate motto is 'Using free markets to create a richer, freer, happier world'. [40]

Those who see Smith as a promoter of selfish capitalism governed by the invisible hand are unlikely to have spent much, if any, time studying and thoughtfully interpreting his work and understanding his thinking, instead grabbing soundbites that fit a cognitive bias of what is good and what is bad in economic policy and for society. Serious scholars of Smith's work argue that he saw it as impossible to separate what is good and bad for the economy from what is good and bad for society. They go hand-in-glove, as Joseph Stiglitz argues in his book *The Road to Freedom: Economics and the Good Society*

40 Adam Smith Institute. https://www.adamsmith.org

(2024). Stiglitz's emphasis on a 'good society' aligns with Adam Smith's core philosophy.

Those who have studied Smith's work – such as Deirdre McCloskey, Isaiah Berlin Chair in Liberal Thought at the Washington-based Cato Institute and Emerita Professor of Economics at the University of Illinois Chicago – describe Smith as deeply egalitarian, as the first true liberal and a moral philosopher first and foremost. There is little dispute that Adam Smith has significantly contributed to contemporary political theory, framing how we should understand key normative concepts such as justice, liberty and equality. As this book will argue, while Smith favoured *capitalism*, he was much more guarded when it came to *capitalists*, and the form of capitalism we see today in Australia and elsewhere would surely cause Smith to turn in his grave.

Smith the economist

Adam Smith is arguably the best-known economist of all time – the father of economics – despite competition from the likes of Thomas Malthus, David Ricardo, John Stuart Mill, Alfred Marshall, Karl Marx, John Maynard Keynes, Friedrich Hayek, Joseph Schumpeter, Ronald Coase, Milton Friedman, Hernando de Soto, Paul Samuelson, Joseph Stiglitz and many others mentioned throughout this book. Smith was the first great economist to understand that individual self-interest operating in competitive markets can achieve the best economic outcomes for the benefit of society.

Although the term 'oeconomy' (meaning 'the thrifty management of the household' – *oikos* being the Greek word for 'household') was in existence during Smith's era, 'economics' and 'economists' were not terms that were established.[41] In *The Wealth of Nations*, Smith blends history, ethics and political philosophy.[42] His approach to the political economy was free from the highly mathematical and sometimes abstract nature of the economics we know today, which often seeks the credibility of scientific precision at the expense of understanding human behaviour and the complexity of society. If economics is a science, it is more a social science than a natural science. Alfred Marshall famously said mathematics in economics was 'at best a useful piece of scaffolding which should be removed in the presentation of final arguments'. Marshall understood economics in the way that Smith did. In Marshall's classic 19th-century textbook *Principles of Economics* – a book which also made a seminal contribution to the way economics is taught today – he started the book by writing, 'Political economy or economics is a study of mankind in the ordinary business of life'.[43] Joseph Stiglitz echoed this sentiment when he wrote, 'All economics is supposed to be about behaviour; it's supposed to describe how people actually behave'.[44] Perhaps the greatest 20th-century economist, John Maynard Keynes, expressed a similar view in a letter to Roy Harrod in 1938 when he wrote, 'I want to emphasise strongly the point about economics being a moral science'.[45] The words of these great economists are classic Smithian, and they so eloquently capture how his two classic works complement each other.

---

41 Conlin, J (2018), p22.

42 Sagar, P (2018). *The Opinion of Mankind: Sociability and the theory of the state from Hobbes to Smith*. Princeton University Press, pp66-71.

43 Marshall, A (1890). *Principles of Economics*. 8th edn. Macmillan.

44 Stiglitz, JE (2024), p147.

45 Montes, L (2004), *Adam Smith in Context: A critical reassessment of some central components of his thought*. Palgrave-MacMillan, p144.

The role of economics through the eyes of Smith, Marshall and Keynes may appear at odds with Milton Friedman's vigour in arguing that facts must replace values, that subjectivity should be purged from the rigours of economic analysis and policy, and that economists should think of themselves as scientists.[46] In fairness to Friedman, though, he saw the strength of mathematical economics as greater precision in assumptions and analysis. He believed in 'positive economics' in contrast to 'normative economics', which suggests that he would not let the maths or the model rule over observations or evidence. In this regard, he was aligned with a contemporary Chicago economist of his time, the great Dutch econometrician Professor Henri Theil, who, while an expert in economic modelling, had a nuanced view of the accuracy of models, and was acutely aware of their limitations and the uncertainty associated with them. These limitations were brought to life during the GFC when the US Federal Reserve Chairman, Alan Greenspan, said, 'The Federal Reserve has got the most elaborate econometric model, which incorporates all the new-fangled models of how the world works – and it missed it (GFC) completely.'[47]

In sharp contrast, Smith understood that a healthy society is a product of a strong community, where gift-giving, volunteering, caregiving and reciprocity are important. These valuable contributions to the economy and society go unmeasured in traditional economic metrics of prosperity. Yet, if measured, they are likely to account for between 20 to 30 per cent of GDP.[48]

---

46 Conlin, J (2018), pp171-173.
47 Greenspan, A. Testimony before the House Committee on Oversight & Government Reform. 23 October 2008. https://www.pbs.org/newshour/show/greenspan-admits-flaw-to-congress-predicts-more-economic-problems
48 Stiglitz, JE (2024), p38.

Smithian economists know that it is an underinvestment, or breakdown, in these unmeasured aspects of society that is at the root of many societal problems, including the growing propensity for depression, which research has linked in large part to a breakdown in family and community values. Johann Hari brilliantly examines this issue in his bestselling book *Lost Connections* (2019).[49] There is also growing evidence that physical health problems can be attributed to an unhealthy society. Traditionally, medicine has separated the mind from the body, the person from their environment. The biopsychosocial view of medicine was first promoted by the psychiatrist George Engel,[50, 51] who convincingly argues that there is an interconnection between biology, psychology and socioenvironmental factors in understanding human wellness and health and, thus, use for a holistic approach to primary care for family doctors and psychiatrists.[52] The ideas that emphasise these important attributes of a healthy society come straight out of the pages of *The Theory of Moral Sentiments*.[53]

Despite the significant progress in economics over the centuries, the discipline still operates in the shadow of Adam Smith. While pursuing its credentials as a hard science rather than a social science, economics has, in the eyes of many, become detached from the real world as it espouses rationality,

---

49 Hari, J (2018). *Lost Connections: Why you're depressed and how to find hope.* Bloomsbury.

50 Engel, GL. 'The need for a new medical model: a challenge for biomedicine'. *Science*, vol. 196, no. 4286, 8 April 1977, pp129-136.

51 Engel, GL. 'The clinical application of the biopsychosocial model'. *The American Journal of Psychiatry*, vol. 137, no. 5, May 1980, pp535-544.

52 Kusnanto, H, Agustian, D & Hilmanto, D. 'Biopsychosocial model of illness in primary care: a hermeneutic literature review'. *Journal of Family Medicine and Primary Care*, vol. 7, no. 3, May–June 2018, pp497-500.

53 Norman, J (2018). *Adam Smith: Father of economics*, p307.

values-free decision-making, self-regulation and the overuse of mathematical models to support forecasts. Yet, virtually every great economist of the past two centuries has claimed the influence of Adam Smith, and all the distinctive branches of modern economics can trace their lineage back to Smith.[54] Importantly, Smith believed that economic understanding had to be set in the context of politics, sociology, psychology, morals, ethics, culture and society; to separate these linked components of the jigsaw would be to miss critical information and, consequently, result in a poor understanding of economic outcomes.

Few would disagree with the great economist John Maynard Keynes when he said to the effect that as economic theorists strive for their unique contribution to the evolution of science, none should compare themselves to Adam Smith. Adding weight to Keynes's views of Smith, Friedrich Hayek argued that Smith's work surpasses all modern insights into what influences human behaviour and shapes society.[55] These and many other reasons help justify the claim that Adam Smith's views matter, and the passage of time has not dimmed them. If anything, it has given them fresh importance and relevance.

Smith on trade

Adam Smith's early environment influenced him greatly in his championing of trade and his belief that nations would prosper if merchants were allowed to freely trade across borders, unburdened by the dead weight and heavy hand of government intervention and restrictions such as tariffs or self-interested business lobby groups seeking protection from foreign

54 Ibid., p161.
55 Boettke, PJ (2024).

competition under the convenient guise of 'national interest'. He saw the imposition of laws to restrict trade or taxes on imports as having a consequence of encouraging entrepreneurs to find ways to avoid these restrictions, and, in the extreme, of creating smugglers who became victims in the sense of criminalising honest men.

To highlight his views on trade, Smith wrote:[56]

> *By means of glasses, hotbeds, and hotwalls, very good grapes can be raised in Scotland, and very good wine too can be made of them at about thirty times the expense for which at least equally good can be brought from foreign countries. Would it be a reasonable law to prohibit the importation of all foreign wines merely to encourage the making of claret and burgundy in Scotland?*

Like Smith, the great classic economist David Ricardo knew, more than two centuries ago, that businesses struggling in the face of foreign competition would lobby the government to restrict imports. They would argue then, as they do today, that foreign nations' economies would prosper at the expense of the domestic economy. Smith emphasised in *The Wealth of Nations* that countries were not sustainably rich or poor simply out of geographical luck, climate and resources; their sustainable success was a function of how they organised and educated their labour, innovated, and grew productivity.[57]

Like Smith, Ricardo also saw the logic of encouraging free trade, even when other countries impose barriers, as residents in nations that promote free trade enjoy lower prices and greater choice. Ricardo believed that countries should focus on

56 Smith, A (1776). *The Wealth of Nations.*
57 Phillips-Fein, K (2023).

producing goods where they had a comparative advantage and, through trade, enjoy the benefits of nations that focused on goods where they had a comparative advantage. In Smith's eyes, trade was a win-win for consumers and for the domestic economy. When barriers are introduced, prices rise, choices are reduced and inefficient businesses are protected.

Despite their commitment to free trade, Smith and Ricardo are arguably unlikely to support China's trade policy today. There is an argument – and the source of much angst amongst nations such as the US – that a nation running a trade surplus of $150 billion per month, as China does, which also produces 31 per cent of the world's manufacturing goods but accounts for only 13 per cent of world consumption, is predatory in nature and can be seen as damaging to employment in other countries.[58] China's trade policy has resulted in an aggressive tariff response by the US government under President Trump.

Smith would be perplexed by the macroeconomic logic in the argument presented by President Trump in 2025 that the US trade deficit with other countries is evidence of those countries cheating the US. Smith would argue that a nation's trade deficit is the result of their choice of excess spending over income – and so Trump's argument is akin to an individual blaming the credit card company for a large credit card debt caused by that individual's spending habits.

Much aligned with Smith's philosophy, Harvard's Michael Porter argued in *The Competitive Advantage of Nations* (1990) that a nation's sustainable prosperity is created, not inherited. It does not sustain itself out of a country's natural endowments, its labour pools, its interest rates or its currency value, as some

58 Evans-Pritchard, A. 'China's third plenum is almost a declaration of economic war'. *The Telegraph (UK)*, 24 July 2024.

economists might argue. Instead, a nation's competitiveness depends on the capacity of its businesses to invest and innovate. Companies gain an advantage against the world's best because of the benefits of having strong domestic competition, highly efficient and strong supply chains, and demanding local customers. In many ways, the success of the US has been shaped by the ingredients described by Porter. Countries blessed with abundant resources can also be cursed by complacency and underinvestment in innovation. This often translates into declining productivity. In today's framing, Smith knew that the only way to increase real income is through real productivity growth, which has been one of the major challenges facing modern Australia, as Professor Ross Garnaut AC eloquently argued in his 2023 Bannerman Competition Lecture and in his book *Let's Tax Carbon: And Other Ideas for a Better Australia* (2024).[59, 60]

Many aspects of the 'mercantile system' were a concern to Smith. His concerns centred on how the mercantile system, focusing on state control of economic activities to promote national interests by restricting trade with the aim of accumulating overseas reserves, protected the business elite, who controlled monopolies, oligopolies and other powerful industry clusters that characterised many of the major European economies at that time (and arguably still do today). Smith was concerned about the power these private-sector actors exercised through their lobbying of governments to curry favour in the protection of monopolies, including implementing tariffs and trade restrictions. He feared that they, in essence, captured

59 Garnaut, R, 2023 Bannerman Competition Lecture, 3 May 2023.
60 Garnaut, R (2024). *Let's Tax Carbon: And other ideas for a better Australia.* La Trobe University Press.

the state to serve their advantage. He saw this most vividly with the East India Company, where he attacked the privileges and resulting abuses that defined that company:

> *By a perpetual monopoly, all other subjects of the state are taxed very absurdly in two different ways: first, by the high prices of goods, which, in the case of free trade, they could buy much cheaper; and, secondly, by their total exclusion from a branch of business which it might be both convenient and profitable for many of them to carry on.*[61]

The East India Company was a trading company incorporated by royal charter in 1600 that had extracted exclusive privileges from the British government. It then used its powers for the benefit of the few and at the expense, in the case of a famine in India caused by the company's actions, of the lives of many. (The emergence of the East India Company and the unrelated Dutch East India Company in 1602 was, in many ways, the beginning of globalisation.)

Smith and labour movements

Adam Smith cared deeply about employees' plight and rights, and the benefits of forming unions (trade unions) to effect bargaining power. He understood that in the ordinary course, bargaining power heavily favoured the company – or 'masters', as he described management. In *The Wealth of Nations*, he wrote:[62]

> *What are the common wages of labour, depends everywhere upon the contract usually between those two*

61 Smith, A (1776). *The Wealth of Nations*, B.IV, ch.2, iv.2.15.

62 Ibid., I:VIII.

> *parties, whose interests are by no means the same. It is not, however, difficult to foresee which of the two parties must, upon all ordinary occasions, have the advantage in the dispute, and force the other into compliance with their terms. The masters, being fewer in number, can combine much more easily … In all such disputes, the masters can hold out much longer.*

He went on to remark:

> *Masters are always and everywhere in a sort of tacit, but constant and uniform combination, not to raise wages of labour above their actual rate … Masters, too, sometimes enter into particular combinations to sink the wages of labour even below this rate. These are always conducted with the utmost silence and secrecy.*

What is remarkable about these passages – written more than 250 years ago, well before the Industrial Revolution, let alone our modern era – is that they still ring true.[63] Employers continue to have much power over their workers, and as I discuss in Chapter 3, some businesses exploit that power even in today's enlightened times. Smith would, however, also be concerned about the abuse of power that some modern trade unions can exercise through industry monopolies, such as that seen in the conduct of the Construction, Forestry and Maritime Employees Union (CFMEU).[64]

---

63 Stiglitz, JE (2024), pp89-90.

64 Martin-Guzman, D. 'CFMEU administrator, launches "culture of violence" probe in Queensland'. *Financial Review*, 4 February 2025.

Smith on the role of government

On the role of government, Smith was very clear. He saw that the proper role of government in promoting the wealth of nations was largely limited to three functions:

1. protecting society from the violence and invasion of other nations – in other words, to ensure that a nation had the capacity and capabilities to defend itself
2. protecting citizens from injustice or oppression from others and ensuring an effective structure of institutions for the fair administration of justice
3. establishing and maintaining public institutions and public works to ensure the orderly operation of civil society.

Smith emphasised the defence of the nation as the first duty of government. He wrote:

> *The first duty of the sovereign, that of protecting the society from violence and invasion of other independent societies, can be performed only by means of military force. But the expense both of preparing this military force in time of peace and of employing it in time of war is very different in the different states of society.*[65]

He went on to add:

> *An industrious, and upon that account wealthy nation, is of all nations the most likely to be attacked; and unless the state takes some new measures for the public defence, the natural habit of the people render them altogether incapable of defending themselves.*[66]

---

65 Smith, A (1776). *The Wealth of Nations*, B. V, ch.1 V.1.0.
66 Ibid., ch.1, V.1.14.

While creating the conditions for markets to flourish and wealth to be created, he was clear that 'defence, however, is of much more importance than opulence'.[67] Smith knew that the national defence is funded by taxation, and that increased taxation can decrease productivity and wealth creation. Therefore, he saw it as important that a nation grow its wealth to support increased expenditure on defence.[68]

Smith also understood that a market economy functions best within a clear constitutional and legal framework, including laws relating to contract enforcement, land title ownership and transferability, insolvency and competition.

As I discuss in the next chapter, Smith warned about the dangers of politicians with grand ideas and the cost and damage they can inflict on society. He would have agreed with the British politician Rory Stewart, who wrote in his memoir, *Politics on the Edge*, 'Our life as politicians has rewired our synapses, just as profoundly as the study of London streets has enlarged the hippocampus of London cabbies'.[69]

Smith's misgivings on an oversized state – a problem that Australia and other rich countries grapple with today – is captured by what he wrote in *The Wealth of Nations*:

> *In every great monarchy in Europe, the sale of the Crown lands would deliver a much greater revenue than any which these lands ever afforded to the Crown … When the Crown lands have become private property, they would, in the course of a few years, become well improved and well cultivated.*[70]

---

67 Ibid., IV.ii.30.
68 Ibid., II.iii.2.
69 Stewart, R (2024). *Politics on the Edge*. Vintage, p4.
70 Smith, A (1776). *The Wealth of Nations*.

While Smith believed that government should have a limited role in the economy and society and did not favour 'big government', it would be a disservice to argue, as some have, that he was anti-government. His philosophy on the role of government was similar to that of John Stuart Mill, who saw the government's role as that of the 'night-watchman', while being small and competent and not the bloated, omnipresent nanny.[71] Smith criticised intrusive regulation, particularly on trade, and the waste often associated with a large public sector (which he labelled 'unproductive hands'). He saw the need for government intervention in some markets, such as banking, where there is clear evidence of market failure or in sectors where market manipulation was evident in the pursuit of economic rent extraction. As discussed in the book, this is a chronic problem in Australia.

Smith also saw it as important that the government was incorruptible in ensuring that the rule of law is enforced, and to, as Milton Friedman emphasises, 'set the rules of the game and act as an umpire in enforcing them'.[72] Setting the game's rules in areas of competition policy, for example, is something only government can do. As mentioned, Smith was particularly concerned about how powerful business and lobby groups could influence and capture government policy at a cost to society;[73] the role of cronyism involving political favours is a common problem and a topic I return to in Chapter 2.

---

71 Micklethwait, J & Wooldridge, A (2015). *The Fourth Revolution: The Global Race to Reinvent the State*. Penguin Press, pp7-9.

72 Friedman, M (2002). *Capitalism and Freedom: Fortieth Anniversary Edition*. University of Chicago Press, p25.

73 Barrett, J, '"We are already the honey pot": scam victims say powerful banking lobby is blocking compensation'. *The Guardian*, 4 August 2024. https://www.theguardian.com/money/article/2024/aug/04/we-are-already-the-honey-pot-scam-victims-say-powerful-banking-lobby-is-blocking-compensation

Smith on taxation

A role of government that Smith believed in was to raise taxes, which should be levied fairly, efficiently and equitably. There is evidence in his writings that Smith supported a progressive taxation system in which the tax rate increases with the taxable amount, as is the case in Australia. In other words, the burden of taxation should fall heaviest upon the rich. Taxes should reflect the ability to pay, and those who benefit most from society should pay the most. He believed that taxes should be simple to understand and collect, and that they should be predictable and not imposed in a way that would hamper economic growth. Importantly, the burden of taxation should not discourage hard work and innovation.

Smith was wary of government excesses in spending other people's money on political projects, such as in Australia with taxpayer funds being used to build sports stadiums instead of hospitals,[74] and the punitive nature of personal income tax.

Adam Smith prophetically understood this when he wrote, 'There is no art which one government sooner learns of another, than that of draining money from the pockets of people'.[75]

Smith believed that taxes should be used to fund essential public services – defence, infrastructure, and in today's world he would surely have added health care – and, most importantly, education, while acknowledging, consequently, government would necessarily be somewhat bigger than true of his day.

---

74 Morton, A. 'The devils and the detail of the $715m AFL stadium dividing Tasmania'. *The Guardian*. 11 June 2023. https://www.theguardian.com/australia-news/2023/jun/11/the-devils-and-the-detail-of-the-715m-afl-stadium-dividing-tasmania

75 Smith, A (1776). *The Wealth of Nations*, II, p346.

Smith and education

Given his background, it is perhaps little surprise that Adam Smith was passionate about universal education. Education is a central theme in all of his key works.[76] Smith had a wide-reaching view of education that was not confined to formal learning in the sense of academic study. This is an important theme I discuss more fully in Chapter 5. Smith viewed social learning on moral conduct through social interactions as fundamental to living a happy life.[77] Without reverence for the rules of moral conduct, Smith saw the potential of a breakdown of social order and the economy: 'society would crumble into nothing'.[78]

Adam Smith cared deeply about the quality of education, as evident in criticism of his experience at Balliol College, Oxford. He saw education as a social good, a public good, and that government should directly cover the costs of educating those unable to fund themselves.[79] Eighteenth-century Scotland was a unique era, but Smith believed education should be accessible and affordable, and he believed strongly in the virtues of the Scottish educational model.[80] This emphasis on government support for education was arguably in conflict with his belief in small government, but quickly reconciled in the context of education's economic and social value to the individual and the economy. In keeping with the Scottish philosophy on education, from his *The Theory of Moral Sentiments*, Smith is clear that education should be viewed broadly as the learning

76 Rauwald, JLZ (2024). 'Adam Smith on the public provision of education'. *History of European Ideas*, vol. 50, no. 5, pp733-749.
77 Ibid.
78 Smith, A (1759). *The Theory of Moral Sentiments*, ch.IV.
79 Ibid.
80 Ibid.

of 'wisdom' and 'moral sentiments', both of which are central to a healthy society.

Smith's passion for a broad-based education as a force for economic and social development is an important topic I return to in Chapter 5. Clear evidence of his legacy was the popularity of the philosophy, politics and economics (PPE) degree, first launched by Oxford University in the early 1920s and now taught at several leading universities across the world, including the University of Sydney, the University of Melbourne and Australian National University (ANU), as well as other Australian universities. An Oxford PPE degree has become a staple diet for aspiring politicians the world over – an astonishing proportion of Britain's elite are PPE graduates from Balliol College, Oxford, as are several former Australian prime ministers, including Tony Abbott, Malcolm Fraser and Bob Hawke, and other former senior government figures such as former foreign minister Gareth Evans.

Smith's contribution to the PPE curriculum was acknowledged by Ryan Patrick Hanley (2017), who notes, 'Smith not only distinguished himself as an early practitioner of what we today identify with PPE, but he also provides a useful point of reference for those doing PPE today'. In his writings, Smith contributed to political theory by providing a framework for understanding key normative concepts such as justice, liberty and equality. His polymath qualities allowed him to see patterns and linkages across various fields, guiding his intellectual curiosity.

Smith wrote that 'a philosopher and a common street porter' might display 'the most dissimilar characters', but the difference was essentially 'not so much from nature, as from habit, customer and education'.[81] As is true today, in Smith's era, the main determinant of a child's future prosperity was its parents' income, not intelligence or 'genius'. I discuss this important theme in Chapter 5; as Smith would have foreseen, the education system remains at the centre of many challenges and opportunities facing our society and economy today.

Smith and psychology

I want to round off the discussion of 'Who is Adam Smith?' by looking at Smith as a moral philosopher and, as I argue, a psychologist. We have already acknowledged that his instinctive understanding of human behaviour would justify him to be regarded as a founding father of psychology. An example was his emphasis on forming a deep understanding of human interaction and self-reflection. In *The Theory of Moral Sentiments*, he describes how he creates the impartial spectator by dividing himself into two, 'myself and my social self', adopting a 'someone might be watching' test on his behaviour. He wrote:

> *When I endeavour to examine my own conduct … I divide myself, as it were, into two persons … The first is the spectator, whose sentiments with regard to my own conduct I endeavour to enter into, by placing myself in his situation, and by considering how it would appear to me, when seen from that particular point of view. The second is the agent, the person who I properly call myself … The first is the judge; the second the person judged of.*[82]

---

81 Smith Adam (1776), *The Wealth of Nations*, p28.
82 Smith, A (1759). *The Theory of Moral Sentiments*, p183.

Smith, just like Harvard philosopher John Rawls, who described the 'veil of ignorance' in his *A Theory of Justice* (1971)[83], is essentially saying that we must use our values in examining our conduct as if our behaviour is subject to the scrutiny of others. Interestingly, Smith does not bring a religious prism to this judgement in that it is not the judgement of God but that of our fellow humans. Smith believed that man's instincts were a function of 'nature' rather than a set of divine commandments revealed to certain prophets by God, as some believe the Ten Commandments were revealed to Moses.[84] Conceptually, this philosophy is very similar to Sigmund Freud's psychoanalytical theory of the ego and superego. The ego is the decisions we make based on conscious and unconscious beliefs and values to fulfil perceived needs; the superego plays the moralising role that can act as a handbrake on decisions or actions that might not be in our interests or that of the community. It is, in many ways, the impartial spectator.

If we are satisfied that our impartial spectator test stands up to scrutiny, then our actions are well-intended and defendable. As a result, we sleep well at night, while the business executive, politician or sportsperson who behaves in a way that he or she hopes is never found out – in an unethical and potentially illegal way – will sleep less peacefully. Think here about those past and present partners of accounting firm PwC, embroiled in the tax scandal that blew up in 2023 and which I discuss later in the book, or the sports stars, such as the cyclist Lance Armstrong, caught with illegal or banned performance-enhancing drugs in their system.

83 Rawls, J (1971). *A Theory of Justice*. Harvard University Press.
84 Conlin, J (2018), p25.

To better understand others' motives and concerns, Smith believed in the importance of putting oneself in their shoes and trying to see things as they do.[85] In doing this, Smith exhibits his understanding of cognitive science and what psychologists call the 'theory of mind', which is the ability to attribute mental states to oneself and others and, in so doing, understand that others may have beliefs, desires, intentions and views different from one's own. Having a theory of mind can be important as it provides the ability to predict and interpret the behaviour of others. Smith's natural skills in what we know as psychology today are evident throughout his works, as I highlight in several places throughout this book. Psychology is the study of the human mind, its mental processes, and how it functions and affects our understanding and behaviour. In *The Theory of Moral Sentiments*, Smith argued that the desire for wealth and status motivates the effort to achieve self-improvement. In contrast, Smith argues in *The Wealth of Nations* that people are fundamentally self-interested (which is not the same as selfish). Smith also understood that for most people, the greatest happiness fundamentally comes from having a good reputation, which results from behaviour and values exhibited over a long time.[86] He implicitly knew that a good reputation is built slowly, as in the speed of the travelling tortoise, and can be lost quickly, as in the speed of the galloping horse.

Many economists sometimes lose sight of the fact that Smith did not believe in unbridled selfishness. In *The Theory of Moral*

---

85 Oslington, P & Hart, DM (2023). 'Adam Smith and why he matters today: essays on the relevance of Smith after 300 years'. *Occasional Paper 199*. The Centre for Independent Studies.

86 Norman, J (2018). *Adam Smith: Father of economics*, p302.

Sentiments, he wrote about the importance of the compassion we feel for others:

> *How selfish soever man may be supposed, there are evidently some principles in his nature, which interest him in the fortune of others, and render their happiness necessary to him, though he derives nothing from it, except the pleasure of seeing it. Of this kind is pity or compassion, the emotion which we feel for the misery of others, when we either see it, or are made to conceive it in a very lively manner. That we often derive sorrow from the sorrow of others, is a matter of fact too obvious to require any instance to prove it; for this sentiment, like all the other original passions of human nature, is by no means confined to the virtuous and humane, though they perhaps may feel it with the most exquisite sensibility. The greater the ruffian, the most hardened violators of the law in society, is not altogether without it.*[87]

*

In my introduction to Adam Smith, I have touched upon several themes I return to throughout the book. In the next chapter, we look at some of these through a modern lens as we understand why Adam Smith matters to us.

87 Smith, A (1759). *The Theory of Moral Sentiments.*

2

Why Adam Smith Matters to Us

Given how the world and our understanding of economics and society have changed since Smith wrote his classic works in the late 18th century, some readers might naturally and understandably question their relevance to our complex modern world. In response, I will demonstrate that just as the foundational works of Shakespeare (1564 to 1616), our great religions and the basis of much common law have stood the test of time, so have the important principles espoused by Adam Smith. And just as many of the problems plaguing our world today can be understood, in part, by how we have drifted away from the true meaning of earlier teachings of our great religions, for example, so too it is the case that many economic, governance and social problems of today exist because the principles outlined by Smith have been forgotten, ignored or bastardised. He remains a prophet of our time. In this chapter, I reflect on why Adam Smith matters to us (or 'you', the modern reader).

Adam Smith matters today because he is unique among many great minds that have shaped our world. This was the central argument in Professor Peter Boettke's excellent paper 'Why Read Adam Smith Today?'[88] Students of physics are not sent to read Newton's *Philosophiae Naturalis Principia Mathematics* (1687) or Einstein's 'Cosmological Considerations in the General Theory of Relativity' (1917) as it is assumed that modern literature has embedded what is valuable from the past and disregarded ideas that have not stood the test of time, often superseded by fresh insights. So, why should Smith be any different, given the quantum leap in the science of economics? Boettke argues that Smith is different because his insights are as relevant to the world today as they were close to 300 years ago. Yet, in an unstructured and more anecdotal survey of more than 40 friends and acquaintances who graduated in economics, including those practising as economists, none had assiduously studied *The Wealth of Nations* in any detail – relying largely on lecture notes instead – and none had given any thought to *The Theory of Moral Sentiments*, considering it out of scope in the study of economics in most universities.

An enduring influence on both sides of politics

Part of the wonderful mystique of Adam Smith and the great curiosity about his work is that it is still living with us today, well beyond the hallowed halls of the University of Chicago and

88 Boettke, PJ (2024).

other great universities. A key reason Smith matters today is that much of what he has written appeals to both the right and the left in our political world. Most recently, Smith has been credited with influencing the views of former Democratic US president Barack Obama.[89] Before this, the influence Smith had on the views of great economists such as Friedrich Hayek from the 'Austrian School' (which included Carl Menger, Ludwig von Mises and others), which in turn influenced George Stigler, Milton Friedman and others from the 'Chicago School', who went on to greatly influence much of the small-government, privatisation, deregulation and free-market political agenda in the era of Ronald Reagan and Margaret Thatcher. Most interesting is that there is also much evidence Smith significantly influenced the communist theories espoused by Karl Marx that shaped the old Soviet Union, China and some other countries.

Some of Marx's worldviews were shaped by Georg Wilhelm Friedrich Hegel, who in turn was greatly influenced by Smith. In *The Formation of the Economic Thought of Karl Marx*, Ernest Mandel (1971) noted, 'Hegel has been profoundly affected in his youth by economic studies, in particular by the work of Adam Smith.'[90] In a series of lectures between 1803 and 1806, Hegel acknowledged the influence of Smith, notably his magnum opus, *The Wealth of Nations*. This masterpiece of Smith greatly influenced Karl Marx, which is evident in Marx's *Economic and Philosophic Manuscripts* (1844). Mandel reaffirmed

89 Riach, K & Roy, G (2023), 'Adam Smith's return to Glasgow University, 300 years on', in in Mullins, R, Smith, C & Mochrie, R (eds.). *Adam Smith: The Kirkcaldy papers*. Adam Smith Global Foundation, pp55-59.

90 Mandel, E (1971). *The Formation of the Economic Thought of Karl Marx*. Pearce, B (trans.). Monthly Review Press.

Smith's continuing influence on Hegel, who turned to Smith for a deeper understanding of the political economy and society.[91]

While Smith influenced the work of Marx, there were fundamental differences between the two men – just as there were between Marx and Hegel, who differed significantly on topics such as the utilisation of property ownership. Through his belief in central planning, Marx would have been a strong advocate of the 'man of system', a concept that Smith was wary of, as we will discuss later. Smith believed strongly in the actions of individuals, while socialist theories view the self-serving decisions of individuals to be at odds with the collective good and not in the interest of society. Smith argued that the 'greatest aggregation of wisdom was contained in the decentralised decisions of individuals trying ... to obtain the most from their separate capitals'.[92] He believed that when individuals are free to choose when their 'natural liberty' is unconstrained, the best outcome for society would result. In contrast, when individuals are directed to do something ostensibly in the interest of society, a suboptimal outcome is achieved for the economy and society. The modern history of socialism would strongly support this thesis. Yet, since the GFC, the pendulum has been swinging toward a larger state, with critics of capitalism and advocates for greater intervention in the ascendance, as I discuss in Chapter 3.

Smith saw that society benefits most when resources are employed to generate rewards for the business owner and that

---

91 Henderson, JP & Davis, JB (1991). 'Adam Smith's influence on Hegel's philosophical writings'. *Journal of the History of Economic Thought*, vol.13, no. 2, pp184-204.

92 West, EG (1990). *Adam Smith and Modern Economics*. Edward Elgar Publishing, pp26-35.

businesses will organise their affairs optimising their outcome, ultimately for the benefit of the consumer where product markets are competitive: 'by directing that industry in such a manner as its produce may be of the greatest value, he intends only his own gain, and he is in this … led by the invisible hand to promote an end which was no part of his intention'.[93] Smith, demonstrating his psychology credentials, saw no merit in the argument that an individual works harder in the best interest of society before their self-interest. When personal interests are subordinate to the public good, innovation, productivity and 'free rider' problems emerge. There is little or no motivation for risk-taking, innovation and wealth creation. This reality was captured by a highly respected advisor to the Chinese leader President Xi Jinping. Professor Zhou Qiren in advising Xi commented that during his time toiling in the countryside during the Chinese Cultural Revolution, he observed that 'the same farmer worked like two different persons on his private plot versus on collective land'.[94]

Unlike Marx, Smith saw the importance of protecting property rights and how property as a form of capital – or a potential source of capital, as Hernando de Soto powerfully argues in his book *The Mystery of Capital* – is central to a capitalist economy. He argues that poor countries are held back by a failure to release potential capital through the private ownership of land subject to over-regulation.[95] This issue is also a feature of some rich countries, such as Australia, where the

---

93 Smith, A (1776). *The Wealth of Nations*, p268.

94 *The Economist*, 'Xi Jinping's surprising new source of economic advice', 1 June 2024.

95 de Soto, H (2003). *The Mystery of Capital: Why capitalism triumphs in the west and fails everywhere else.* Basic Books.

new housing supply is constrained by an onerous regulatory and bureaucratic regime governing land release for development; ironically, Australia was a world leader in the system of Torrens title to land, a conclusive, secure and transparent public register of land ownership used in many developed countries and designed by an Australian, Sir Robert Torrens (1812 to 1884). In de Soto's words, land trapped in government ownership, subject to an inconclusive ownership registration system or privately held but constrained by regulatory systems, is 'dead capital'.

These issues over dead capital are prevalent in socialist societies, which would please Marx but not Smith. (Hernando de Soto owned two pet dogs, Marx and Engels, and named them so because 'they are German and have no respect for property'.[96])

Smith would certainly not agree with the government's extensive involvement in the affairs of the economy in the way that Marxism and its close cousin socialism would advocate. Smith argued that when the government attempts to help a business, it can often do so at the expense of other businesses and consumers. The example of the government's decision to restrict international airlines from entering or expanding in the Australian market assists only the incumbent at the cost to the consumer. 'National interest' (along with the growing use of 'national security') excuses are often offered up as justification, but this can more often reflect 'state capture' by powerful business interests that care little about the public interest and focus only on profit maximisation, generating economic rents and executive rewards (more on this later in the chapter).

96 *The Economist*, 'The economist versus the terrorist', 30 January 2003.

Education as a driver of economic growth

Smith believed in education as a key driver of economic growth. Australia's current standards in education and policies around it could perhaps contribute to explaining our recent poor productivity. Productivity is only one marker of economic growth; however, it is a startling statistic that over the decade to 2024, productivity in Australia increased by just 0.4 per cent annually, marking the lowest growth rate since the 1950s. Do Smith's views on education matter to modern-day Australia? Let's start to explore this question now, and we revisit it later in Chapter 5.

Taking the lead from Smith, the emphasis on education as a driver of economic growth was central to the arguments of the University of Chicago's Professor Gary Becker, who in the 1960s said that education directly increased the stock of 'human capital' productivity, increased earnings and economic growth.[97] Becker argued that more years spent studying would increase earning potential, all other things remaining equal. His arguments, and those of others, led to the creation of a branch of economics called 'human capital theory'.

As I discuss in Chapter 5, the education world has developed significantly. Still, the emphasis on university education has arguably gone too far, creating a sense that a university degree is essential for a better future, even though there are many critics of the quality of university education.[98] At the same time, there is much evidence that education has markedly

97 Becker, GS. 'Investment in human capital: a theoretical analysis'. *Journal of Political Economy*, vol. 70, no. 5, October 1962, pp9-49.

98 Cassidy, C, '"Nobody is blind to it": mass cheating through AI puts integrity of Australian universities at risk, academics claim'. *The Guardian*, 31 July 2024. https://www.theguardian.com/australia-news/article/2024/jul/31/universities-australia-cheating-issues-ai-chatgpt

deteriorated regarding the fundamentals. This is a key finding from the 2024 National Assessment Program on Literacy and Numeracy (NAPLAN). The NAPLAN scores paint a sobering picture of Australia's schooling system, with one in three students performing below literacy and numeracy benchmarks, and the problems are persistent.[99]

The education experience for many in Australia has become somewhat of a lottery when we compare the state of public education to that on offer in the private sector, to those who can afford that choice. Smith would be concerned about how the Australian system favours the wealthy because there is a higher per capita allocation of taxpayer funding to private schools over state schools. Consistent with the 2011 Gonski report, which highlighted the taxpayer over-funding of private schools and under-funding of public schools,[100] the Productivity Commission's 2024 report on education services revealed that private school funding increased by 15 per cent in 2021–22, compared to 7 per cent in the public system.[101] In 2023, 20 private schools with the wealthiest parents received $130 million of taxpayer funding, while public schools struggled.[102] The 2015 Programme for International Student Assessment (PISA)

---

99 Hunter, J & Parkinson, N. 'Three ways to end NAPLAN mediocrity in our schools'. *Financial Review*, 14 August 2024. https://www.afr.com/policy/economy/three-ways-to-end-naplan-mediocrity-in-our-schools-20240812-p5k1li

100 Gonski, D et al., *Review of Funding for Schooling—Final Report*, Australian Government Department of Education, 2011.

101 Productivity Commission. *A path to universal early childhood education and care: inquiry report*. Australian Government, September 2024. https://www.pc.gov.au/inquiries/completed/childhood/report

102 Cassidy, C. 'Twenty private schools with wealthiest parents received $130m total in Australian public funds in 2023'. *The Guardian*. 4 December 2024. https://www.theguardian.com/australia-news/2024/dec/04/twenty-private-schools-with-wealthiest-parents-received-130m-total-in-australian-public-funds-in-2023.

report which compared educational outcomes across OECD countries, stated that social segregation was felt acutely in the school system with an ever-widening gap between advantaged and disadvantaged children in Australia.[103] The education system plays an important role in reinforcing stigma, discrimination and social inequality, with the victims being those from poorer and disadvantaged socioeconomic backgrounds. The economic cost of this alone is substantial, as the distinguished international economist and Columbia University Professor Jeffrey Sachs emphasised when he said that the sustainable success of economies everywhere will be heavily correlated to the quality of education, and that these costs go well beyond economic measures but to the health of society.[104]

Early decisions between public and private education can be life-defining, as Princeton University Professors Anne Case and Sir Angus Deaton highlight in their book *Deaths of Despair and the Future of Capitalism*, which I discuss in more detail in Chapter 5. The 2024 NAPLAN tests highlighted a concerning but not surprising gap between the results of Australia's wealthier private and state-controlled public schools.[105] Children from high-income families were over-represented in the highest-performing groups, while those from poor families were predominant in the lowest-performing quartile.[106] This is an important theme discussed in Chapters 5 and 6.

---

103 Hare, J. 'NAPLAN is a measure of wealth, not student ability'. *Financial Review*, 14 August 2024. https://www.afr.com/work-and-careers/education/naplan-is-a-measure-of-wealth-not-student-ability-20240813-p5k206

104 Sachs, JD. *Education Above All*. 17 September 2023. https://www.jeffsachs.org/recorded-lectures/education-above-all-talk.

105 Hare, J (2024).

106 Hare, J. 'One in three pupils fails to meet baseline literacy, numeracy'. *Financial Review*. 14 August 2024. https://www.afr.com/work-and-careers/education/one-in-three-pupils-fails-to-meet-baseline-literacy-numeracy-20240811-p5k1hv

Father of behavioural economics

Behavioural economics has been an important topic in understanding how people make decisions and what satisfies their needs. It has become an important branch of economics which crosses over into psychology.

The psychologist Daniel Kahneman has been given much credit – and the 2002 Nobel Prize in Economic Sciences – for 'integrating insights from psychological research into economic science, especially concerning human judgement and decision-making under uncertainty'.[107] Kahneman demonstrated that the psychology of judgement and decision-making was more a case of systematic biases than rational thinking in the face of risk and uncertainty. People prefer their sources of information to be highly correlated and consistent. With fellow psychologist Amos Tversky, Kahneman developed 'prospect theory', which argued that an individual's well-being responds to *changes* in wealth more than levels. In pursuing gains, people are risk averse, preferring the certainty of a $100 win over a 50 per cent chance of winning $500. This theory, which Kahneman outlined in his bestselling book *Thinking, Fast and Slow* (2012), flew in the face of the theory of rational decision-making, which had become a cornerstone belief in economics (a view also criticised by Nobel laureate Joseph Stiglitz in his book *The Road to Freedom*, in which he argues 'individuals differ markedly from the way they are depicted in standard economic theory. They are less rational').[108] Kahneman's work, collaborating with Tversky, was to later

---

107 Jones, C. 'Nobel Prize-winning psychologist Daniel Kahneman dies, aged 90'. *Financial Times*, 28 March 2024. https://www.ft.com/content/c1a7f8d1-ffd3-4454-b93e-6007d4579018

108 Stiglitz, JE (2024).

influence Richard Thaler, who went on to popularise and bring to life a 'new' branch of economics – behavioural economics. Behavioural economics is the modern rebranding of economic psychology – the Venn diagram intersection, or, as Professor Russ Roberts describes it, the border between psychology and economics.[109]

Kahneman and Tversky are often credited as the 'founding fathers' of behavioural economics, yet their theory on decision-making was evident throughout the work of Adam Smith. In *The Theory of Moral Sentiments*, Smith demonstrates that people do not behave robotically but dynamically in response to circumstances, biases and incentives. In *The Wealth of Nations*, he illustrates many areas that debunk the view that people behave rationally. Smith was unquestionably the father of behavioural economics, while Kahneman, Tversky and Thaler deserve great credit for popularising an important branch of economics.

The individual and self-interest are central to a healthy society

In the previous chapter, we discussed Smith as a moral philosopher and psychologist. Smith's psychology credentials were evident in his emphasis on moral values, which was central to his worldview. He did not argue that self-interest was an endearing quality but that public spirit, care and natural justice were more important, thereby imposing guardrails around how markets should function and capitalism flourish. Highlighting Christian values of the time, Smith emphasised empathy for

109 Roberts, R (2015). *How Adam Smith Can Change Your Life: An unexpected guide to human nature and happiness.* Penguin General UK, p11.

others, or the importance of putting ourselves in another person's shoes, thereby appreciating how they see things. He saw the importance of treating people with dignity and respect, not simply as subjects ruled or resources to be hired and fired.[110] Self-control, therefore, was important to Smith as a virtue. He believed a more considered and holistic approach to how markets should function is called for, and the dignity of the individual is central to a healthy society – as important today as it was 300 years ago. A prerequisite to a well-functioning society, as also argued by David Hume in his *A Treatise of Human Nature* (1740), was the establishment of a clearly defined system of the rule of law, which protected property rights, respected and enforced contracts, and individual liberty.[111]

A central tenet of Smith's views is the power of self-interest, though he never supposed that we are all driven solely by self-interest in a material sense; people have other motives that influence behaviour. However, self-interest is a powerful motivator, which he captured brilliantly when he famously said, 'It is not from the benevolence of the butcher, the brewer, or the baker, that we expect our dinner, but from their regard of their own interest. We address ourselves, not to their humanity but to their self-love, and never talk to them of our own necessities but of their advantages.'[112] It is from these words that the metaphor of the 'invisible hand' is brought to life. (As I noted earlier, while this metaphor is widely seen as defining Smith, it was mentioned just three times in *The Wealth of Nations*, and that was near the end of his close-to-1,000-page work.)

110 Boettke, PJ (2024).
111 Hume, D (1978). *A Treatise of Human Nature*. 2nd edn. Oxford University Press.
112 Smith, A (1776). *The Wealth of Nations*, p288.

While the reference to the butcher, the brewer and the baker is a much-quoted passage, what is not quoted as frequently, if at all, is something that Smith says earlier in the same paragraph: 'In civilised society, man stands at all times in need of the co-operation and assistance of great multitudes.'[113] Here, again, the value of relationships or community is emphasised as important context for understanding the individual's motivation.

Equally, as is often done, it would be wrong to characterise Smith's views as equating self-interest with a sense of a 'rational economic man' in pursuit of utility maximisation. Rather, he sees humans as also motivated by self-love. This concept of self-love or self-interest, guided by the 'invisible hand', leads to outcomes that benefit society. Smith eloquently captured this in *The Wealth of Nations*:

> *As every individual, therefore, endeavours as much as he can both to employ his capital in the support of domestic industry, and so to direct that industry that its produce may be of the greatest value; every individual necessarily labours to render the annual revenue of the society as great as he can. He generally, indeed, neither intends to promote the public interest nor knows how much he is promoting it. By preferring the support of domestic to that foreign industry, he intends only his security; and by directing that industry in such a manner as its produce may be of the greatest value, he intends only his own gain, and he is in this, as in many other cases, led by the invisible hand to promote an end which was no part of his intention. Nor is it always the worse for society that it was no part of it.*

113 Smith, A (1759). *The Theory of Moral Sentiments*, pp86-87.

By pursuing his own interest, he frequently promotes that of the society more effectually than when he really intends to promote it.[114]

A strong proponent of promoting human endeavour, what Smith was saying is that left to their own, people in serving their interests will produce goods and services that others will buy, and that in competitive markets, demand and supply will determine the price of those goods and services. Businesspeople working this way serve the public interest even though that is never their primary intent. Their primary intent is 'self-love', or to enrich themselves, which motivates self-improvement and achieving their goals, as if guided by an invisible hand.

While his ideas champion individual liberty and are not to be confused with socialist ideas, Smith was clear in his writings that the public good, or the common good, should always trump private self-interest: 'The wise and virtuous man is at all times willing that his own private interest should be sacrificed to the public interest.'[115] Moreover, when the interests of the wealthy and poor clash, Smith's writings consistently demonstrate that he favoured the poor.[116] In his writings, Smith reveals a deep and abiding dislike for nobility, aristocracy and the leisured rich. He felt these people influenced politics in ways that betrayed the public interest. The 'butcher, the brewer and the baker' were the people he felt mattered most. Smith's impulses were emphatically egalitarian.[117]

114 Smith, A (1776). *The Wealth of Nations*, p249.
115 Norman, J (2018). *Adam Smith: Father of economics*, p183.
116 Ibid., p186.
117 Ibid.

Money, power and fame don't lead to happiness

Smith would be aghast at how self-interest has created harmful excesses in modern society and led to considerable inequality. Professor Deirdre McCloskey, in her book *The Bourgeois Virtues* (2006), highlighted just how material progress and consumerism have created a society measured by what we own and how individuals measure their worth on material possessions.

Throughout his work, Smith is clear that money, power and fame don't lead to happiness. This is something many in the modern world still do not accept. Smith captured the true meaning of human happiness when he wrote, 'Man naturally desires, not only to be loved, but to be lovely'.[118] What Smith meant in this simple, content-rich sentence differs from what we think of 'loved' and 'lovely' today. He meant we all want to be liked, trusted and respected, and have others care about us. 'Lovely' is a precondition to being 'loved', meaning we are worthy of being loved in that others see us as authentic, caring and always acting with a high level of integrity, and we care deeply about our reputation. The consequence of all this is true happiness,[119] the happiness that allows us to sleep well at night. Smith also talked about the human desire for praise and the desire to be worthy of that praise – praiseworthy – and the need to be wary of those seeking praise without being praiseworthy.

Being respected and respectable matters deeply. The value and happiness individuals derive from a good reputation are equivalent to a hard-earned property asset. This helps explain why individuals naturally tend to screen out or wish away information or events that threaten their self-image or

---

118 Roberts, R (2015), p40.
119 Ibid, p43.

reputation – cognitive dissonance behaviour. Social psychologists Carol Tavris and Elliot Aronson wrote an excellent book on how successful people justify bad decisions and poor behaviour: *Mistakes Were Made (but Not by Me)*.[120] Such people do not acknowledge their mistakes because they have persuaded themselves that they did not make them or were unaware of what was happening. Think of the CEO of a professional services firm earning $3 million per year who claims that he did not know of unethical or illegal conduct within the firm even though this was well documented in emails and flagged to him by the firm's client. Either the CEO was blatantly lying – no doubt under legal advice – or he was suffering from a classic case of cognitive dissonance.

People lacking authenticity and integrity, and who are prone to doing 'whatever it takes', may be temporarily 'loved' or 'praised' but are rarely 'lovely' or 'praiseworthy'. When they lose whatever positional power they may have had, any sense of being 'loved' is also lost. The political and business worlds are littered with examples of people whose reputations have not stood the test of time. Whatever success, financial or other, they may have achieved is not worth the cost of being seen as unethical, cheating or bullying their way through life. Success through unethical behaviour is a very shallow success, if it can ever be described in this way. Think of the financial riches of Alan Bond, Christopher Skase, Robert Maxwell, Rodney Adler and Ivan Boesky in the 1980s, and in more recent times, Elizabeth Holmes, Bernie Madoff, Prince Andrew, Jeffrey Epstein, Harvey Weinstein, Adam Neumann, Sam

120 Tavris, C & Aronson, E (2007). *Mistakes Were Made (But Not by Me):Why we justify foolish beliefs, bad decisions, and hurtful acts*. Houghton Mifflin.

Bankman-Fried and the Sackler family exposed in the brilliant Netflix series *Dopesick*. Think of the highly paid bank CEOs in Australia whose reputations were damaged by the conduct of their banks through the Hayne Royal Commission in 2018, or those who took their organisations close to the wall in late 1980s and early 1990s (such as ANZ Bank and Westpac). Think of the highly publicised criticism of former Qantas CEO Alan Joyce in 2023, or the methods employed by Lex Greensill of Greensill Capital in creating his wealth, as described in Duncan Mavin's book *The Pyramid of Lies: The prime minister, the banker and the billion pound scandal* (2022).[121] The list goes on and on.

Smith writes in *The Theory of Moral Sentiments* on happiness, 'What can be added to the happiness of the man who is in health, who is out of debt, and has a clear conscience?'[122] There's no mention of financial riches!

In *The Theory of Moral Sentiments*, Smith tells a story from *Plutarch's Parallel Lives*, various modern versions of which have been recounted many times in other books, such as *How Adam Smith Can Change Your Life* by Russ Roberts (2014). In the Australian context, the parable may be told as follows:

> *A successful Australian businessman visits a small New Zealand village near Queenstown on the South Island. The Australian businessman notices an art gallery staffed by the artist owner and his assistant. The gallery has a splendid exhibition of unique and distinctive art. The Australian compliments the gallery owner on his work*

121 Mavin, D (2022). *Pyramid of Lies: The prime minister, the banker and the billion pound scandal.* Macmillan.

122 Smith, A (1759). *The Theory of Moral Sentiments*, p78.

and asks about the gallery's opening hours as he is keen to return with his wife to buy some art. The gallery owner says the gallery is open for only three hours, three days a week. The Australian businessman asks the gallery owner how he spends the rest of his time.

'I sleep late every day, go for a long walk every morning often up Queenstown Hill, then I paint two days a week, but only for a few hours. I like to go horse riding or fishing most days. I am always home when the children return from school, and I love playing with them and helping with their homework. I try to have lunch with my wife every day, and it is great when friends join us. After family dinner, some evenings, I enjoy a stroll down to the Irish bar for a Guinness and listen to live music. It is great when my wife and I can do that together and catch up with friends. I have a very full and busy life.'

The Australian replied, 'I work for a global management consulting firm and have an MBA from a leading business school. I can help you grow this business and make you and your family very wealthy. You should spend more time painting and hire staff to man the gallery, which should be open seven days a week. You should consider opening other galleries, particularly in Australia, advertising the business more actively and building a brand. The potential here is exciting. I can help promote you in Sydney, Melbourne, Perth, Brisbane and Canberra. You would need to spend much of your time promoting your work in Australia, and we could then look at international markets. Ten years from now, this could be an amazing business we could look to sell. You could be very, very rich.'

'But then what?' asked the Kiwi gallery owner.

The Australian businessman quickly replied, 'Then you can retire and move back to this tranquil village, where you can paint, fish, ride your horse, spend time with your family and friends, enjoy the product of your success and just think about how content you will be on your evening stroll down to the Irish bar for that well-earned Guinness…'.

A version of this tale has been told many times over centuries, but the meaning and message never age. Stephen Schwarzman – the co-founder of the Blackstone Group, the world's largest alternative asset management business – tells a similar story of when he tried to convince his father to expand nationally the successful draper business he had in Frankford, Philadelphia. Armed with his Harvard MBA, the young Schwarzman became one of the world's most powerful businessmen and saw great potential for geographical expansion and the riches that would bestow. Schwarzman senior said, 'Steve, I am a very happy man. We have a nice house. We have two cars. I have enough money to send you and your brothers to college. What more do I need?'[123]

The relentless pursuit of financial success is a trap that so many fall into, only to discover that it doesn't bring happiness and can often result in much sadness, disappointment and untold stress to individuals and their families. Smith understood this trap, and it is why he emphasised that happiness is largely a product of 'being loved and being lovely'.

Yet, despite the evidence that the relationship between wealth and happiness is tenuous at best, most of us cling to the notion that the world would feel much better and many

123 Schwarzman, SA (2019). *What It Takes: Lessons in the pursuit of excellence.* Simon & Schuster, p12.

problems would disappear if we had more money.[124] The evidence, however, is that the pursuit of wealth can come at a high opportunity cost – a problem that high-achieving and ambitious business and professional people know well. That opportunity cost can involve less time for important relationships, family, friendships, health, spiritual well-being and other satisfying pursuits.

The psychologist Mihaly Csikszentmihalyi identified several reasons for the tenuous link between wealth and happiness. Two of the reasons are sociocultural: the growing disparity in wealth makes reasonably well-off people feel less successful, or as John Stuart Mill put it, 'men do not desire to be rich, but richer than other men';[125] and this feeling is exacerbated by a lack of alternative values or meaning in life. Two of the reasons are psychological: when we evaluate success, our minds reset expectations, so we are always looking to achieve more and are never fully satisfied; and as we psychologically place more emphasis on material goals, less priority or value is given to pursuing other goals necessary for a meaningful and balanced life.[126]

This is why the great English philosopher John Locke cautioned people not to mistake imaginary happiness for real happiness.[127]

The wisdom of John Locke and Adam Smith was in many ways captured in a book by Australian palliative care nurse

---

124 Csikszentmihalyi, M. 'If we are so rich, why aren't we happy?' *American Psychologist*, vol. 54, no. 10, October 1999, pp821-827.

125 Leigh, A (2024). *Battlers & Billionaires: The updated story of inequality in Australia*. Black Inc., p102.

126 Csikszentmihalyi, M (1999).

127 Locke, J (1690). 'An essay concerning human understanding'. Nidditch, PH (ed.; 1975). Oxford University Press.

Bronnie Ware titled *The Top Five Regrets of the Dying* (2011). The book lists the five most common regrets of people nearing death:

1. 'I wish I'd had the courage to live a life true to myself, not the life others expected of me.'
2. 'I wish I hadn't worked so hard.'
3. 'I wish I'd had the courage to express my feelings.'
4. 'I wish I had stayed in touch with my friends.'
5. 'I wish that I had let myself be happier.'[128]

Other studies have revealed similar regrets, and nowhere in those regrets is a wish to have had a more material life or to have been richer. Very few people die wishing they had worked harder – though hard work is an important ingredient of success in life's endeavours – or earned more and owned more property. Stephen Schwarzman's father had the right philosophy about what constitutes a fulfilled life.

This problem and trap that people fall into is in part the inability to distinguish between short-term pleasure and long-term happiness, which is pervasive throughout society. And while Smith instinctively knew this, he did not know that neuroscience explains this through the differences between two key neurotransmitters (chemicals that make the brain work – or, sometimes, not): dopamine, which works mainly in the reward neural network, and serotonin, which primarily regulates mood but in short supply can be a factor in mental health problems such as depression and anxiety. (There is controversy in the medical field as to the veracity of the serotonin theory

128 Ware, B (2012). *The Top Five Regrets of the Dying: A life transformed by the dearly departing*. Hay House.

of depression, with a highly acclaimed paper published in 2022 arguing 'that the serotonin theory of depression is not empirically substantiated'.)[129]

Excessive levels of dopamine can drive behaviours focused on short-term pleasure that is individualistic in nature, which can lead to addictions of various kinds, some ultimately very harmful. Serotonin can help adjust these behaviours and help people make choices that emphasise long-term happiness, community and team goals over destructive, largely individualistic, short-term pleasure. Imbalances in these neurotransmitters can be a factor in behaviour or thinking that, if left untreated, can be harmful long term. Depression, for example, is most often treated with a drug category known as SRRIs (selective serotonin reuptake inhibitors).

Dr Anna Lembke's book *Dopamine Nation* (2021) brilliantly explains a curse at the root of many of society's problems and the costs of a society that has drifted away from the wisdom of Adam Smith.[130] It argues that we have allowed ourselves to be captured by a fast-paced consumer culture where we are constantly in pursuit of instant gratification, stimuli and pleasure, which in turn is making us sick and weakening the fabric of society. From the promotion of compulsive overconsumption by the internet to constant texting, the bombardment of social media, fast foods, drugs, gambling, excessive shopping and a whole range of other forms of addiction may create short-term pleasure hits but cause long-term damage to individuals, friends and family and the very fabric of communities. They impact the way that we value ourselves and how we see others. Sociologists call

129 Moncrieff, J et al. 'The serotonin theory of depression: a systematic umbrella review of the evidence'. *Molecular Psychiatry*, vol. 28, July 2022, pp3243-3256.

130 Lembke, A (2021). *Dopamine Nation*. Headline Book Publishing.

this 'status anxiety'. Psychologists and psychiatrists dealing with damaging addictive behaviour understand this problem. As I discuss in Chapter 6, these phenomena seriously threaten our individual and societal well-being, which Adam Smith prophetically understood and warned against.

A greater share of the pie

Moving away from the discussion of the individual, let's uncover more reasons why Smith matters to us by considering Smith's thinking on society, business and the role of government.

Smith acknowledged that differences in education, skills, motivation and natural talents inevitably result in variation in income and wealth, and that this was a natural outcome of a market economy.

However, he expressed concern about extreme disparities in income and wealth. He saw how that could lead to social disharmony, how concentrated wealth could lead to power and the exertion of undue influence on government, and how that might undermine democracy. Smith never promoted a winner-takes-all society where inequality became the norm, as is the case today. He did not believe that inequality should be a by-product or a trade-off for a more wealthy and prosperous society.[131] He made his views clear when he wrote that everyone should be able to lead a decent life with dignity:

> *No society can surely be flourishing and happy, of which the greater part of the members are poor and miserable. It is but equity, besides, that they who feed, clothe and lodge*

---

131 Boucoyannis, D (2013). 'The equalizing hand: why Adam Smith thought the market should produce wealth without steep inequality'. *Perspectives on Politics*, vol. 11, no. 4, pp1051-1070.

> *the whole body of the people, should have such a share of the produce of their labour as to be themselves tolerably well fed, clothed and lodged.*[132]

As I discuss in Chapter 3, the story of the capitalist system over the last 40 years has been of rewards disproportionately flowing to capital or investors, then executives in the form of remuneration structures, then trickling down to employees and workers. George Orwell's words in *Animal Farm* might be an apt description of how the few have disproportionately captured rewards:

> *Comrades! You do not imagine, I hope, that we pigs are doing this in a spirit of selfishness and privilege? Many of us actually dislike milk and apples … Our sole object in taking these things is to preserve our health. Milk and apples (this has been proven by science, comrades) contain substances absolutely necessary to the well-being of a pig. We pigs are brainworkers. The whole management and organisation of this farm depend on us. Day and night we are watching over your welfare. It is for YOUR sake that we drink that milk and eat those apples.*[133]

In a Smithian world, the benefits of capitalism would be distributed more widely, with a more significant share of a firm's profits being paid in the form of wages to employees. CEOs would show great sensitivity to social expectations of how they are paid for the value they bring and the real risks that they take. Smith argued that legislation favouring higher wages for workers is 'always just and equitable'.[134] Yet, in Australia, there have been

132 Norman, J (2018). *Adam Smith: Father of economics*, p117.
133 Orwell, G (1945). *Animal Farm: A fairy story*. Secker & Warburg.
134 Smith, A (1776). *The Wealth of Nations*, p188.

high-profile cases of 'wage theft' where businesses have systematically underpaid their employees. Some of Australia's biggest employers and institutions – Qantas, BHP, NAB, the Commonwealth Bank of Australia (CBA), Woolworths, Super Retail Group and the Australian Broadcasting Corporation (ABC) – have exposed their employees to large-scale underpayments (albeit in some cases unintentionally).[135]

As discussed in Chapter 1, Smith was pragmatic enough to understand, though not necessarily agree with, the reality that the masters or employers would often have the upper hand when negotiating with the government and its agencies on employee-related matters. The demise of trade unions has only exacerbated this problem – the unionisation rate of workers in Australia is approximately 13 per cent, slightly higher than the 10 per cent rate in the US,[136] while the UK has a trade union participation rate of 24 per cent and Canada 30 per cent. The demise of trade unions is partly a function of their political agenda, which saw them increasingly drift away from their original genesis and legitimacy, with little accountability to members and much abuse of power.[137] In his book on growing inequality in Australia, Andrew Leigh points to a study highlighting that up to a third of the change in inequality during the 1980s and 1990s was due to the collapse of trade union membership.[138]

---

135 Herbert, B. 'Employees have clawed back $1 billion in stolen wages and entitlements – but there could be more out there'. *ABC News*, 4 June 2024. https://www.abc.net.au/news/2024-06-04/work-wage-theft-claims-rising-legal-aid-firms-report/103869286

136 Leigh, A (2024), p80.

137 *Financial Review*. 'CFMEU's industrial power has corrupted'. 18 July 2024. https://www.afr.com/policy/economy/cfmeu-s-industrial-power-has-corrupted-20240715-p5jtn3

138 Leigh, A (2024), p80.

At the same time, a greater share of the economic pie has flowed to capital at the expense of labour (workers), a point brilliantly argued by the economist Thomas Piketty, which I discuss in Chapter 4. With the current exciting developments in technology, particularly in AI (artificial intelligence), the situation is likely to deteriorate further for workers. An example of this is Telstra's announcement in 2024 that it would axe 2,800 employees (9 per cent of its workforce) given its push to adopt AI.[139] CBA is also exploring how AI can replace call centre staff.[140] The trend of replacing many mid- and high-level managers with technology seems irreversible, because banks have started replacing bankers with algorithms in lending decisions. And this trend will not be confined to what might be viewed as lower-level roles. The management consulting firm McKinsey & Company wrote:

> *A range of back-office functions to be automated, include financial reporting … insurance claim processing … loan approvals, and tax calculations. Computer algorithms and 'robotic process automation' can drastically reduce the time and manpower devoted to these activities.*[141]

In other words, in the future many degree-qualified, so-called knowledge workers will no longer be needed (a discussion I take up again in Chapter 5).

---

139 Lynch, J & Lam, J. 'Telstra to axe 2800 workers, or 9pc of workforce as part of $400m cost cuts'. *The Australian*, 21 May 2024.

140 Smith, P. 'CBA explores replacing local call centre staff with AI'. *Financial Review*, 17 September 2024. https://www.afr.com/technology/cba-explores-replacing-local-call-centre-staff-with-ai-20240913-p5kafb

141 Bughin, J et al. 'Skill shift: automation and the future of the workforce'. *McKinsey Global Institute*, 23 May 2018. https://www.mckinsey.com/featured-insights/future-of-work/skill-shift-automation-and-the-future-of-the-workforce

The curse of cronyism and lobbying

Adam Smith was the first to present a comprehensive picture and analysis of cronyism and why it can damage business and government. He clearly saw how skilful businesspeople can manipulate politicians. He detested what we now call 'crony capitalism' and would be mortified if proponents of this approach to business saw a kindred spirit in him.[142]

Businesses and trade unions know there can be extraordinary payoffs from the relatively small investment in lobbying the government. Those payoffs can have a higher value when political donations are part of the lobbying strategy. The economics of lobbying can be enormously enriching, even when it is done at the expense of the public interest. Think tanks make a healthy contribution to democracy, but it is worth remembering that some think tanks are no more than 'advocacy tanks' – often lobbyists in disguise rather than genuine contributors to the democratic process. And some lobbyists, as I discuss later, can be very damaging to the democratic process and to the national interest, mainly when they are acting as de facto agents for foreign government interests or powerful industry groups, which is an acute problem in the US and an emerging one in Australia.

In many ways, while the powerful business groups (and trade unions) are motivated by the invisible hand of self-interest, this is emphatically not what Smith had in mind. He would advocate for constraints or restrictions on those powerful groups so that they are less able to work against the public interest and corrupt political decisions on matters such as climate change. While Smith was not a champion of state intervention, he was

142 Norman, J (2018). *Adam Smith: Father of economics*, pp268-270.

less of a champion of state capture. When there is state capture by business groups or trade unions, consumers are forced to pay higher prices than they might otherwise have had to and to accept inferior goods and services. The close ties between the state and powerful business groups and trade unions remain a feature of modern society and are prevalent in Australia today.

Adam Smith disliked large businesses exercising political influence, often in market structures of weak competition and sometimes holding their hand out for state assistance, which Qantas, for example, is known to be highly adept at.[143] Qantas was skilled at threatening to cut its workforce if competition were allowed, and then allegedly doing so even though the government came to protect them from competition, such as denying Singapore Airlines access to the lucrative trans-Pacific route between Australia's east coast and the US.[144] Smith believed that a competitive market should suffice for almost all things, so the role of government is to create minimal facilitative conditions and then step back. He believed that commercial privileges and natural monopolies should be regulated or abolished. Market imperfections should be treated on an ad hoc basis as they arise.

The political appointments to government agencies illustrate a dimension of cronyism. A study by The Australia Institute in 2022, which claimed to be the 'largest and most comprehensive domestic study of the practice of cronyism in relation to appointments to a government agency ever conducted', in

143 Aston, J (2024). *The Chairman's Lounge: The inside story of how Qantas sold us out.* Scribner Australia, p227.

144 *Aviation Pros*, 'Australia refuses Singapore Airline access to route'. 15 June 2025. https://www.aviationpros.com/home/news/10434499/australia-refuses-singapore-airline-access-to-route

reviewing appointments to the Commonwealth Administrative Appeals Tribunal (AAT) highlighted that in the Howard and Rudd/Gillard/Rudd administrations, political appointees accounted for between 5 and 6 per cent of all appointees. By contrast, during the Abbott, Turnbull and Morrison administrations that followed, political appointees accounted for 32 per cent of all new appointments, an increase that was particularly accelerated under the Morrison administration. A governance norm for such appointments is that candidates have a legal qualification. That criterion was allowed to be relaxed, and appointees from a political background – overwhelmingly aligned to the government making the appointment – were more likely to be appointed full-time (47 per cent of all such appointments) compared to those from a non-political background (22 per cent were full-time). The report noted:

> *There was considerable variability in the qualifications and experience of political appointees [from 1996 to 2022]. While some political appointees had legal qualifications and significant legal experience, others had low education levels and no professional experience.*[145]

Smith would also almost certainly detest the ethical standards motivating the behaviour that can result in an abuse of privileges, such as the conduct of the accounting firm PwC when it allegedly sought to use confidential information provided by a government department to help its clients, many of whom were foreign, to avoid potential tax liabilities associated with a proposed change in the law, and then allegedly sought to

145 Wilkinson, D & Morison, E. *Cronyism in appointments to the AAT: An empirical analysis.* The Australia Institute, May 2022. https://australiainstitute.org.au/report/cronyism-in-appointments-to-the-aat/

cover up its conduct.[146] PwC had developed close government ties and enjoyed a share in the significant increase in taxpayer funds spent on 'Big Four' accounting (a theme I return to in Chapter 6). The data on taxpayer funds flowing to the Big Four is both eyewatering and staggering: the federal government alone paid close to $6 billion to the Big Four in the five years to 2022 – KPMG $1.9 billion, Deloitte $1.5 billion, PwC $1.4 billion and EY $1.1 billion[147] – in addition to $2 billion spent by state governments (NSW spent $504 million, Victoria $844 million and Western Australia $582 million). And this spending is understated, as the reported figures only include specific contracts costing more than $400,000.[148] In return, the Big Four have donated millions of dollars to the two major political parties, with a larger allocation to the Liberal Party.[149]

A classic example of apparent corruption associated with cronyism is the Leppington Triangle case. In 2018, the Australian government purchased a 12-hectare parcel of land adjacent to the proposed Western Sydney Airport. Independent valuers assessed the land worth $3 million, but the government agreed to pay the landowners – Tony and Ron Perich, who were

---

146 Kruger, C. 'Senate committee lashes PwC over tax scandal, alleges cover-up'. *Sydney Morning Herald*, 27 March 2024. https://www.smh.com.au/business/the-economy/senate-committee-lashes-pwc-over-tax-scandal-alleges-cover-up-20240321-p5feah.html

147 Harcourt, T, '"Royal Commission": KPMG whistleblower isn't holding back'. *The Australian*, 4 July 2023.

148 Ferguson, A. 'How the big four accounting firms infiltrated governments, earning more than $10b over a decade while taxpayers are in the dark'. *ABC News*, 17 July 2023. https://www.abc.net.au/news/2023-07-17/pwc-ey-kpmg-deloitte-government-10-billion/102602370

149 Beresford, Q (2023). *Rogue Corporations: Inside Australia's biggest business scandals*. NewSouth, p362.

big donors to the Liberal and National Parties[150] – $30 million without justification or public accountability.[151]

The much-publicised case of former NSW Premier Gladys Berejiklian is another example of a senior politician who was found guilty of 'serious corrupt conduct' between 2016 and 2018 when she participated in the award of multimillion-dollar grants to two marginal projects in the then Wagga Wagga electorate of the Liberal MP Daryl Maguire, without disclosing that the pair were in a close personal relationship, which continued until late 2020.[152] This corrupting influence extended to jurisprudence and interferences or biases in the interpretation and execution of the law. There are numerous examples of crimes committed by the privileged, including their offspring, resulting in lesser or no punishment than those administered to the less privileged.[153]

Cronyism is also prevalent in the dealings between government and trade unions. There are numerous examples of this in modern Australia, such as when the Albanese government scrapped the Australian Building and Construction Commission, which investigated the conduct of the CFMEU. Since the scrapping of the commission, no further action has been taken against the powerful trade union despite mounting

150 Middleton, K. 'Buying the Leppington Triangle'. *The Saturday Paper*, 7 August 2021. https://www.thesaturdaypaper.com.au/news/politics/2021/08/07/buying-the-leppington-triangle/162825840012230

151 Murray, CK & Frijters, P (2022). *Rigged: How networks of powerful mates rip off everyday Australians*. Allen & Unwin, p21.

152 Whitbourn, M. 'Gladys Berejiklian defends her leadership after losing ICAC court challenge'. *The Sydney Morning Herald*, 26 July 2024. https://www.smh.com.au/national/nsw/gladys-berejiklian-loses-icac-court-challenge-20240311-p5fbfl.html

153 Cohen, A. 'How the Supreme Court favors the rich and powerful'. *Time*, 3 March 2020. https://time.com/5793956/supreme-court-loves-rich/

evidence of corruption and alleged criminal activity.[154] The CFMEU is the biggest single donor to the Australian Labor Party (ALP), making a $4.3m donation ahead of the 2022 general election.[155] Nothing is necessarily illegal or corrupt about these developments, but in the words of former attorney-general George Brandis, corruption has an insidious cousin called cronyism.[156]

Although Smith largely saw value in trade unions, he would be appalled at some of their well-publicised scandals and antisocial behaviour, including the nature of some of the lobbying tactics many trade unions employ today. The tragedy is that the conduct of some high-profile unions – such as the CFMEU, the Australian Workers Union (AWU), the Transport Workers Union (TWU) and the Health Services Union (HSU), which have variously been subject to allegations of fraud, misuse of members funds and unlawful donations to the Labor Party[157] – has raised public concerns about trade union oversight and governance and has come at a cost to workers who see membership of a trade union as less attractive than it once was, which is no doubt a factor in explaining why real wages have declined over the past decade.

---

154 Remeikis, A & Kolovos, B. 'Alleged crime links and the CFMEU: what to know about the political furore over the construction union'. *The Guardian*, 20 July 2024. https://www.theguardian.com/australia-news/article/2024/jul/20/alleged-links-and-the-cfmeu-what-to-know-about-the-political-furore-over-the-construction-union

155 Source: Australian Electoral Commission

156 Brandis, G. 'It's not corruption, but the Albanese government is guilty of cronyism'. *The Sydney Morning Herald*. 6 May 2024. https://www.smh.com.au/politics/federal/it-s-not-corruption-but-the-albanese-government-is-guilty-of-cronyism-20240505-p5foyn.html

157 *SBS News*, 'Five unions named in royal commission', 10 February 2014. https://www.sbs.com.au/news/article/five-unions-named-in-royal-commission/4612ffo3o

The problems with the market

I dedicate much discussion in this book to what Smith argued were problems with the market, which in turn cause social problems more widely. The fact that many of these problems still exist or have been amplified in modern Australia is one of the reasons why Smith still matters to us. I explore some of these further in the remainder of this chapter and later in the book.

Smith was critical of the 'rentier' outcomes of the privileged and powerful few and how this distorts economic outcomes and social equity. Economic rents differ from what we normally associate with 'rent'. A business earns an economic rent when it generates profits greater than its risk-adjusted cost of capital. Businesses are 'rent-seeking' when they use their market power to increase profits. In competitive markets, it should be difficult for a business to earn more than its risk-adjusted cost of capital. Sadly, this is not the case today, as I discuss later in Chapter 3, where I also show how the explosion in executive salaries can be viewed as a sharing of economic rents between executives and shareholders rather than as a reflection of effort.

One obvious place to start the analysis of the problem of markets dominated by 'rent-seeking' firms is to look at how weak competitive forces in key industries allow incumbent firms to achieve high profits and high economic rents. Where a business is earning economic rents, this is normally associated with market power (such as Qantas, the Big Four banks, the major food retailers and the energy companies) or other privileges granted to that business and protected by the government.

In his 2023 Bannerman Competition Lecture and his book *Let's Tax Carbon* (2024), Professor Ross Garnaut AC highlighted how big a problem rent extraction is in many critical industries, which are characterised by weak competition, high profits and a declining share of wages. He points to a 'large increase in the rent component of total income' and the evidence of 'much scope for oligopolistic pricing'. Garnaut summed up the evidence when he added, 'In Australia, a high and increasing proportion of incomes has emanated from rent-heavy sectors'.[158] The banking sector's conduct clearly illustrated this when it seemed to move in a coordinated manner in cutting deposit rates without any signalling of rate cuts from the Reserve Bank of Australia (RBA). A headline in *The Sydney Morning Herald*, 'Banks make sneaky cash grab as deposit rates trimmed',[159] captured the behaviour nicely, as did an ABC headline reporting that CBA was considering charging its customers $3 each time they accessed their own cash.[160] A thematically similar headline in *The Australian* captured many people's frustration with the conduct of the powerful major banks: 'Big banks' abysmal record on rate cuts in focus'.[161]

As a general principle, Smith was very wary of government policies, no matter how well intended, that would distort the effective functioning of markets. There were exceptions to

---

158 Garnaut, R (2023).

159 Knight, E. 'Banks make sneaky cash grab as deposit rates trimmed', *The Sydney Morning Herald*, 20 August 2024. https://www.smh.com.au/business/banking-and-finance/banks-make-sneaky-cash-grab-as-deposit-rates-trimmed-20240820-p5k3se.html

160 Ainsworth, K. 'Commonwealth Bank unveils account changes that will charge customers $3 "withdrawal fee"'. *ABC News*, 3 December 2024. https://www.abc.net.au/news/2024-12-03/commonwealth-bank-account-changes-charge-customers-withdraw-cash/104676716

161 Moullakis, J. 'Big banks' abysmal record on rate cuts in focus'. *The Australian*, 16 February 2025. https://www.theaustralian.com.au/business/financial-services/big-banks-abysmal-record-on-passing-through-rate-cuts-in-focus-as-reserve-bank-board-meets/news-story/a613c13d2add88a750731c94b24d43db

this general principle, particularly concerning banking. Smith strongly believed in competition in banking and that banks should be regulated, given the moral hazard risk of banks behaving recklessly, believing that the taxpayer would bail them out.[162] Adam Smith understood this when he wrote in 1776:

> *Though the principles of the banking trade may appear somewhat abstruse, the practice is capable of being reduced to strict rules. To depart upon any occasion from these rules, in consequence of some flattering speculation of extraordinary gain, is almost always extremely dangerous and frequently fatal to the banking company which attempts it.*[163]

Smith understood the risks posed to society by banks and supported regulation to constrain their activities:

> *Such regulation may, no doubt, be considered as in some respect a violation of natural liberty. But those exertions of the natural liberty of a few individuals, which might endanger the security of the whole society, are, and ought to be, restrained by the laws of all governments: of the most free, as well as of the most despotical. The obligation of building party walls, in order to prevent the communication of fire, is a violation of natural liberty, exactly of the same kind with the regulations of the banking trade which are here proposed.*[164]

Smith's wisdom was conveniently ignored in the lead-up to the GFC in 2008 in favour of the private interest view, which had

162 Cassidy, J (2009). *How Markets Fail: The logic of economic calamities*. Picador.
163 Smith, A (1776). *The Wealth of Nations*, B.II, ch.2, II.2.94.
164 Ibid., B. II, ch.2, II.2.94.

become the dominant ideology in capitalist economies. This was when the ideology of the 'Chicago school', as interpreted by many, was at its peak, fuelled by the belief that the ideology was reinforced with the collapse of the USSR and the fall of the Berlin Wall. This superiority mindset was very much in line with the philosophy of Alan Greenspan (the 'Greenspan Doctrine'). Greenspan argued that the self-interest of financial institutions was enough to protect shareholder equity and that regulators had a limited role. Post the crisis, he acknowledged, 'Those of us who have looked for the self-interest of lending institutions to protect shareholder's equity, myself included, are in a state of shocked disbelief'.[165] He recognised that government and central bank policies created the conditions for the excesses of the banks, and that banks could not be trusted to self-regulate in a prudent manner.

In the UK, there was sustained political emphasis on the need for the regulator to take a light touch 'in order to retain the international competitiveness of the UK's financial system'. The regulatory report investigating the collapse of the Scottish bank HBOS quotes the then British Chancellor Gordon Brown as saying in 2005, 'There is no inspection without justification, no form filling without notification. Not just light touch but a limited touch.'[166] Brown had bought into the Greenspan Doctrine on regulation hook, line and sinker. The story of what happened to the UK banking sector during the GFC is well documented elsewhere, as are the resultant austerity costs

165 Greenspan, A (2008).

166 Bank of England Prudential Regulation Authority. *The failure of HBOS plc (HBOS): A report by the Financial Conduct Authority (FCA) and the Prudential Regulation Authority (PRA).* November 2015. https://www.bankofengland.co.uk/-/media/boe/files/prudential-regulation/publication/hbos-complete-report.pdf

that still plague that economy more than a decade later. The fact that Gordon Brown, a Labour politician with a strong social conscience and 'left'-leaning sentiment on the political economy, should espouse such a view is testimony to the strength of the laissez-faire ideology at that time and the legacy of Thatcher and Reagan influenced by the 'Chicago school'.[167] However, it was not a view that Smith would have advocated. Despite the obvious and serious problems of moral hazard – highlighted by the GFC, when taxpayers bailed out banks in many countries[168] – strong regulation of banks and banking is important to a healthy economy. Andrew Haldane, Executive Director of the Bank of England, estimated that the cumulative loss of income due to the GFC was close to US$32 trillion, or nearly one year's world GDP pre-crisis.

Smith understood the risk of speculative lending by banks, having witnessed this almost 300 years ago in the crash of the Ayr Bank in 1772 and the damage that was to follow. Smith was to observe that banking was an area in which a 'few individuals' could 'endanger the security of the whole society' through reckless conduct.[169] If only the great and the good running major economies before the GFC had remembered Adam Smith's wise counsel, we would be in a different world today.

As I highlighted in Chapter 1, Smith's emphasis on free trade was a statement on the power of internationalism and an open mind. He would be horrified at the move by many rich countries towards greater populism motivated and encouraged by nationalism and anti-trade policies, which

---

167 Healy, J (2019). *Breaking the Banks: What went wrong with Australian banking?* Impact Press.
168 Ibid.
169 Smith, A (1776). *The Wealth of Nations*, ll.ii pp94-95.

promoted populist campaigns such as Trump's 'Make America Great Again' and the Brexit slogan 'take back control'. Once the bastion of globalisation, the US under the first and second Trump administrations fervently promoted nationalism by claiming that 'Countries are taking advantage of us … They've been doing it for many, many years, and we want to end it'.[170] The criticism of China's trade policy, which I touch on in Chapter 1, is arguably legitimate. Still, Trump has little to say about how the US greatly benefited from free trade, or about the damaging influence of the US in many parts of the world as it pursued its global hegemon, often insensitive to cultures outside of Western norms.

Together with Hayek, Smith argued that the moral demands of a great society must guard against those seeking to advocate nationalism, religious fundamentalism and other characteristics of closed thinking and group identity biases.[171] It would be a profound error to roll back the frontiers of globalisation. Trade has been one of the single most significant contributors to the prosperity of developed and developing economies. Trade was a major factor in taking close to 600 million Chinese people from rural poverty to one of the fastest-growing middle-class populations on earth, and the same is now true of India. The idea of self-sufficiency is delusional, argues the respected *Financial Times* writer and author Martin Wolf.[172]

In contrast to the anti-trade policies of recent times, the importance of trade and the folly of protectionism was captured

---

170 Wolf, M. 'Martin Wolf: in defence of democratic capitalism', *Financial Times*, 20 January 2023. https://www.ft.com/content/877d1a2d-67df-46a4-a3af-8e28198b944a

171 Boettke, PJ (2024).

172 Wolf, M (2023).

in the words of arguably one of the greatest presidents of the United States, Franklin Roosevelt, who said:

> *Trade is fundamental to the prosperity of Nations, as it is of individuals. All of us earn our living by producing for some market, and all of us buy in some market most of the things we need. We do better, both as producers and consumers, when markets upon which we depend are as large and rich and various and competitive as possible. The same is true of nations.*
>
> *We have not always understood this, in the United States or in any other country. We have tried often to protect some special interest by excluding strangers' goods from the competition. In the long run, everyone has suffered.*[173]

Maintaining unproductive hands

Smith shares his concerns about society's problems, but who does he suggest we look to for answers? Is it the government? In Smith's view, what is the government's role in securing a nation's wealth and the health of its society? I offered an overview of Smith's thinking on the markets in Chapter 1, and I'll expand on this here through the lens of lessons for our modern world.

Consistent with the words famously uttered by former US president Ronald Reagan, 'The nine most terrifying words in the English language are, "I'm from the government and I'm here to help" … Government is not the solution to our

173 Roosevelt, FD, *Message to congress on the Trade Agreements Act*, 26 March 1945. https://www.presidency.ucsb.edu/documents/message-congress-the-trade-agreements-act

problem; government is the problem,'[174] throughout *The Wealth of Nations*, Smith makes it clear that he sees a limited role for the state. He was not particularly trusting of politicians, whom he saw as an 'insidious and crafty animal'.[175] Smith was suspicious of the growth in the public sector and the waste routinely associated with such a situation, which he characterised as 'unproductive hands'. He wrote:

> *Great nations are never impoverished by private, though they sometimes are by public, prodigality and misconduct. The whole or almost the whole public revenue is, in most countries, employed in maintaining unproductive hands.*[176]

Smith would have disapproved of government efforts to directly interfere with industry, as the Labor government under Prime Minister Anthony Albanese proposes by offering subsidies and incentives designed to bolster domestic manufacturing under a 'Future Made in Australia' act.[177] The fundamental belief underpinning his move is that the market can no longer be relied upon. This is not a new view; it has formed the foundation of socialist thinking forever. These views are part of a trend in many rich economies of moving away from liberal values towards a 'homeland economics' policy – a mistaken belief that it is necessary and better to mesh economic policy with notions of 'national security' (or 'national interest') and greater self-sufficiency, particularly about key supply chain dependencies. This nationalism and protectionism appeals to

---

174 Stiglitz, JE (2024), p279.
175 Boettke, PJ (2024).
176 Norman, J (2018). *Adam Smith: Father of economics*, p111.
177 Coorey, P. 'Protection is the "new competition"'. *Financial Review*, 10 April 2024. https://www.afr.com/politics/federal/protection-is-the-new-competition-20240409-p5figs

popular sentiment in many countries, even though, in the long term, they are unlikely to achieve better societal or economic outcomes. This reflects the reality that, led by the US, economic liberalism is currently in retreat across the political spectrum, but at what future costs? Even challenging matters conveniently deemed 'national security' can expose an individual to criticism tantamount to treason or being beholden to foreign interest (Chinese – never American).

Smith was very wary of government overreach into areas that are the legitimate domain of business and in how capital should be invested:

> *The statesman, who should attempt to direct private people in what manner they ought to employ their capitals, would not only load himself with most unnecessary attention but assume an authority which could safely be trusted, not only to no single person, but no council or senate whatever, and which would be nowhere so dangerous as in the hands of a man who had folly and presumption enough to fancy himself fit to exercise it.*[178]

Milton Friedman made comment, which Smith would surely agree with, that there is nothing more permanent than a temporary government program or a temporary tax. He is also on record as saying that 'if you put the federal government in charge of the Sahara Desert, in five years there'd be a shortage of sand'.[179]

As I discuss in Chapter 3, the reality is that governments have come to play much more than a limited role in the operations of the economy, largely through their weak protection of

---

178 Smith, A (1776). *The Wealth of Nations*, I, 421.
179 Friedman, M (2002), p45.

competitive markets by a willingness, for example, to endorse anti-competitive strategies, sometimes rationalised as being in the 'national interest' (or pertaining to 'national security'), but more often than not as a result of lobbying and personal relationships that can create conflicts of interest, resulting in policy outcomes that work against the public interest. The acquisition of Suncorp Bank by ANZ in 2024 was never in the Queensland public's interest, even in applying a simple 'pub test', yet it was approved by the competition authorities on appeal, having initially been rejected.

If alive today, Smith would point to the widening gap in economic performance between the US and the big five European economies – Germany, France, Italy, Spain and the UK. According to Ruchir Sharma, the chair of Rockefeller International and author of *What Went Wrong with Capitalism* (2024), the US economy has grown twice as fast as these five European-based economies since 2010. Sharma argues that the government's role can help explain why the European nations have fallen behind.[180] He argues that while governments in the OECD have generally extended their influence over capitalist economies, this has been done most markedly in the European nations mentioned, and the increasing role of government has been a factor in productivity stagnation, evident in the significant increase in public debt and the size of public spending relative to GDP – a significant contribution to growth in 'unproductive hands'. Like Australian businesses, Europeans cite regulation as a significant obstacle to starting or expanding businesses, with many examples of how the burden

180 Sharma, R. 'Capitalism is in worse shape in Europe'. *Financial Times*, 1 July 2024. https://www.ft.com/content/5d12c8ed-c184-4d15-af6d-6523f7f875c8

of regulation increases and becomes more costly as businesses grow – more on this in Chapters 6 and 7.

So, while wary of government intervention in matters the market is best placed to manage, Smith believed in government intervention designed to improve market efficiency, address market failures and promote competition.

Politicians and regulators believed Smith could be captured by what he called a 'spirit of system', which sees them captivated with abstract plans, such as significant reforms to taxes or industrial relations, or championing certain industries. While Smith acknowledged that such plans might be well intended with the aim of improving society, or parts thereof, such as the 'Voice' referendum in Australia in 2023 and the banning of social media for those under 16 years – which is idealistically a very good move, given the mental health implications of social media[181] – the problem was that the 'spirit of the system' blinded its sponsors to the practical challenges of execution in the real world. In *The Theory of Moral Sentiments*, Smith outlined his concerns:

> *The Man of System ... is apt to be very wise in his own conceit; and is often so enamoured with the supposed beauty of his own ideal plan of government, that he cannot suffer the smallest deviation from any part of it. He goes on to establish it completely, and in all its parts, without any regard either to the greater interest, or to imagine that he can arrange the different members of society with as much ease as the hand arranges the different pieces upon*

181 'Australia's under-16 ban puts social media on notice'. *Financial Times*, 25 November 2024. https://www.ft.com/content/2f2f3ef1-f18c-4778-9b2b-cc5aba8f49db

> *a chessboard. He does not consider that in the great chess-board of human society, every single piece has a principle of its own, altogether different from that which the legitimate might choose to impress upon it.*[182]

The 'Man of System' was very much in the mould of Marx and Friedrich Engels, but Smith highlights that the politics of any predetermined grand plan may not, in practice, prove workable, and therefore, politicians need to take great care in advancing such grand plans. These words highlight the age-old problem with major reforms and why governments, fearing a negative reaction from the public, tend to shy away from embarking on them. Smith also highlights the power of human nature and democracy and why grand plans, such as central planning in communist systems, rarely succeed, nor do major reforms – such as the highly unpopular poll tax undertaken by the Thatcher government in 1980s Britain, which ultimately failed and was a significant factor in Thatcher's eventual demise – rarely sustain successful outcomes. A similar example occurred when John Hewson, the former leader of the Liberal Party in Australia and an impressive and well-credential economist, misread the public mood in his handling of the introduction of a goods and services tax (GST) as a major policy initiative. Hewson ultimately lost the election to Paul Keating's Labor Party. Adam Smith argues that ideology and meaningful change can be a complex combination with a low probability of success, no matter how attractive the abstract plan is in the mind of the 'Man of System'. Hence, Smith's advice that we should be sceptical and wary of such initiatives – and, in that context, programs such as the 'Future Made in Australia' act – must be

182 Smith, A (1759). The Theory of Moral Sentiments, pp342-343.

carefully and fully debated given the high probability of failure at great cost to the taxpayer.

An example of how inept governments can be in addressing major social problems is highlighted in the US in the proliferation of illicit drugs and the shocking fatalities associated with this problem. Ever since US President Nixon launched the 'war on drugs', declaring drug abuse as 'public enemy number one' on 17 June 1971, US spending on drug prevention has grown each year. Various programs – such as the Drug Abuse Resistance Education, or DARE, in which police officers visit schools and tell children to 'just say no' to drugs – have little or no impact. In 2023, America had at least 6 million opioid addicts.[183]

The fundamental issue here, as I will discuss in Chapter 6, is not the drugs per se but the social conditions that result in people feeling marginalised by society, as described in graphic detail in the sobering book *Deaths of Despair and the Future of Capitalism* by Professors Anne Case and Angus Deaton, and in US Vice-President JD Vance's book *Hillbilly Elegy: A Memoir of a Family and Culture in Crisis*. Politicians with grand ideas for solving big problems often lose touch with the reality of community sentiment, the underlying causes of societal problems and economic realities.

When it came to over-regulation, red tape and mindless bureaucracy, Smith also saw that the complexity and obscurity of some laws could undermine the personal liberty of many to the advantage of a few. Ironically, bank regulation is an example of how powerful incumbents benefit from complex regulation, as

183 *The Economist*, 'America's fentanyl epidemic, explained in six charts', 14 March 2024. https://www.economist.com/graphic-detail/2024/03/14/americas-fentanyl-epidemic-explained-in-six-charts

it acts as a barrier to entry to aspiring competitors. Banks lobby extensively against new regulation, yet are adept at embracing and benefiting from it. With their access to sophisticated legal resources, powerful groups' influence creates an environment in which such abuses can flourish and natural justice for the less privileged is curtailed. The employment of former politicians in lobbying government and leveraging relationships and networks intended for the public good is one example Smith described as 'men who tyrannize the government', which he considered to be a form of corrupting influence for the benefit of the powerful and privileged.

Yet there is little doubt that the growth in regulation and crippling bureaucracy in both the private and public sector has come at great cost to economic growth and personal freedom. Like in other rich countries, the Australian economy has become entangled in red tape in areas like house building and innovation. Over-regulation particularly hurts small businesses. President Trump is tackling this problem in the US by creating the Department of Government Efficiency (DOGE) – the federal code in the US runs to 180,000 pages, up from 20,000 in the 1960s.[184] In 2024, the New Zealand government set up a 'ministry for regulation' to which people can report 'red-tape issues'. These moves, and others, are part of a campaign in many countries to tackle the stifling cost of regulation, the march of a 'Man of System' culture and the growth in 'unproductive hands' that built momentum after the GFC.

In the continuing debate over the competitiveness of nations, no topic engenders more reaction than that of the role

184 *The Economist*. 'The revolt against regulation'. 1 February 2025. https://www.economist.com/weeklyedition/2025-02-01

of government. Those who advocate for limited government and the promotion of 'free markets' ignore the legitimate role that government must play in shaping the context and institutional structure surrounding businesses. This is essential for innovation to flourish, and governments must intervene in the case of market failure or when customer interests are hostage to rent-seeking behaviour. There is, however, much evidence of state overreach and political ineptness in the conduct of markets, which has been a major factor in the crisis that capitalism faces today. More on this in the next chapter.

One contentious role of government is in taxation and public expenditure policy. As I discussed in Chapter 1, Adam Smith had clear principles on taxation: taxes should be fair, efficient and equitable. Applying these principles to the Australian tax system highlights how our system desperately needs repair. A report in 2024 by Prosper Australia, a think tank founded in 1890 with philosophical roots in the thinking of Adam Smith, John Stuart Mill and Henry George, highlighted just how the current tax system overtaxes, and has a heavy reliance on taxes on job creation because of earned income by individuals and businesses – from 'honest work' – and lets off relatively lightly income earned on property ownership by investors and economic rents earned in sectors of the economy such as the resources sector.[185]

A central problem with the Australian tax system is the inequity caused by negative gearing (discussed more fully in Chapter 6). One of the causes of personal income being taxed too highly is the preferential treatment given to income-derived

185 Helm, T. 'Buying better income taxes with better land taxes'. Prosper Australia, 17 February 2025. https://www.prosper.org.au/2025/02/buying-better-income-taxes-with-better-land-taxes-2/

property and other real asset investments, and the absence of any form of inheritance tax. This distortion has many economic and social implications, including failing to recognise that productivity growth is driven more by people working harder for higher disposable income than passive investments. Owners of multiple properties are given more favourable tax incentives than individuals working hard to improve their standing who pay tax on all they earn. If they are lucky enough, through hard endeavour, to earn more than $250,000 per annum, they are then taxed at 45 per cent in the dollar for every dollar earned over $190,000, which means, with Medicare levy added, that they are working for the taxman for half the working week. It is much smarter to be self-employed, focus on property investment and minimise tax liability through negative gearing.

Adam Smith would be horrified at the policy framework dictating the approach that successive Australian governments have taken to tax reform, with little political leadership appetite for risking political capital in addressing a problem (and opportunity) obvious to many. There has not been meaningful political leadership on tax reform since the 1990s and early 2000s, when Paul Keating and then Peter Costello were treasurers, demonstrating political bravery and masterful communication skills to drive through necessary reform.

The examples discussed in this chapter on why Adam Smith matters to us highlight evidence of how far we have strayed from his philosophy and wisdom. This problem is most acutely evident in how capitalism has evolved in Australia (and elsewhere), which is the subject of the next chapter.

3

This is not Adam Smith's Capitalism

Despite its remarkable strengths and undoubted superior qualities compared to alternative ideologies, such as socialism and communism, faith in capitalism has plummeted.[186] There is a palpable anger and distrust of capitalism and the role of business in society today across most, if not all, rich nations, certainly Anglo-Saxon economies.[187] While business leaders complain about regulation and other government interventions, they fail to understand that mistrust of business leaders is profound, pervasive and persistent due to their behaviour.[188]

186 Sharma, R. 'What went wrong with capitalism?'. *Financial Times*, 25 May 2024. https://www.ft.com/content/7650d057-be19-45ce-9a4e-b5ac0418d5c4

187 Hunt, V, Simpson, B and Yamada, Y. 'The case for stakeholder capitalism'. McKinsey & Company, 12 November 2020. https://www.mckinsey.com/business-functions/strategy-and-corporate-finance/our-insights/the-case-for-stakeholder-capitalism

188 Mayer, C (2024), p4.

Since the GFC, which was in many ways an inflection point, there has been a dramatic shift in the climate of opinion, with a growing sense that the capitalist ideas, which have undoubtedly spurred economic growth and created so much prosperity, are under siege and have become discredited. When the banks got in trouble during the GFC, the taxpayers came to bail them out, and the individual wealth of most bankers was largely unaffected by the consequences of the trauma inflicted on the economy. This is a classic illustration of the moral hazard problem as it was a case of socialism for bankers – including in Australia – and austerity for everyone else, particularly the less well-off in countries like Britain and the US.[189]

The GFC was, in so many ways, compelling evidence of how capitalism had lost touch with Adam Smith and particularly his warnings on banks, and was corrupted by what was the financialisation of capitalism: the value of the global financial system (debt and equity) grew from a ratio of 1:1 with global GDP in 1990 to over 6:1 by 2006.[190] In 2022, that ratio was down to 4:1.

Rod Sims, the chairman of the Australian Competition and Consumer Commission (ACCC) summed up the reputation problem facing businesses today: 'Too many firms mislead their customers or treat them unconscionably, and the incentives that encourage bad behaviour often outweigh incentives to put the customer first.'[191]

189 Healy, J (2019).
190 Ibid.
191 O'Dowd, C. 'ACCC takes aim at bonuses, short-term targets', *The Australian*, 14 July 2018. https://www.theaustralian.com.au/business/accc-takes-aim-at-bonuses-shortterm-targets/news-story/1d1358ab3c35d71ee5af077b340509e4?amp

This has led to a breakdown of trust. There are numerous reasons for this breakdown, which can be traced back to the debate in the late 20th century that centred on a 'battle' between two apparently conflicting ideas on the role of business: the stakeholder idea, which argues that firms are responsible for a wide range of stakeholders, and the shareholder idea, which argues that the firm has a primary responsibility to its shareholders. The concept of 'shareholder value', which has dominated the business landscape since the 1970s, if not earlier, has been largely discredited in the minds of many, though the reality is that it remains today the 'invisible hand' in the motivation of most businesses, certainly those listed on a public market. This dichotomy has been the source of much of the loss of confidence and trust that many in society have for the business community.

How and why has this unsatisfactory and unsustainable situation been allowed to develop?

A social responsibility of business to increase profits

To answer this question, it is helpful to go back to 13 September 1970, when the controversial free-market economist Milton Friedman asked and answered a fundamental question: what is the role of business in society? Friedman was clear in his answer that the only social responsibility of business was to increase profits:

> *In a free-enterprise, private property system, there is one and only one social responsibility of business—to use its resources and engage in activities designed to increase its profits, so long as it stays within the rules of the game,*

> *which is to say, engages in open and free competition without deception or fraud and conforms to the basic rules of society, both those embodied in law and those embodied in ethical custom.*[192]

Particularly since the GFC, this philosophy, which had become known as the 'Friedman Doctrine', has been the subject of criticism and attack – see, for example, Joseph Stiglitz's book *The Road to Freedom* (2024) – with many ardent supporters of Friedman's view long since abandoning their support, at least publicly. It would take a very brave CEO, business commentator, academic or politician to stand up in defence of this perceived narrow and highly controversial view on the purpose of business. But let me have a go!

Friedman and Smith had much in common, including their scepticism of the role of the 'merchant class' or businesses seeking to manipulate the government to gain privileges at the cost of society. The emphasis I give to Friedman here is, in many ways, an attempt to bring Smith's work to life in more modern times through the lens of a great economist while noting some fundamental philosophical differences in how Smith and Friedman saw the world. The Friedman Doctrine is viewed by many as the foundation of the shareholder-value emphasis of capitalism and 'unfettered markets' – which Friedman critics often describe as markets without rules and regulations.[193] Smith would not have agreed with this emphasis, and the contrast and understanding of what Friedman meant in his famous essay on 'the purpose of business' provides

---

192 Friedman, M (1962). Capitalism and Freedom. University of Chicago Press, p133.
193 Stiglitz, JE (2024), p10.

essential insights into how views can be bastardised and turned into shallow slogans in a way that was never intended.

Some commentators view the emergence of the 'Chicago School of Economics' in the second part of the 20th century – influenced by the earlier thinking of Friedrich Hayek, and led by Milton Friedman and George Stigler – as superseding the works of Adam Smith. This view fails to appreciate, as Glory M Liu argues in her book *Adam Smith's America* that the 'Chicago School' produced a 'radically simplified version of Smith.'[194] In truth, Milton Friedman embraced Smith, and in his lectures at the University of Chicago, Friedman was often seen wearing a tie emblazoned with portraits of Smith, and George Stigler often donned a T-shirt that read 'Adam Smith's Best Friend.'[195]

What Friedman sought to achieve in expressing the now-contrarian Friedman Doctrine was to clarify purpose as essential to business legitimacy in a capitalist economy. But he also saw the need for important qualifications in defining the role of business, primarily that there are competitive markets, and that businesses behave ethically and legally and conform to the 'rules of the game', or the 'basic rules of society'. The 'basic rules of society' embody the laws, regulations and ethical customs of the environment in which a company operates. He was not advocating, as Stiglitz and others argue, 'unfettered capitalism.'[196] Friedman also emphasised that abiding by 'ethical customs was one of the basic rules of society' and that these rules should be a natural constraint on business owners' desire to

194 Liu, GM (2022). *Adam Smith's America: How a Scottish philosopher became an icon of American capitalism*, Princeton University Press, p4.
195 Phillips-Fein, K (2023).
196 Stiglitz, JE (2024), p10.

'make as much money as possible'.[197] The famous management guru Peter Drucker also emphasised the importance of ethics and integrity as the foundation of a healthy business.[198]

So, by the important qualifying criteria of both Friedman and Drucker, businesses should not promote misinformation on climate change or the environment; companies should not seek to avoid taxes that they are obligated to pay, nor look to use tax havens to avoid taxes; lobbying to create privileges that work against the public interest is not conforming to the 'basic rules of society'; and companies should not promote drugs that can be dangerous to the public due to their addictive powers, promote gambling knowing the damage it can do to vulnerable people and their families, insult consumers by promoting 'fake discounts', or sell products that they know are damaging to their customers. In other words, businesses should have as their purpose a goal of solving problems and creating opportunities for good, and not have as their implicit purpose a goal of creating societal problems, hurting their customers and imposing costs on the health system, for example. It is ethically and morally wrong that businesses should profit at the expense of others in this way, but in practice, so many businesses do.

It is not the fault of Friedman and his emphasis on shareholder value that many businesses engage in activities that violate the 'basic rules of society' with impunity despite dedicating volumes of pages in their annual reports to environmental, social and governance (ESG), corporate social responsibility

---

197 Friedman, M (1962), p130.

198 Hill, A. 'He's an Oxford-trained philosopher of war: CEO's can't get enough of him'. *Financial Times*. 10 July 2024. https://www.ft.com/content/f6f153b7-25c0-4e39-a760-d278a094879c

(CSR), diversity, equity and inclusion (DEI), and the importance of ethics – topics for discussion in Chapter 4.

Another problem with the interpretation of what Friedman had to say is that it has become tied to profit maximisation in the short term versus the long term – the classic 'short-termism' criticism made of many businesses. Too many businesses make suboptimal decisions, cut corners and are liberal in their interpretation of some of the 'basic rules of society' because of the impact on short-term profits. Friedman never advocated short-termism, and like Smith would be mortified that business leaders thought this a sustainable way to grow wealth and be good corporate citizens.

Ironically, contrary to Friedman's philosophy, public equity markets argue that they are long-term focused, yet company shares are actively traded daily. The market often punishes short-term blips in performance, causing many businesses to underinvest and weaken long-term prospects. Growth depends on investment, which implies allocating capital and expense to potential future revenues, which, by definition, lowers short-term results.

Basic rules of society

Perhaps the biggest problem with the critical interpretation of Friedman's edict is the weak response of governments and regulators to frame the 'basic rules of society' better and then punish those who violate those rules. It is not the job of businesses to define those rules, though they are incentivised to lobby and influence politicians, which they do. It is the job of politicians and policymakers to define those rules, and businesses must operate within them and do so ethically, not game them. In democracies, governments set the rules, not corporations. But have governments lost their way when it comes to enforcing them?

What have been the consequences for the following: the alleged shocking conduct of PwC when it was providing advice to the Federal Treasury on how to prevent global corporations from minimising their Australian tax, then allegedly sharing that information with those global corporations likely to be impacted (conduct that Smith or Friedman would not have condoned but would have seen as damaging to capitalism); the appalling conduct of some banks, allowed in part by weak regulatory intervention, as highlighted by the Hayne Royal Commission in 2018; the galling conduct of Qantas in selling seats on cancelled flights and then making it tortuous for customers to get their money back or use future flight credits; the disgraceful conduct of James Hardie Industries in the administration of asbestos claims in the late 1990s; the bewildering conduct of Crown Resorts in violating laws in China and Australia, with its competitor The Star Entertainment Group and its well-publicised cultural and legal problems; or the exploitation of its employees by 7-Eleven.[199] Then there are the price-gouging practices across several key industries highlighted in a 2024 report by Professor Allan Fels AO, which I discuss in Chapter 6,[200] and the misconduct of the giant food retailers in promoting 'fake discounts'.[201] The list in Australia alone is endless.

---

199 Beresford, Q (2023).

200 Fels, A. *Inquiry into price gouging and unfair pricing practices: final report.* Australian Council of Trade Unions, February 2024. https://pricegouginginquiry.actu.org.au/

201 Johnston, E. '"Fake discounts" a serious test of trust for Coles, Woolies'. *The Australian*. 24 September 2024. https://www.theaustralian.com.au/business/companies/supermarkets-coles-woolies-to-test-trust-with-zombie-discounts-claims/news-story/2e3eec2a49b6bc62b81cb9166ee9f154

A common problem when businesses are caught conducting their affairs in morally, ethically and sometimes legally violating ways, as was highlighted by the 2018 Royal Commission into Misconduct in the Banking, Superannuation and Financial Services Industry (otherwise known as the Hayne Royal Commission),[202] is the propensity for leaders to exhibit, as discussed earlier, the psychological phenomenon of cognitive dissonance, which is the tendency to rationalise their actions as being right all along despite the conflicting evidence and criticism from others, which can be acknowledged but rationalised in a way to downplay the issue, and a belief that a mere apology will suffice for what is rationalised as a 'misunderstanding' or 'I can't recall'. The propensity for cognitive dissonance in leaders in both the public and private sectors is commonplace, as is the self-belief that it will 'all blow over and be forgotten about'. Another speeding ticket. No big deal. It will pass on. We carry on.

The criticism of capitalism in Australia is the theme of the book, *Rogue Corporations: Inside Australia's biggest business scandals* (2023) by Quentin Beresford, which argues that the root cause of business scandals is the pursuit of shareholder value and that 'Australia has been plagued by narcissistically inclined CEOs, toothless regulators, timid governments and shockingly negligent boards'.[203] Beresford makes many excellent points, but it would be wrong to extend the wrongs to all businesses or to imply that these issues are unique to Australia. Equally, the pursuit of shareholder value is not wrong when it is done ethically. It is also wrong to point the finger of blame solely at business and not at weak government and regulatory

202 Healy, J (2019).
203 Beresford, Q (2023), p7.

policy over many decades, which allows abuse to go largely without meaningful penalty.

The government's role is to introduce penalties that create a huge disincentive for businesses to conduct their affairs in this way, and for regulators to ensure that punishment is severe. It is equally the role of government to ensure that key industries are not dominated by a few businesses that extract economic rents to the disadvantage of society. The days of businesses operating to a self-designed code of conduct should be consigned to the past, and the personal consequences of offending executives should be material, if not career-ending.

So, why does the government need harsher penalties (or for penalties to be enforced) given modern-day businesses' commitments to shared-value ESG, CSR and DEI?

Harvard Business Review summarised the dilemma neatly when citing the popular fable of the scorpion and the frog.[204] In this fable, the scorpion asks the frog for a ride on his back across the river. The frog was initially hesitant for fear of being stung to death. The scorpion, in response, argued that his interests are only served by getting to the other side safely and not drowning, so what incentive does he have to sting the frog? Halfway across the river, the scorpion stings the frog. As he dies, the frog asks why he was stung, and the scorpion replies, 'It's in my nature; I couldn't help myself'. Is capitalism and its distorted interpretation of the Friedman Doctrine on shareholder value, and Smith's emphasis on the 'invisible hand', the scorpion? Some evidence that embedded behaviours, criticised and rejected in the past, can resurface, assisted by

---

204 LaPierre, S. 'Does capitalism need reform – or revolution? *Harvard Business Review*, March–April 2024. https://hbr.org/2024/03/does-capitalism-need-reform-or-revolution

cognitive dissonance that 'this time is different' when profits are under pressure, was evident in the decision by the CBA to step back from the recommendation in the Hayne Royal Commission to place a cap on mortgage volume bonuses,[205, 206] or the case of Crown Resorts and its countless breaches of anti-money-laundering laws despite historical commitments to address weaknesses in its controls and its culture. As Justice Lee, sitting in the Federal Court, noted, 'Contrition means more than saying sorry when you get caught. It means a state of mind of people who have done wrong to play with a straight bat in the future.'[207]

Shareholder value is important in a market economy and should be celebrated. The problem lies not with the idea but with weak laws, regulations, corporate governance and ethical and moral values that have allowed abuses and sometimes eye-watering scandals. In a contemporary sense, the ongoing lip service from some businesses to environmental issues and concerns is one example of businesses not being in step with society. The prominence of profit growth taking precedence over all other considerations highlights how out of step things have become with Adam Smith's philosophy and why he distinguished between 'capitalism' and 'capitalists'. At the heart

205 Duran, P. 'ASIC "disappointed" as CBA scraps bonus caps for home loan bankers'. *The Australian*, 29 April 2024. https://www.theaustralian.com.au/business/financial-services/asic-disappointed-as-cba-scraps-bonus-caps-for-home-loan-bankers/news-story/400bc0a73122333f38f69758e228ca68

206 'CBA ignored ASIC on scrapping banker bonus cap.' *The Australian*, 8 July 2024. https://www.theaustralian.com.au/business/financial-services/cba-ignored-asic-after-regulator-raised-the-scrapping-of-banker-bonus-cap-with-board-and-ceo/news-story/13352aec5323411777b78eba1e8f704e

207 Bolza, M. '"More than saying sorry when you get caught": judge questions Crown's contrition'. *The Sydney Morning Herald*, 10 July 2023. https://www.smh.com.au/business/companies/more-than-saying-sorry-when-you-get-caught-judge-questions-crown-s-contrition-20230710-p5dn6x.html

of this are two important factors: weak forms of corporate governance, which I return to in the next chapter, and capture by powerful industry groups of the political policy agenda at both federal and state levels, which did not serve the broader public interest well.

The curse of the industry lobby groups

As mentioned in the previous chapter, Smith was sceptical about how industry groups work against the public interest. In *The Wealth of Nations*, he wrote:

> *People of the same trade seldom meet together, even for merriment and diversion, but the conversation ends in a conspiracy against the publick, or in some contrivance to raise prices. It is impossible indeed to prevent such meetings, by any law which either could be executed, or would be consistent with liberty and justice. But though the law cannot hinder people of the same trade from sometimes assembling together, it ought to do nothing to facilitate such assemblies; much less render them necessary.*[208]

There are numerous modern-day examples, from banking industry lobby group the Australian Banking Association (ABA) to the gaming industry, of those who use their power to influence government policy, often at the cost of society. An example of this practice was the success of the gambling industry in avoiding the government's ban on gambling advertisements across television, radio, newspapers and online media channels in 2024. Various community groups were

208 Smith, A (1776). *The Wealth of Nations*, B.I, ch.10, I.10.82.

pushing the government to impose a ban given the severe problem of gambling in Australian society, which attracts young, impressionable people to gambling given its close association with sport. Australia's gambling advertising has tripled over a decade, and this growth mirrors the damage to individuals, families and communities from gambling. Critics of gambling advertising include former prime ministers John Howard and Malcolm Turnbull, who, in a public declaration of protest, pointed out that Australians lose $25 billion per annum, which results in 'escalating devasting social harm including financial loss, health and mental issues, partner violence, family break-up and suicide'. The criticism also called out, 'There is strong evidence that gambling companies are now grooming our kids by targeting children as young as 14 through social media. Our children are also being targeted by a tsunami of gambling ads that assault our screens, especially around coverage of our major sporting codes. It is ensnaring a whole new generation of gamblers'.[209] The development of new digital apps and techniques based on neuroscience marketing will only further fuel a ruinous addiction. The business model of the gambling industry is based mainly on human suffering – and this has been normalised.

To date, the lobbyists for the gambling industry have won out due to weak government.

The scandals surrounding Qantas, PwC, the gambling industry and others highlight what independent senator David Pocock described as a need for greater scrutiny of the transparency of the influence of lobbying. He pointed out, 'This is part

---

209 'Call to ban gambling ads: open letter to the prime minister & opposition'. Alliance for Gambling Reform. https://www.agr.org.au/open-letter-to-the-prime-minister-oppo

of a much broader conversation in Australia about just how ridiculously loose our laws are regarding transparency and lobbying … This system facilitates this cosy relationship between politicians who are meant to make the rules for industry, and industry, who don't want those rules made'.[210] The independent MP Dr Monique Ryan highlighted 'the insidious nature of lobbying' using VIP airport lounge memberships handed out to politicians and the fact that there almost 2,000 lobbyists in Parliament House on every sitting day – ten for every member of the house and the Senate.[211]

Closely aligned to lobby groups exerting undue influence is the role of former politicians using their privileged position as politicians for personal gain. There was an Australian flavour to one of the biggest political lobbying scandals in Britain in modern times when former prime minister David Cameron (now Lord Cameron) used his Westminster network to advance the cause of scandal-marred finance company Greensill Capital, headed by Queenslander Lex Greensill, who had also allegedly commissioned the services of former Foreign Secretary Julie Bishop to do the same in the corridors of Canberra. (Bishop denies she was lobbying for Greensill, despite being appointed Chairwoman of Greensill Asia Pacific and receiving US$600,000 a year in fees through her consultancy practice while acting for

---

210 Gould, C. 'Prime Minister Anthony Albanese denies ever calling Alan Joyce for Qantas upgrades'. *ABC News*, 30 October 2024. https://www.abc.net.au/news/2024-10-30/anthony-albanese-denies-calling-joyce-qantas-upgrades/104539966

211 Ryan, M. 'A lounge membership is a valuable gift. Airlines don't offer them to MPs for no reason'. *The Guardian*, 5 November 2024. https://www.theguardian.com/commentisfree/2024/nov/05/a-lounge-membership-is-a-valuable-gift-airlines-dont-offer-them-to-mps-for-no-reason

Greensill.)[212] These former politicians' lack of business savvy was exposed with the collapse of Greensill Capital.

Milton Friedman on lobbying

Milton Friedman's main motivation in emphasising the profit motive as the 'only one social responsibility for business' was concern over how many business leaders were increasingly becoming entangled in the political process and distracted by the idea of influencing the political process to their advantage, such as by restricting competition. Principal–agent problems arise when one party, the principal or owner, delegates decision-making authority to another party, the agent or manager, but cannot fully monitor the agent's actions. Such problems flourish if executives feel that their status as a business leader gives them a licence to focus on activities that are not relevant or legitimate to the business they are responsible for. Towards the end of his life in 2006, Friedman was clear on his concern about businesses seeking to curry favour with politicians: 'It's always been true that business is not a friend of a free market … It's in the self-interest of the business community to get government on its side … businessmen are the chief enemies and greatest threat to the preservation of free enterprise.'[213] As Smith did, Friedman understood that businessmen were incentivised to engage in anticompetitive behaviour if left unchecked. Being aligned with the government was one of the best ways of achieving this. We saw this vividly in how the so-called

212 Butler, B. 'Attorney general's department asks Julie Bishop to clarify role at collapsed Greensill Capital'. *The Guardian*, 11 June 2021. https://www.theguardian.com/australia-news/2021/jun/11/attorney-generals-department-asks-julie-bishop-to-clarify-role-at-collapsed-greensill-capital

213 Roberts, R. 'An interview with Milton Friedman'. EconLib, 4 September 2006. https://www.econlib.org/library/columns/y2006/Friedmantranscript.html.

'tech bros' (the billionaires who control the technology industry in the US) and Wall Street CEOs – including many who were trenchantly critical of Trump during his first term – lined up to kiss the presidential ring in the lead-up to his inauguration in 2025. The existence of monopolies and other concentrated industry structures is dependent on political support. By narrowing their focus on (ethically and legally) creating profits, Friedman believed that this would constrain their other ambitions, and decision-making would not be dominated by political motives and influence or by social objectives unaligned to the legitimate purpose of the business. Friedman, like Smith, saw this as dangerous and damaging.[214]

Part of the danger in Friedman's words was that a generation of businesses narrowly interpreted them to mean that they were now justified in relentlessly pursuing profits regardless of the social costs,[215] just in the same way that many distil Smith's contribution to economics as that of the 'invisible hand'. Businesses mastered the craft of promoting public interest and social responsibility to mask their anticompetitive strategies operating through the state.[216] Friedman summed up the problem well when he said, 'Monopoly flourishes most when it can get positive support of the government in enforcing restrictive agreements'. Businesses can rig the regulatory game under the guise of social responsibility to defend monopoly power.[217] A similar view was presented by the great free-market

214 Chan Smith, D. 'How Milton Friedman read his Adam Smith: the neoliberal suspicion of business and the critique of corporate social responsibility'. 31 August 2020. https://ssrn.com/abstratcs=3674604

215 Ibid., p3.

216 Ibid., p12.

217 Ibid, p19.

economist Friedrich Hayek, who argued at a Mont Pelerin Society gathering in 1947 that 'many pretending defenders of free enterprise are defenders of privileges and advocates of government activity in their favour'.[218] Friedman was consistent, however, in saying that social responsibility strategies were valid if they aligned with the business's interests.

Despite its many blemishes, shareholder value remains one of the most influential ideas in business. It represents a philosophy understood and practised by the best-managed firms in the world. This is despite the public support for stakeholder capitalism echoed in most major economies yet lacking precision and clarity of purpose. The powerful Business Roundtable, a 200-strong group of chief executives at some of the US's biggest companies, declared publicly in 2019 their commitment to stakeholder capitalism. Yet, like the proverbial scorpion, it is difficult for them to help themselves from driving towards great year-on-year profitability.

Professors Paul Collier and Sir John Kay articulated a more accurate framing of Friedman's views when they argued that 'the responsibility of those who direct companies is to build great businesses'.[219] A great business must meet a wider set of criteria, including profitability, sustainability and good corporate citizenship.

218 Ibid, p16.
219 Collier, P & Kay, J. 'Letter: Friedman set a standard for judging management', *Financial Times*. 15 December 2020. https://www.ft.com/content/82a08a9c-0a14-4ea4-b66f-88ab6d19dee9

The powerful CEO

Long before Harvard's Michael Jensen discussed the principal–agent problem inherent in public company models,[220] Adam Smith highlighted the risks of directors' and managers' priorities not aligning with those of business owners. This risk is amplified in the era of powerful CEOs, evident in the salaries (and economic rents) they can extract from their boards.

The fact that a market economy has led to inequality is indisputable, a reality that no one would argue against. The real issue is the degree or scale of inequality. This is starkly evident in the wages paid to chief executives relative to the average wage to workers in the same firm. The gap in this measure has been a major failure in the form of capitalism that Smith had in mind. In 2024, a CEO in an ASX 300 company is on a median wage of $2.7 million per annum (including variable incentives), up to 55 times what the average worker earns. In the 1990s, the figure was 17 times the average earnings.[221] In the US, CEO remuneration rose from 30 times the median worker in the 1990s to 400 times by 2023, when stock options are included.[222]

In many cases, CEOs hold a very small exposure to the equity of the business on the ASX, and only in a very few cases have they invested their own money (following the example of former ANZ Bank CEO John McFarlane, who, during his stewardship of the bank between 1997 and 2007, invested all

220 Phan PH & Jensen, MC (2002). 'A theory of the firm: governance, residual claims, and organizational forms'. *Administrative Science Quarterly*, vol. 47, no. 2, p387.

221 Nicholas, J & Barrett, J, 'Interactive: pick an Australian CEO and compare their salary with a childcare worker, nurse or teacher'. *The Guardian*, 3 September 2024. https://www.theguardian.com/australia-news/datablog/article/2024/aug/31/australian-executives-pay-jumped-in-the-last-year-so-did-the-gulf-between-ceos-and-the-average-worker

222 Sharma, R (2024). *What Went Wrong with Capitalism*. Simon & Schuster, p226.

his salary in the banks' equity (except for $46 to pay for his membership of the bank's social club). (When I was CEO of Judo Bank, a bank I co-founded, I reinvested my gross salary back into the equity of the company once it had become listed on the ASX, and at the time of my departure from the company in early 2024, I held approximately 3.5 per cent of the company's equity – at that time, a top ten shareholder.)

Many business leaders have strong and distinctive personalities. Their effectiveness is often based on unusual self-confidence, drive and resilience. However, there is a growing risk that, over time, the very attributes that have been the foundation of their achievements can turn into destructive tendencies.[223]

The corporate landscape in Australia is littered with such examples; you don't have to try hard to think of examples of CEOs who have become confident of their own invincibility and addicted to the trappings of power and status. At the extreme, that can demonstrate damaging narcissistic behaviours – a highly inflated sense of self-importance, a constant need for attention and admiration, and a lack of empathy towards others. Over-powerful chairs or CEOs can become destructive to businesses, hence the importance of a strong board. This is a theme that I discuss in the case of Qantas in the next chapter, which is not a unique illustration of a deeply ingrained flaw with our corporate governance model.

The corrosive effects of power on the behaviour of the powerful are well documented in political history but less discussed in the business world. Allowing too much power

223 MWM Consulting. *Taming Narcissus: Managing behavioural risk in top business leaders.*

in the hands of individuals invites outcomes that could be terminally damaging to businesses. There are plenty of warning signs, such as the gradual hollowing out of management talent that may be seen as a threat and replacement by sycophant followers, many of whom have been loyal in the past;[224] an ego that subconsciously emphasises the 'I' and not the 'we'; and the constant self-promotion in pursuit of a 'rock star' profile, to name a few characteristics of narcissistic behaviour.

The risks associated with too much power are exacerbated by the environment in which CEOs can find themselves. Powers of internal and external patronage are greatly extended – not only to people but also in relation to ideas. Aggressive merger and acquisition (M&A) strategies might be pursued, often lacking economic and strategic logic. The likely effect of this on the ego can be toxic. A run of success, perhaps down to luck in the timing of market conditions, can cause a CEO to fall victim to the delusions of grandeur nourished by adoring media commentary. There are many examples: think of Fred Goodwin at the Royal Bank of Scotland and Jeffrey Skilling at Enron. Think also about the many Australian examples beyond Alan Joyce at Qantas, such as the well-publicised alleged scandals that embroiled the founder and CEO at Mineral Resources, Chris Ellison[225] and that which WiseTech founder and CEO Richard White faced.[226]

224 Ibid.

225 Thomson, J. 'MinRes board fails the pub test. Again'. *Financial Review*, 19 November 2024. https://www.afr.com/chanticleer/minres-board-s-handling-of-property-deal-doesn-t-pass-the-pub-test-20241118-p5krlw

226 Mason, M, McClymont, K & McKenzie, N. 'WiseTech chief executive Richard White quits amid scandal'. *Financial Review*, 24 October 2024. https://www.afr.com/technology/wisetech-chief-executive-richard-white-quits-amid-scandal-20241024-p5kl4b

It is essential to be clear that, in part, the discrediting of shareholder value is because it is associated with CEO greed, short-termism, underinvestment, corporate scandals, and business practices that are insensitive to society's concerns about, for example, climate change. Neither Smith nor Friedman would likely be sympathetic – and would most probably be very critical – of such behaviour. CEO salaries are often a share of economic rent rather than market-based compensation for effort expended. More on that in a moment.

Given the behaviour of so many businesses, there is the view that businesses are fundamentally psychopathic, run by psychopaths.[227] They are run to maximise profit and sometimes engage in exploitative and manipulative behaviour, creating products that harm their consumers. Yet, outside their professional roles, most business leaders are honest, ethical, community-minded and caring – normal people. This leads to the conclusion that the problem is with the system's values and how it causes people to develop an almost split personality, which results in behaviour and decisions in a working environment that they would not make in their personal lives.

Rentier capitalism

I earlier touched on rentier capitalism in Australia, citing the 2023 Bannerman Competition Lecture by Professor Ross Garnaut AC, and I will return to the theme in Chapter 6. Rentier capitalism was given prominence in Thomas Piketty's *Capital in the Twenty-First Century*, particularly in how it exacerbates the problem of growing inequality in society. Piketty argues that in many countries, the problem of inequality is set to

227 Mayer, C (2024), p69.

inexorably rise because of the $r>g$ formula, where g represents the rate of economic growth and r represents the rate of return on capital – or, in some cases, the rate at which economic rents can be earned from existing assets.[228] A reframing of Piketty's thesis is that uncompetitive industry sectors and privileges following the owners of capital will always allow r to exceed g $(r>g)$, so inequality continues to grow.

A broader but equally important problem is that economies marked by key industries dominated by a small number of businesses, each of which enjoys economic rents, are often subject to weak growth and poor productivity due to a lack of competition. This underlying growth problem can be masked by important sectors such as mining, and strong population growth, which Australia has enjoyed. However, as discussed in this book, Australia faces a chronic productivity problem.

In their important and well-researched book *The Myth of Capitalism: Monopolies and the death of competition* (2018), Jonathan Tepper and Denise Hearn argue that slowing growth and rising inequality have become a toxic combination. While many blame an excess of free market capitalism for this politically dangerous mix, Tepper and Hearn convincingly argue that the opposite is true. A predatory form of monopoly capitalism has emerged. The market, they argue, needs a resurgence of antitrust law, not just to protect consumers but to protect competition itself.[229] For example, this book could have been written solely on the Australian banking, food retail, telco and air travel markets, and its central thesis would remain

228 Piketty, T (2013). *Capital in the Twenty-First Century*. Belknap Press.
229 Tepper, J & Hearn, D (2018). *The Myth of Capitalism: Monopolies and the death of competition*. Wiley.

unchanged. The scale of rentier capitalism is evident in the returns on equity earned by significant banks, or the close to 20 per cent earned by the big mining companies Rio Tinto and BHP, with the giant retailers Coles and Woolworths earning returns on equity exceeding 25 per cent.[230] The two giant food retailers showed their ethical virtues when charged with promoting 'fake discounts' on hundreds of food items by the ACCC, allegedly deceptive behaviour in promoting discounts on food items when, in fact, the prices were higher than before the promotions.[231]

Capitalism ruined

The fundamental reason capitalism has a poor reputation largely centres on market abuses, cronyism, rentier capitalism, weak corporate governance, businesses that inflict more harm than good, and privileges granted to a few that are abused. The curse of privileges undermines confidence in the market economy and the nature of democracy. This is a problem in many Western economies and a serious one in Australia, according to one of the country's most respected economists, Professor Ross Garnaut AC, who argues that Australia is increasingly dominated by powerful firms that are extracting

230 Martin, P. 'The Greens want a super-profits tax. Labor and business used to like the idea too'. *ABC News/The Conversation*. 4 September 2024. https://www.abc.net.au/news/2024-09-04/labor-and-business-history-on-greens-super-profits-company-tax/104305404

231 LaFrenz, C, McIlroy, T & Mizen, R. 'Woolworths, Coles faked discounts on hundreds of products, says ACCC'. *Financial Review*. 23 September 2024. https://www.afr.com/companies/retail/accc-alleges-woolworths-coles-faked-discounts-on-everyday-goods-20240923-p5kcn9

economic rents from the economy and society, and Australians have been 'in denial' about this problem.[232]

This problem is, of course, not unique to Australia. Perhaps the most striking example of privilege in recent times, argues the respected *Financial Times* columnist Martin Wolf,[233] was the treatment of the members of the Sackler family who ran Purdue Pharma. They bear heavy responsibility for the mass prescription of opioids in the US, which was arguably the worst drug-related scandal since Britain's Opium Wars on China in the mid-19th century. The promotion of opioids by the Sacklers resulted in the deaths of hundreds of thousands of people in the US, yet the family was protected from prosecution due to their wealth – a wealth created by the drugs they sold. The Sacklers walk free while over 374,000 people are in prison for minor drug crimes in the US, the vast majority of whom are from underprivileged communities. Wealth can contaminate the political and legal systems for the privileged few, and this is not confined to the US.

German car manufacturer Volkswagen provides another example of how widespread this problem is. In 2015, Volkswagen publicly admitted that it had cheated on US emission tests to make its vehicles appear less polluting. Volkswagen used a 'defeat device' mechanism that causes a vehicle to behave differently during an emission test than on the road. The 'defeat device' component used by Volkswagen was supplied by Bosch, who was fined US$328 million in a civil settlement for its role

232 Hutchens, G. 'Australia would be raising $70 billion a year from carbon price if it wasn't dismantled, Ross Garnaut says'. *ABC News*, 17 September 2023. https://www.abc.net.au/news/2023-09-17/ross-garnaut-70-billion-from-carbon-price-economic-rent/102850464

233 Wolf, M (2023).

in this shameful behaviour that was totally devoid of integrity or ethical standards.[234]

Andrew Leigh, in his book *Battlers and Billionaires*, highlights how one of Australia's esteemed business leaders, the late Richard Pratt, was found in 2007 to have operated what the Federal Court called 'the most serious cartel case to come before the Court in the 30-plus years in which price fixing has been prohibited by statute'.[235]

As I discussed earlier in this chapter, a fundamental reason for capitalism's failings in Australia lies with poor government policy. Only the government develops the rules and an enforcement regime that causes businesses to address their character failings. Self-developed and policed 'codes of conduct' never pass the test of protecting the public interest. Never.

Smith, like Friedman, knew that unbridled capitalism was not in the interest of society or free markets. In *The Wealth of Nations*, he noted caustically:

> *The proposal of any new law or regulation which comes from [businessmen] ought always to be listened to with great precaution and ought never to be adopted till after having been long and carefully examined, not only with the most scrupulous but with the most suspicious attention. It comes from an order of men whose interest is never exactly the same with that of the public, who have generally an interest to deceive and even to oppress the public, and accordingly have upon many occasions both deceived and oppressed it.*[236]

---

234 Mayer, C (2024), p31.
235 Leigh, A (2024), p64.
236 Smith, A (1776). *The Wealth of Nations*, B.V, ch.1, V.1.45.

As a champion of the market, Smith did not see politicians as having any credibility in allocating resources in a commercial sense for societal benefit. Still, he saw politicians as essential in protecting the public from business abuse by setting 'the rules of the game' and enforcing them. The key is to strike a balance so businesses operating in competitive markets can pursue their legitimate commercial objectives. At the same time, abuse of customers through price gouging and anti-competitive practices is punished meaningfully. Giving powerful business leaders free rein would be the equivalent of putting the foxes in charge of the chicken coup.

Critics of capitalism, instead of pointing the finger at their interpretation of the Friedman Doctrine to justify their case, should look to the father or patron saint of capitalism, Adam Smith, and learn again the true spirit of capitalism – ethical capitalism. Let's look more at this in the next chapter.

4
Ethical Capitalism

Capitalism has progressively morphed in a way that Adam Smith had never intended. Modern sentiment on this is very similar to that espoused back in 1935 by former US President Teddy Roosevelt, who proclaimed, 'I believe in corporations; they are indispensable instruments of modern civilisations; but I believe that they should be supervised and so regulated that they shall act in the interests of the community as a whole.'[237]

Roosevelt alluded to the importance of 'ethical capitalism'. Ethical capitalism is a market-based economy in which ethical considerations are a factor in businesses' decisions. It is closely aligned with a stakeholder view of how businesses should operate, recognising that businesses are responsible to a wide range of stakeholders, including shareholders, that CSR is

---

237 Micklethwait, J & Wooldridge, A (2003). *The Company: A short history of a revolutionary idea.* Modern Library, p182.

important and not sacrificed at the altar of profit maximisation, and that businesses certainly do not engage in activities that damage the well-being of customers.

A true understanding of what Adam Smith stood for and how he viewed capitalism reveals that he was much more than a free-market economist; he was passionate about the well-being of the less well-off. In *The Theory of Moral Sentiments*, he placed great value on the notion of the impartial spectator, asking that people have an internal conversation on moral values: 'What would you do?'[238] There is little doubt that Smith would be appalled at the immorality and unethical nature of much of what is conducted today in the name of capitalism; examples abound despite the emphasis of businesses on ESG, DEI and CSR. An eye-opening example in 2024 was the accusation that the multinational tobacco company Philip Morris International (PMI), based on leaked internal documents, 'was manipulating science for profit' to promote its new heated tobacco product targeted at non-smokers. PMI was accused of paying researchers to influence scientific research's conduct, publication and reach, and concealing unhelpful findings.'[239]

There is no debate on the fact that capitalism has its flaws. To believe that all capitalists will behave honourably just because they are engaged in capitalism is akin to believing that all drivers of cars will drive safely just because they have a driving licence; the vast majority are safe and operate within the spirit as well as the letter of the law, but some drivers are reckless,

---

238 Smith, A (1759). *The Theory of Moral Sentiments*.

239 Lay, K. 'Tobacco giant accused of "manipulating science" to attract non-smokers'. *The Guardian*, 28 June 2024. https://www.theguardian.com/global-development/article/2024/jun/28/tobacco-giant-philip-morris-pmi-accused-manipulating-science-attract-nonsmokers-iqos-targeting-politicians-doctors-tokyo-olympics

and some cause injury and even fatalities. The challenge is to mitigate capitalism's wasteful, damaging and corrupting features through effective corporate governance and regulatory and legal deterrents, making truly competitive markets that act in the community's interests.

Ethics and profits – which comes first?

Central to Smith's philosophy was the importance of ethics. Virtually all businesses espouse their conviction in ethics – and many put their people through online and in-person ethics training courses – yet the reality is that profit-seeking behaviour can trump ethical values, even in an era when ESG is championed by every public and many non-public entities. This was brilliantly highlighted in Joe Aston's book on Qantas, *The Chairman's Lounge: The inside story of how Qantas sold us out.*[240]

Think about fast food companies, the gaming industry, the alcohol industry, the pharmaceutical industry, the natural resources industry – the list goes on. None of these industries or the businesses within them would admit that they intend to promote their products and services to harm our environment or customers. Yet, many of their practices strongly suggest that they *don't* care. They don't set out to hurt or kill customers, but they implicitly don't care if they die. Fast food, alcohol, soft drinks, gaming and pharmaceuticals harm public health and can often be the cause of premature deaths. Ironically, governments tolerate companies that profit from the costs they ultimately impose on our underfunded and under-resourced health system. Many businesses, for example, have

240 Aston, J (2024).

become skilled in neuromarketing, the study of how people's brains respond to brand-related promotions. Neuromarketing techniques are used to study the brain to predict consumer decision-making behaviour and exploit it accordingly, regardless of ethical considerations. This is very prevalent in the gambling industry and in other business sectors that thrive on the addictive behaviour of consumers. For them, profits are what matter the most.

As Dr Mark Cross writes in his book *Mental State: The insanity of Australia's mental health system – and how to fix it* (2024) on the role of business in fuelling the mental health crisis in Australia:

> *I can only imagine what we could achieve if those corporations that profit from the sale of nicotine products, alcohol, sugar drinks and processed food placed the nation's health above shareholder dividends and CEO bonuses.*[241]

Ethical dilemmas are but one reason why society has become disillusioned by big business and its power to exert influence on government policy. As I discussed earlier, powerful industry groups greatly influence many democracies, as illustrated by the gambling industry in Australia. According to the Grattan Institute, Australia's gambling industry is amongst the biggest in the world, with estimated gambling losses (spending on gambling minus the payouts) of $24 billion, or $1,635 per adult, in 2022[242] – the highest per adult losses in the world, twice the level of the US and three times the level of New Zealand,

---

241 Cross, M (2024). *Mental State: The insanity of Australia's mental health system – and how to fix it*. ABC Books, p13.

242 Sathanapally, A, Griffiths, K & Baldwin, E. *A better bet: how Australia should prevent gambling harm*. Grattan Institute, 4 September 2024. https://grattan.edu.au/report/a-better-bet-how-australia-should-prevent-gambling-harm/

with slot machines (or 'pokies') being the biggest single source of losses. The losses were greater in poorer socioeconomic communities, with residents of Fairfield in Sydney, for example, losing $3,967 a year.[243] New South Wales (NSW) is second only to Nevada – home to Las Vegas – regarding the number of 'pokies': NSW has nearly 90,000 machines, equivalent to one for every 88 people, whereas Nevada, with a population of 3.1 million, has about one machine per 120,000 people.[244]

But the issue is not confined to NSW. Australia has less than 1 per cent of the world's population and 18 per cent of the world's 'pokies'. The world's biggest poker-machine manufacturer is an Australian company called Aristocrat.[245] In 2010, a government advisory board estimated that the social costs of gambling were $4.7 billion a year and characterised 'pokies' as 'electronic cocaine'. Given that in the eight years to 2022, rates of regular gambling rose by over 50 per cent among men aged 18 to 34,[246] it is fair to assume that these 'social costs' will be significantly higher today, given the increase in advertising and marketing of the gambling industry. The burden of these 'social costs' is evident in job losses, fraud, broken relationships, family violence, self-harm through substance abuse and, ultimately, suicide rates. It is a reasonable

243 Remeikis, A. 'Call for action to address gambling harm as report finds Australians lose an average of $1,600 a year'. *The Guardian*, 5 September 2024. https://www.theguardian.com/australia-news/article/2024/sep/05/grattan-institute-gambling-harm-report-australia-ad-ban

244 Sullivan, H. 'How Australians became the world's biggest gamblers'. *The Guardian*, 8 September 2024. https://www.theguardian.com/australia-news/article/2024/sep/08/how-australians-became-the-worlds-biggest-gamblers

245 Ibid.

246 Sathanapally, A. 'It's time Australia put the guardrails on its gambling habit'. *Financial Review*, 5 September 2024. https://www.afr.com/companies/games-and-wagering/it-s-time-australia-put-the-guardrails-on-its-gambling-habit-20240902-p5k71j

assumption that the attempts to quantify 'social costs' are likely to be materially understated given the human costs of an addiction that skilfully manipulates the most vulnerable. Despite this, local governments are reluctant to tamper with current practices, as they benefit from associated taxes to the tune of at least $6 billion a year based on 2022 figures. Adding to the irony surrounding the gambling industry is that it received $90 million worth of 'research' tax credits in the financial year 2021–22 – research that may ostensibly be aimed at extracting greater revenues from vulnerable people.[247]

Despite the antisocial nature of pokies and the strong family ethos of sporting codes such as the Australian Football League (AFL) and the National Rugby League (NRL), they have become material contributors to the finances of most AFL and NRL clubs, sometimes accounting for over a third of club revenues. Both these major football codes actively lobbied the government not to introduce a gambling advertising ban in 2024.[248] The AFL enriches itself through gambling advertising revenue and receives 10 per cent of all dollars corporate bookmakers make on the game.[249] This generates an annual income of $40 million, a figure that the AFL is looking

247 Middleton, K. 'Chalmers says it's "problematic" gambling companies claimed $90m worth of research tax credits in one year'. *The Guardian*, 28 October 2024. https://www.theguardian.com/australia-news/2024/oct/28/chalmers-says-its-problematic-gambling-companies-claimed-90m-worth-of-research-tax-credits-in-one-year

248 Mizen, R. 'NRL, AFL personally lobbied Anthony Albanese against gambling ad ban'. *Financial Review*, 18 October 2024. https://www.afr.com/politics/federal/nrl-afl-personally-lobbied-anthony-albanese-against-gambling-ad-ban-20241017-p5kjaw

249 Costello, T. 'The AFL and NRL are pushing aside gambling harm to profit at their fans' expense'. *The Guardian*, 30 September 2024. https://www.theguardian.com/commentisfree/2024/sep/30/the-afl-and-nrl-are-pushing-aside-gambling-harm-to-profit-at-their-fans-expense

to increase to match the more than $50 million per annum received by the NRL.[250] The inextricable ties between the two major football codes and the gaming industry exist despite the harm caused to many in the community who are loyal to the codes. The former AFL chief executive Andrew Demetriou became a board member at the then scandal-ridden Crown Resorts and was on the record as saying in 2019, 'The values of the AFL are not dissimilar to the values of Crown'; shortly thereafter, Crown was found not suitable to hold a Sydney casino licence, and other scandals were to follow.[251]

The dangers of wokeism

In competitive markets, as Smith would have envisaged and as Milton Friedman alluded to, profits come from 'doing the right thing' by producing goods that society values. Smith's view on capitalism, 'ethical capitalism', is not what passes for capitalism today, which has prompted such societal backlash.

Business-school historians will look back on the period since the GFC as a watershed in corporate communications, with a shift in emphasis from return on equity (ROE) and shareholder value to CSR, ESG and DEI. These acronyms have become punching bags for critics who argue that they are an attempt by the political left to redefine the purpose of business, and that in complying with the reporting obligations on these topics

250 Samios, Z. '$40m not enough: The AFL'S plan to grab more gambling money'. *Financial Review*, 28 January 2025. https://www.afr.com/companies/games-and-wagering/afl-seeks-bigger-slice-of-gambler-money-in-talks-with-bookmakers-20250127-p5l7ji

251 Kehoe, J. 'How the AFL got hooked on harmful gambling'. *Financial Review*, 26 June 2024. https://www.afr.com/companies/games-and-wagering/how-the-afl-got-itself-hooked-on-harmful-gambling-20240624-p5jo3r

many businesses have engaged in 'greenwashing' – the practice of overstating ESG, CSR and DEI activities and achievements.

To criticise the degree to which businesses must conform to the expectations placed on them would expose any CEO and chair to vitriolic attack and the potential of becoming political targets. At the same time, these terms have become the favoured whipping boys of the political right, which equates them with left-wing 'woke capitalism'.[252] Corporate activists promote ESG and DEI priorities for businesses, which point to virtue signalling to protect profit margins and market power.[253]

Unsurprisingly, many business leaders feel trapped between a rock and a hard place in navigating the confusing minefield that CSR, ESG and DEI have become, which can create a sense of corporate insanity. Yet, few leaders would disagree with Professor Robert Eccles, who argues that at its core, ESG – primarily 'E' – is the fundamental question of the corporation's role in society.[254]

In a modern world in which 'wokeism' – which I mean to cover virtue signalling, political correctness, censorship and cancel culture – flourishes, people are counselled not to be judgemental and to avoid any language that could be interpreted as implying discrimination. Zealots of wokeism – 'woke warriors' – are on the lookout for offenders and victims.[255]

---

252 Tett, G. 'The stakeholder doctrine is flourishing despite attacks on ESG'. *Financial Times*. 6 September 2024. https://www.ft.com/content/cd5f86b4-9d83-43c5-8474-ed4ebc632de6

253 Burn-Murdoch, J. 'Yes, CEOs are moving left, but "woke capitalism" is not the whole story'. *Financial Times*, 18 October 2024. https://www.ft.com/content/29426c31-b8f9-49da-bc8b-e6c860935694

254 Eccles, RG. 'Moving beyond ESG'. *Harvard Business Review*, September–October 2024. https://hbr.org/2024/09/moving-beyond-esg

255 *The Economist*. 'After peak woke, what's next?', 19 September 2024. https://www.economist.com/leaders/2024/09/19/after-peak-woke-what-next

Yet, while Smith argued that being judgemental makes us who we are as human beings, as moral beings, he surely would have argued that in being judgemental, we should do no harm to others.

Despite the rhetoric, because of the loose and ever-expanding nature of ESG, there seems little doubt that the public equity markets place an unwavering weight on profits and profitability, even if that comes at a cost of climate change, which some may silently view as tomorrow's problem to which a scientific solution may emerge. It is disappointing that the importance of 'E' in ESG can be lost as a measurable focus in the confusion surrounding what ESG means, with its remit ever expanding in the eyes of some of its more fervent warriors.[256] The impact of business activities on the environment is a legitimate business concern even if it impacts profits. Businesses should be clear on how their activities create value for shareholders and how their ESG initiatives contribute. They need to be equally clear on what their business cannot do with ESG, given that some issues are outside the legitimate business domain and belong in the realm of public policy.

In achieving universal commitment to ESG principles, and primarily 'E', there is also an element of 'prisoner dilemma' in that businesses hesitate to take necessary moves for fear that others may not and that they will be disadvantaged as a result. This is evident in the more than 1,000 companies representing US$23 trillion in market capitalisation that committed to a goal of net zero emissions by 2039, at the UN COP26 climate

---

256 Trinca, H. 'Corporates stay the course on the voice as ESG debate picks up'. *The Australian*, 30 June 2023. https://www.theaustralian.com.au/commentary/larry-fink-culture-wars-and-the-trouble-with-esg/news-story/5ab5b249c1cdd6123ca9be390b197272

summit in Glasgow in 2021, and then gradually stepped back from their commitments, blaming governments for having not created the policy framework for them to meet the emissions reduction targets.[257]

Criticism of business attitude to climate commitments was voiced by former BP CEO Lord John Browne, who urged business leaders to consider Aesop's fable of the rider who stops feeding his horse in peacetime, only to find it lame when war comes. Browne argued that if we want something – the environment – to serve us longer, we must constantly take good care of it. He argued that 'the hard truth is that we've done a poor job of reconciling corporate actions with the interests of society and the planet in a balanced way. Yet the urgent need to do so is undiminished'. Browne's remarks reflect frustration that some large corporations have either dropped or missed goals to cut emissions or to reduce ties with the most polluting sectors. Many businesses are simply skipping over their promise to improve,[258] including many large Australian businesses, largely due to the pressures of delivering short-term profit growth for shareholders and the incentive rewards of senior executives. The decision by BP to 'pivot back to oil and gas after "misplaced" faith in renewable and green energy' was but one example of companies buckling to the pressure of the equity market and their CEO declaring

257 'Companies take step back from making climate target promises'. *Financial Times*, 15 March 2024. https://www.ft.com/content/3ebc5b56-a8f0-4fcd-99dd-9023d7a20013

258 'How companies are starting to back away from green targets'. *Financial Times*, 20 June 2024. https://www.ft.com/content/c9fee776-1471-442c-aae8-8d78fe60faeb

than the pivot was a strategy 'reset' to focus on boosting returns for shareholders.[259]

The Wealth of Nations was, in many ways, a book on CSR and the importance of the public interest.[260] Smith's invisible hand argued that the private search for profit advances the public interest and, thus, CSR.

Read carefully, Friedman's words also remind us that the debate on CSR is not new. He argued that the notion of CSR – as are the notions of ESG and DEI – is analytically very loose and vague and can result in businesses drifting into the domain that is legitimately the area of government, politicians and special interest groups – things that shareholders can choose to do acting in a private capacity. The CSR, DEI and ESG language has morphed into an impractical laundry list of concepts that are very difficult for businesses to digest and comply with. Still, Friedman and his acolytes must accept some blame for this. In their advocacy of the economic model free from subjective values and other societal biases, they created a vacuum into which the intellectual left has stepped, creating a tsunami of rules, policies, regulations and laws that have overwhelmed the corporate governance agenda in many businesses, crowding out more fundamental business matters, often then leading to corporate governance failures, which I explore later in this chapter.

In this context, the rise of wokeism and 'cancel culture' has added pressure to expand the legitimate business domain.

---

259 'BP pivots back to oil and gas after "misplaced" faith in green energy.' *Financial Times*, 26 February 2025. https://www.ft.com/content/8bcf131f-c820-493f-8ea6-6a35440facd3

260 *The Economist*, 'Profit and the public good', 22 January 2005. https://www.economist.com/special-report/2005/01/22/profit-and-the-public-good

This has resulted in many business leaders becoming actively vocal, using company resources to promote issues that, essential as they are, are not the natural domain of business, such as supporting the Voice and gay marriage referendums in recent times. The vagueness of social responsibility creates conflicts that can damage one stakeholder over another. For example, the board of a business heading into difficult times may decide that the right thing to do is to cut the workforce to meet short-term profit expectations. In doing so, there may be community implications, but not doing so may result in greater societal costs in the long term. How can this dilemma be solved without clarity on the primary purpose of business? But equally, a business should not pursue profitable activities if there is resulting damage to the environment, for example, regardless of whether it is legal. Equally, as Professor Colin Mayer and Professor Ross Garnaut AC separately argue, businesses should not be allowed to pursue activities that create problems and damage the interests of society.

Smith's wisdom should also be considered regarding growing societal expectations and social pressures to conform to DEI policies. This is not to argue against the importance of fairness and inclusion, but to highlight the need to be cognisant of human nature and ensure that policies are not poorly, or ideologically, defined. Smith argued, 'Every individual is naturally more attached to his particular order or society than to any other. His interest, his vanity, the interest and vanity of his friends and companions … he is zealous to defend them against the encroachment of every other order or society'.[261] What Smith is arguing is what psychologists who have studied

261 Coase, RH (1994).

epigenetics have known for a long time: that behaviours and biases are deeply ingrained by the environment we grew up in. Our brains automatically and unconsciously cause us to be attracted to some things and not to others. As it is promoted within most environments, DEI assumes that a crash course on diversity, unconscious biases or hardwired policies can allow a switch to be flicked that addresses these deeply ingrained preferences. If changing behaviour were that easy, alcohol consumption would be dramatically reduced, gym membership would be near universal and there would be no market for new diets or keep fit books. The reality is that any DEI program that fails to understand the science of neurobiology is doomed to fail, which is true of most such programs rolled out across Australia's public and private sectors and elsewhere. Adam Smith would have understood this.

Many special interest groups would have businesses participate in politically charged debates unrelated to their business's core activities. Activists who point to CSR, DEI and ESG obligations drag the business community into areas unrelated to the legitimate interests of the business. While there is sometimes a legitimate business case for companies to be vocal on specific CSR, DEI and ESG matters, too often businesses can find themselves sleepwalking into topics that only serve to politicise businesses in a way that could ultimately damage the company and its brand. Larry Fink, the head of BlackRock, called for business leaders to take more responsibility for addressing social and economic issues such as environmental challenges, gender and racial inequalities, and the growing crisis in providing pension and health care. He argued that given mounting societal frustration, disillusionment and absence of trust in governments, businesses must fill the void.[262] Fink's comments in his 2019 letter to the CEOs of the S&P 500 captured this: 'Stakeholders are pushing companies to wade into sensitive social and political issues – especially as they see that government is failing to do this effectively.'[263] Fink is highly credible, but his views on the legitimate business domain are wrong and potentially dangerous. As I discussed earlier, it is dangerous partly because ESG and DEI have become poorly defined, often confusing labels used to capture a broad range of matters, some with questionable relevance to business. This has been the curse of a woke culture and its many warriors, many of whom sit within businesses' human resources (HR) and corporate affairs departments and are a challenge to 'doing the right thing'. Some businesses have even appointed 'Chief Diversity Officers' to assist HR functions in righting the wrongs and injustices of an imperfect world.

Clarity of purpose

It is difficult for corporations and organisations to 'do the right thing' without clarity on the primary purpose of business, and as Professor Colin Mayer observed, 'Corporate purpose is much more evident in start-ups than in established firms that frequently lose sight of their fundamental reason for being.'[264]

In a 2022 survey of over 75,000 people in 28 countries, the Edelman Trust Institute looked closely at societal business expectations with clear findings. Of those surveyed, 85 per cent

262 Flood, C. 'BlackRock's Fink urges CEOs to tackle social issues', *Financial Times*, 17 January 2019. https://www.ft.com/content/4d36db4e-1a6b-11e9-9e64-d150b3105d21

263 Sorkin, AR, 'Larry Fink Asks C.E.O.s to Lead a Divided World', *The New York Times*, 17 January 2019. https://www.nytimes.com/2019/01/17/business/dealbook/larry-fink-letter-business-leaders.html

264 Mayer, C (2024), p33.

said that the primary purpose of business is to produce safe and reliable products, create jobs, create wealth, grow the economy and drive innovation. This is terrific clarity of purpose. At the same time, participants emphasised the essential societal duties of business to tackle climate change, address discrimination, support local communities and step in when government is ineffectual. In terms of stakeholders, the interests of employees and customers were prioritised. This seems like a sensible set of expectations, consistent with a shareholder and stakeholder view of the firm. However, asking businesses to step in when government is ineffective is taking matters too far. Business leaders should know that despite Larry Finks's views, taking a public position on controversial matters can result in dire consequences.

Most sensible CEOs would prefer to leave politics to politicians and stay clear of various issues, particularly those associated with 'culture wars'. Business leaders are very poor politicians, and politicians rarely make good business leaders. This truism should be respected if miscalculations are to be avoided. The line between what is a legitimate CSR, DEI and ESG topic for a company to advocate and where it should leave the debate to the political classes and the media must be clearly articulated by each company's board. CEOs and chairs should never be allowed to use their position within a company to prosecute personal-interest agendas. That said, there are many examples of where businesses must be clear on social matters to be good corporate citizens. Examples include a company's carbon footprint and commitment to diversity, family values, work-life balance, and avoiding gender and racial discrimination in hiring and promotion. In doing these things well, businesses positively contribute to society. So, in listening carefully to stakeholders, businesses need to be crystal clear about which societal issues directly affect their business and think clearly and carefully about making statements on unrelated issues – which a sceptical public and workforce increasingly see as virtue signalling, CEO-ego-driven and populism to carry political and media favour. It is important to know where to draw the line, and that politically charged statements can carry much personal risk when the political winds change. Warren Buffett was clear on this when he said, 'I don't believe in imposing my political opinions on the activities of our businesses'.

To strengthen the link between purpose and business activity, Professor Colin Mayer argues that the law should be changed so that directors' duties are more focused on promoting the company's purpose, and that regulation, particularly when it comes to businesses engaged in critical public functions, should be more focused on ensuring that such businesses operate in a manner aligned with their purpose.[265] There is an argument that operating consistently with the business's purpose should be a legally binding commitment, just as prospectus profit forecasts are when a company enters the publicly listed market. More on this in Chapter 7.

Social licence

If Smith were alive today, I believe he would advocate social licences for large businesses with dominant market power or special privileges, such as banks. The concept of social licence – a metaphor, as there is no written contract – should

265 Ibid., p45.

not be uniformly applied to all businesses. Small and medium-sized businesses don't carry the same influence and power as large businesses in critical industry sectors. (This is not to say that small businesses can be excused from bad behaviour and don't need to uphold moral values.)

The standard definition of a social licence to operate is the level of acceptance by communities and stakeholders of an organisation's activities. In essence, a social licence is based on trust. Many professions (lawyers, doctors and accountants), and certain industries such as banking, need a licence. The licence to operate in the case of banks is issued to the institution by a government agency. In contrast, in the case of other professions, the licence is issued to the individual; that is, the doctor, the lawyer and the accountant have a professionally accredited licence to operate.

For a financial services company to describe itself as a 'bank', it must be licensed by the Australian Prudential Regulation Authority (APRA). In addition to this being a form of regulation, the granting of a banking licence is to certify to the public that a bank is subject to certain standards and oversight, ensuring, at least in theory, that the public good is protected and the principal–agent costs are being closely monitored. A social licence to operate goes beyond the approval of a licence by a regulator. Typically, according to The Ethics Centre,[266] a social licence to operate has three components: legitimacy, credibility and trust.

266 The Ethics Centre, 'Ethics explainer: social licence to operate', 22 January 2018. https://ethics.org.au/ethics-explainer-social-license-to-operate/

The special nature of banks has been the subject of many investigations in recent times. For example, the UK financial regulator noted:

> *Banks are different and society has a strong interest in bankers taking a different attitude to the balance between risk and reward to that which applies to the rest of the economy … their failure is of public concern, not just a concern for shareholders.*[267]

When it comes to business, how should we understand whether companies have sufficient social legitimacy to take on the responsibility for delivering essential services such as banking, health services, water, energy and telecommunications? A social licence can never be self-awarded; it requires that the activities of the business have sufficient credibility and trust in addition to legitimacy. There are many examples of social licences having been lost, such as BP in the Gulf of Mexico and Shell in the Niger Delta. Several banks, such as the RBS in the UK and Wells Fargo in the US, had their social licence curtailed in response to scandals. Facebook (or Meta) also faces the risk of its social licence being lost unless it addresses growing concerns around data security and the fact that it allows material to be published on its platform that can be harmful and even dangerous. Facebook and other social media platforms do not intentionally cause harm to others, but their business model allows harm to occur.[268] Society is demanding that this be addressed.

---

267 The Financial Services Authority, *The failure of the Royal Bank of Scotland: Financial Services Authority Board Report*, December 2011, pp4-5.

268 'Facebook must recognise it is more than a platform', *Financial Times*, 3 December 2018. https://www.ft.com/content/fe99f4ea-f31d-11e8-ae55-df4bf40f9d0d

An example of the nature of social licence was evident in the cybersecurity scandal that plagued the telecommunications company Optus in 2023. The scandal ultimately led to the resignation of Optus's talented CEO amidst criticism of poor communication with customers and other stakeholders.[269] The social-licence nature of these events was highlighted by how politicians quickly became embroiled in the hostile public commentary, which can, at times, be excessive and stretch the boundaries of civilised behaviour, as was the case with PM Scott Morrison's highly personal attack, under parliamentary privilege, on Australia Post CEO Christine Holgate over the gift of watches to Australia Post executives.[270] Other examples include the turmoil that plagued Qantas in 2023–24, the conduct of the major food retailers Woolworths and Coles, and the 'wafer thin social licence' held by the scandal-ridden Star Entertainment, the casino group that regulators criticised for its culture and weak corporate governance.[271]

Corporate governance

Despite his misgivings on principal–agent problems, Adam Smith would consider effective corporate governance to be necessary. Contemporary corporate governance, however, has evolved in an overly legalistic manner that places much weight

269 Wiggins, J. 'Optus communications "manifestly inadequate" in 2023 phone outage'. *Financial Review*, 27 September 2024. https://www.afr.com/companies/telecommunications/optus-communications-manifestly-inadequate-in-2023-phone-outage-20240927-p5ke2l

270 Grattan, M. 'View from The Hill: Christine Holgate presents a compelling story of Morrison's bullying'. *The Conversation*, 13 April 2021. https://theconversation.com/view-from-the-hill-christine-holgate-presents-a-compelling-story-of-morrisons-bullying-158895

271 'No tax break bailout for Star's casino racket'. *Financial Review*, 4 September 2024. https://www.afr.com/companies/games-and-wagering/no-tax-break-bailout-for-star-s-casino-racket-20240902-p5k71d

on process and compliance, with most directors in many Anglo-Saxon economies coming from the traditional and conservative fields of accounting, law and banking. The highly respected journalist Tony Boyd wrote in the *Financial Review*:

> *...there is a worrying escalation in the box-ticking, compliance culture in Australian boardrooms ... over the past decade, the nation's boardrooms have gradually transformed into places that are preoccupied with bureaucratic formalities rather than technology-driven strategies. The dismal state of affairs is perpetuated by the dominance of the Australian Institute of Company Directors (AICD), the world's largest membership organisation devoted to teaching compliance-driven governance.*[272]

The public commentary on the quality of boards is largely dominated by gender diversity – one important consideration – but little on directors' quality and real commercial experience. Concerningly, far too many directors have little 'skin in the game' in terms of a meaningful equity stake in the business. Another problem is that some good directors are underpaid and need to build a 'portfolio' to replace the economics of their executive careers. The consequences are that many directors have too many boards, in many cases involved in companies with no domain knowledge beyond the universal legal and accounting principles, which weakens the boards' competency and ability to discharge effective stewardship. Corporate governance standards on board competency, as distinct from board makeup, are viewed by many as a broken model masked

272 Boyd, T. 'The ASX's legal mess reveals deep-rooted problems in boardrooms'. *Financial Review*, 19 August 2024. https://www.afr.com/companies/financial-services/asx-s-legal-mess-points-to-deep-rooted-problems-in-boardrooms-20240816-p5k2y8

by the fact that many significant companies enjoy privileged market positions.[273] As mentioned earlier, in his book *Rogue Corporations* Quentin Beresford identifies a range of common features of poor corporate governance and rogue corporate behaviour: the rise of celebrity CEOs with flawed personalities, excessive CEO remuneration packages, poor corporate culture focused on aggressive pursuit of short-term profits, poorly performing boards, weak regulators, inadequate penalties for bad behaviour, and the corporate capture of government policy processes.

The case study of Qantas illustrates all common corporate governance failures, despite years of case study reviews, reform, regulation and laws. Embroiled in scandals, including breaking the law, the board failed to heed the warnings of 'significant reputational and customer service issues'.[274] The then-chairman of Qantas, Richard Goyder AO, commented, 'I think the Qantas board has been appropriately challenging and certainly had strong governance'.[275] The chairman had previously said about his CEO, Alan Joyce: 'Alan is the best CEO in Australia by the length of a straight – he was unbelievably hardworking, open, transparent and open to challenge'.[276]

The 2024 corporate governance review of Qantas, commissioned by the company under investor pressure in the aftermath

---

273 Beresford, Q (2023).

274 de Kretser, A & Thomson, J. 'Qantas board failed to rein in Joyce's "command and control"'. 8 August 2024. https://www.afr.com/companies/transport/former-qantas-boss-alan-joyce-to-lose-more-than-9m-in-bonuses-20240808-p5k0mq#:~:text=Mr%20Saar's%20review%20found%20there,some%20issues%2C%E2%80%9D%20it%20found.

275 Robin, M. 'Richard Goyder's board was on cruise control'. 8 August 2024. https://www.afr.com/rear-window/qantas-review-finds-board-on-cruise-control-20240808-p5k0qu

276 Ibid.

of the scandals that engulfed the airline, produced uncontested findings diametrically opposed to the views of the then chairman. The review found a dominant 'command and control' CEO and a board with its head firmly in the sand. The review pointed out that the Qantas board had 'too much deference to a long-tenured CEO … the board's mode of engagement … did not always facilitate robust challenge'. The review highlighted a dominant CEO who called all the shots in the face of a weak and complacent board.[277] In a heavily critical statement on the quality of corporate governance as one of Australia's leading companies, Joe Aston, in his book *The Chairman's Lounge*, harshly describes the highly regarded Qantas chairman as 'the zombie chairman'.[278]

Qantas CEO Alan Joyce used that platform and the company's brand to strongly advocate for various social issues, including same-sex marriage and the Indigenous Voice to Parliament.[279] This curried favour with the government of the day but would have potentially made thousands of Qantas employees (and customers), who held a different view, feel intimidated and threatened by the vocal endorsement of their CEO on controversial issues not germane to the business. Such a position by the CEO is hardly inclusive of alternative views.

This list of blemishes, highlighted by Qantas but not confined to the airline, as the 2018 Hayne Royal Commission highlighted, largely reflects directly on the quality of corporate

---

277 Johnston, E. 'The five big mistakes inside the Qantas boardroom'. *The Australian*, 8 August 2024. https://www.theaustralian.com.au/business/companies/alan-joyce-power-at-qantas-and-bonus-structure-led-to-mistakes-inside-weak-boardroom/news-story/04737fd710c1c22ac32041f586f59bd1

278 Aston, J (2024).

279 'How the Qantas board fell for the cult of Alan Joyce'. *Financial Review*, 8 August 2024. https://www.afr.com/chanticleer/how-the-qantas-board-fell-for-the-cult-of-alan-joyce-20240808-p5k0q1

governance and the inherent weaknesses that Adam Smith foreshadowed.

In 1776, Smith prophetically wrote:

> *The directors ... being the managers rather of other people's money than of their own, it cannot well be expected that they should watch over it with the same anxious vigilance with which the partners in a private firm frequently watch over their own. Negligence and profusion, therefore, must always prevail, more or less, in the management of the affairs of such a company.*

Adam Smith and Karl Marx disagreed, but they both thought that the corporate form, in which directors owned very little of the firm they were stewards, was unworkable for remarkably similar reasons.

While modern corporate governance addresses some of the issues inherent in the principal–agent problem, it only scratches the surface. It has arguably been weakened by an overly compliance-driven value system.

Smith's insights into corporate governance, stated almost 300 years ago, highlight that little has changed in corporate governance in a world otherwise changed beyond recognition since the late 18th century. This is a puzzle, and another reason why Milton Friedman sought clarity and a narrow business purpose when he wrote about the social responsibility of business. When you set aside much of the corporate spin of some major businesses, their focus on ROE and executive incentives, together with their disappointing abuse of community trust, means they have been, in their own eyes, exemplars of the Friedman Doctrine that 'the social responsibility of business is to increase its profits'. Yet, as we have discussed, they have done

Milton Friedman a great disservice, as he would never have approved of how his doctrine has been so abused, in the same way that Adam Smith's philosophy is cherry-picked in support of right-leaning ideologies. It is more accurate to say that many businesses create a sense that they have been run more to protect market privileges and optimise senior executive remuneration than in the interests of their customers or shareholders, yet 'shareholder value' has been wrongly tarnished as a legitimate business goal.

Qantas: A case study

Friedman, like Adam Smith, would have been horrified by the behaviour of Qantas when, during the COVID-19 period in 2021 and 2022, it admitted in negotiating a settlement with the ACCC that it misled tens of thousands of customers by selling tickets on flights that had already been cancelled – so-called 'ghost flights' – and then kept the money paid to offer customers future flight credits, which became very difficult to use. The admission of wrongdoing exposed the most risible of defences that customers were not buying a ticket for a specific flight but were buying a 'bundle of contractual rights'. It is incredible that sensible people in senior executive positions and the board of directors overseeing them could consider such a theoretically legalistic defence as anything but embarrassing, humiliating and damaging to the credibility and reputation of the company.[280] The conduct of Qantas was motivated by a management team and board of directors focused on profit

280 'Why didn't ACCC litigate Qantas?' *Financial Review*, 6 May 2024. https://www.afr.com/companies/transport/why-didn-t-accc-litigate-qantas-20240505-p5foyh

maximisation and personal rewards, with the financial year 2022–23 delivering profits of $2.47 billion, and remuneration to the departing CEO was initially announced as $24 million but later reduced by $9.2 million.[281] The company's board was subject to an embarrassing 80 per cent shareholder vote against the airline pay policy,[282] and it also apparently dismissed the fact that according to the ACCC Qantas was the most complained about company in 2021–22 and 2022–23. The company's critics, including employees, pointed to the CEO and the board for 'the destruction of an Australian icon by promoting a "profit at all costs" culture'.[283] Adding to the company's poor reputation, the then-CEO refused to answer senate inquiry questions on its apparent policy of providing Chairman's Lounge membership for politicians' family members.[284] It was widely reported, for example, that Prime Minister Albanese's son was granted membership in the exclusive Chairman's Lounge by Qantas.[285]

Adding to a catalogue of failures in management and of the board, the High Court found the company to have illegally sacked 1,700 workers as it looked to outsource some of its ground operations in violation of the *Fair Work Act 2009*.

The highly deceptive conduct of Qantas followed its behind-the-scenes lobbying of the Albanese government to block additional international flights into Australia by Qatar Airways. This development would have benefited the travelling public with cheaper long-haul flights and greater choice, yet the

---

281 de Kretser, A & Thomson, J (2024).

282 Fildes, N. 'Qantas slashes former boss Joyce's exit pay'. *Financial Times*, 7 August 2024. https://www.ft.com/content/e67bb078-65b6-4b19-b851-e6204c3c1b94

283 Ibid.

284 de Kretser, A & Thomson, J (2024).

285 Aston, J. 'Alan Joyce puts Albo's son in Qantas Chairman's Lounge'. *Financial Review*, 2 August 2023. https://www.afr.com/rear-window/alan-joyce-puts-albo-s-son-in-qantas-chairman-s-lounge-20230802-p5dtf3

government chose to disregard public interest and act in the interest of Qantas. This political lobbying had a long history: in 2013, Qantas lobbied the Gillard Labor government to stop Virgin's foreign shareholders Air New Zealand, Etihad and Singapore Airlines from recapitalising the number-two airline in Australia, complaining that subsidised state-owned airlines were out to destroy Qantas. Yet, Qantas reportedly received $2.7 billion in taxpayer subsidies during the pandemic. The airline also banned the *Financial Review* from its prestigious Chairman's Lounges – effectively punishing its customers – because of the rigorous reporting by the newspaper on the failings and practices of the airline.[286]

Former ACCC chair Professor Allan Fels, in the report *Inquiry into price gouging and unfair pricing practices* sponsored by the Australian Council of Trade Unions (ACTU), accused Qantas of 'price gouging' as it attempted to keep a tight rein on capacity in the face of the enormous post-COVID demand for travel, thereby driving up fares.[287] This type of conduct says everything about corporate culture and governance. Despite Qantas's generous taxpayer-granted financial support during the pandemic, it goes unchallenged mainly by politicians and regulators. It was only with the threat of legal action by the ACCC that Qantas admitted to its misconduct. The civilised face and moral values of capitalism were absent, behaviour that both Smith and Friedman would find abhorrent.

286 'Indispensable Joyce became excess liability for Qantas'. *Financial Review*, 8 August 2024. https://www.afr.com/companies/transport/indispensable-joyce-became-excess-liability-for-qantas-20240806-p5k01s

287 https://www.theaustralian.com.au/business/aviation/qantas-energy-companies-accused-of-price-gouging-in-a-landmark-report-by-allan-fels/news-story/1e7b4b33007a6051799ec258fbdae751

In many ways, this conduct mirrors that of the major banks, which were found during the Hayne Royal Commission to be engaged in activities including charging 'fees for no service', including to the estates of people who had long been deceased. This conduct was not isolated, and the banking industry's reputation was severely damaged due to extensive abuses, all highlighting the industry's cultural and professional decline.[288]

Then there is the telco sector, where Telstra used its dominant position to announce price increases well above the inflation rate, prompting *The Australian* to write, 'Telstra's inflation-stoking move speaks volumes about the lack of competitive spirit in the telco market.'[289]

*

Leaving capitalism and ethics behind for now, let's examine education today and how it compares with Smith's views almost 300 years ago.

288 Healy, J (2019).

289 Johnson, E. 'Why Telstra's price rises are bad for everyone'. *The Australian*, 10 July 2024. https://www.theaustralian.com.au/business/companies/hiking-mobile-plans-by-more-than-cpi-will-hit-rba-customers-alike/news-story/af6dd6f1cba6b9eb0abc235dc5d2b6ae

5

Adam Smith and Education

In my view, and Smith's view, better education is not the sole solution to a fair, ethical and economically robust society, but it plays a crucial role – so much so that I dedicate a chapter to the subject, exploring our modern approach to education and looking at how Smith would have marked our report card. In Chapter 2, we discussed Smith's views on education as a driver of economic growth. In this chapter, I present the findings that education goes much further. It can drive better health outcomes (particularly mental health) and a more effective democracy.

Smith understood the powerful impact of education on the individual and on society, and this is clear from his writing:

But though the common people cannot, in any civilized society, be so well instructed as people of some rank and

> *fortune, the most essential parts of education, however, to read, write and account, can be acquired at so early a period of life, that the greater part of even of those who are to be bred to the lowest occupations have time to acquire them before they can be employed in those occupations. For a very small expense, the public can facilitate, can encourage, and can even impose upon almost the whole body of the people the necessity of acquiring those most essential parts of education.*[290]

With Smith's wisdom in mind, let's recap education's contribution to our economy.

Balancing monotonous work

Adam Smith advocated for universal public education,[291] a publicly funded and compulsory education system.[292] In *The Wealth of Nations*, Smith argues that universal access to education would offset the mundane nature and other harmful effects of the division of labour. He considers an educated workforce 'more decent and orderly than an ignorant and stupid one'. Smith implicitly knows that humans aren't built for routine and monotonous repetition. We are naturally designed to seek exploration and learning. Activities that prevent people from achieving these natural instincts result in a less-than-engaged workforce. We all face this challenge in a world moving at pace towards the dehumanisation of so much of what we do through

290 Smith, A (1776). *The Wealth of Nations*, B.V., ch.1, V.1.182.
291 Rothschild, E (2001). *Economic Sentiments: Adam Smith, Condorcet, and the Enlightenment*. Harvard University Press, p98.
292 Hill, L. (2016). 'Adam Smith and political theory', in Hanley, RP (ed.). *Adam Smith: His Life, Thought, and Legacy*. Princeton University Press., p329.

digitalisation and the increasing role of AI. The human soul is lost, and the nature of work is more routine than Smith feared.

Smith was a strong advocate of the division of labour, using the example of pin-making to illustrate the power of specialisation. He observed that ten workers performing specialist tasks could produce 48,000 pins a day, as opposed to a single worker undertaking all component tasks that might produce a fraction of that number. He argued that the division of labour means 'more work is done upon the whole, and the quantity of science is considerably increased by it'.[293] In Smith's view, specialisation also extended to trade. It was a source of national competitive advantage and wealth creation, a theme discussed earlier that David Ricardo was to build on later. Smith acknowledged, however, that the extent of the market limits specialisation; in other words, small markets don't always lend themselves to specialisation.[294]

Smith's contribution to business strategy, through his emphasis on specialisation at both the level of the firm and nation, is not given the credit it deserves. Credit in this field is more often attributed to Frederick Taylor and his theories of scientific management developed in the US before the First World War. Taylor's emphasis on standardisation and specialisation are seen as the origins of mass production and the surge in productivity. Yet, the intellectual thinking underpinning what Taylor is credited with owes much to Adam Smith. Smith understood that specialisation delivers superior outcomes in all

---

293 Yueh, L (2019). *The Great Economists: How their ideas can help us today.* Penguin General UK.

294 Samuelson, PA (1976). *Economics.* McGraw-Hill.

walks of life.[295] We see this most visibly in the Olympics, when the times and distances achieved by the decathlete gold medal winner are compared to those of the specialist in, say, the 100-metre sprint: the specialist always outperforms the generalist.

Smith also understood that some specialisation, such as pin-making, can be monotonous. In making a pin, one person straightens the wire, another draws it out, someone else cuts it, and another person moulds the head. Through this division of labour and specialisation, as noted earlier, thousands of pins can be produced in a single day, whereas a fraction of this would result from one person doing all the production tasks; however, in this specialisation model, the nature of work is intolerable. Worker education provides an important counterbalance.

To address this problem and many others, Smith called for the government to mitigate this 'torpor of mind' by making education available for all, with a school in every parish.[296] He saw the provision of education as being critical to the development of a nation. He profoundly observed that the difference between 'a philosopher and a common street porter' arose from 'habit, custom and education: more than nature'.[297] This is a very important insight, and consistent with that of British political commentator Polly Mackenzie, who wrote:

> *There are endless debates about whether ability comes from our genes, or the environment in which we are raised. It doesn't matter. The thing those two factors share is that*

---

295 Healy, J & Hornery, D (2023). Black Belt: A masterclass for start-ups and entrepreneurs. Major Street Publishing, p43.
296 Smith, A (1776). *The Wealth of Nations*, p785.
297 Phillips-Fein, K (2023).

> *you have no control over them. My parents gave me my genes, and they gave me my childhood.*[298]

The key is an environment that encourages motivated and talented people to realise their potential; education plays a fundamental role in unlocking that potential. The story of JD Vance, the US Vice-President, is illustrative of this. The poverty and family dysfunctionality in his early life is told in his book *Hillbilly Elegy: A Memoir of a Family and Culture in Crisis.* Vance grew up in an environment plagued by socioeconomic problems, where drug abuse was commonplace, including within his family, with pharmaceutical businesses like Purdue Pharma profiting from those problems. Due to his grandmother's insistence that he get a good education, Vance worked hard and was lucky to escape what destiny might have ordained for him.[299] He also reminds us that so much of what we do is shaped by innate qualities and inherited traits of our genes and early environment – what, as I mentioned earlier, neuroscientists call epigenetics, the study of how the environment can influence our genes.

Balancing society

Long-term government investment in education is critical for developing skills and knowledge central to the bright future of the economy and society. While technology, including AI advancements, will play a pivotal role in the future, this is in so many ways dependent on the investment in human

298 Mackenzie, P. 'The myth of meritocracy', *UnHerd*, 17 April 2019. https://unherd.com./2019/04/the-myth-of-meritocracy

299 Vance, JD (2016). *Hillbilly Elegy: A memoir of a family and culture in crisis.* HarperCollins.

capital. The risk of limiting access to good-quality education is that it will further widen the already widening socioeconomic inequality gap, something that would greatly concern Smith.

Across all OECD countries, member states devote a substantial share of their GDP to primary, secondary and tertiary educational institutions. In Australia, that number is 6.2 per cent of GDP, which compares to 5.1 per cent of GDP on average across all OECD countries. Of the 6.2 per cent, 33 per cent is dedicated to primary education, 35 per cent to secondary education, 2 per cent to post-secondary non-tertiary education, 3 per cent to short-cycle tertiary programs and 27 per cent to bachelor's, master's and doctoral or equivalent programs. As in almost all OECD countries, tertiary degrees provide a significant earnings advantage. In Australia, 25- to 34-year-old workers with a bachelor's degree earn 24 per cent more than their peers who have not attained this level of education, while those with master's or doctoral degrees earn 24 per cent more again.[300] This data is consistent with the human capital theory advocated by Professor Gary Becker, Professor Jeffrey Sachs and others, as discussed in Chapter 2: that historically, the more university-educated you are, the higher your earnings will be.

An obvious and accurate conclusion is that people with a degree will likely have greater career options and earn higher incomes, leading to a better quality of life. Education, therefore, may be an underlying factor in inequality. The data also shows that people with a degree are more likely to find a partner with a similar level of education attainment, leading to

300 OECD (2023). *Education at a Glance 2023 Sources, Methodologies and Technical Notes*, OECD Publishing.

a household with two highly paid salaries. The progress with gender inequality, particularly with more young women going to university, has seen interesting but unsurprising changes in partner selection in marriage. David Goodhart highlights that not that many decades ago, there were far fewer women going to university or entering higher professional jobs; in that world, male doctors often married female nurses, and businessmen sometimes married their secretaries.[301] Today, that choice is still open, but there are far more highly educated women to choose from. *The Economist* summed up this change:

> *In 1970 only 9 per cent of those with bachelor's degrees in America were women, so the vast majority of men with such degrees married women who lacked them. Now the numbers are roughly even (in fact women are earning more degrees) and people tend to pair up with mates of a similar educational background ... So highly educated, double-income power couples have become far more common. The children of such couples have every advantage, but there are not many of them.*[302]

Deaths of despair

An important insight into the links between education and quality of life was documented in the book *Deaths of Despair and the Future of Capitalism* (2020) by Professors Anne Case and Sir Angus Deaton. The book describes the underlying factors that saw life expectancy in the US fall for three years in a row

---

301 Goodhart, D (2020), p70.

302 *The Economist*. 'The rise and rise of the cognitive elite: brains bring ever larger rewards.' 22 January 2011. https://www.economist.com/special-report/2011/01/22/the-rise-and-rise-of-the-cognitive-elite

to 2019 and how, in the two decades prior, deaths from suicide, drug overdose and alcoholism rose dramatically, claiming hundreds of thousands of American lives each year. They call these 'deaths of despair'. In their research, they conclude these deaths were all among those without a bachelor's degree. 'Those with a four-year degree are mostly exempt; those without the degree are at risk'.[303]

To illustrate the magnitude of the problem, Case and Deaton provide data from the state of Kentucky for white people aged 45 to 54. The risk of premature death rose from 37 to 137 per 100,000 people in the ten years to 2005 for those without an undergraduate degree, while the data was flat for those with a degree. They conclude, 'Education is clearly one of the keys to understanding who is dying and why … we need to understand the role education plays in people's lives … For those born in 1980, whites without a bachelor's degree are four times more likely to commit suicide than those with a degree'.[304] Most suicides involve depression and/or other mental illnesses such as substance addictions. These deaths are often labelled 'accidental deaths' when they can better be understood as deaths of despair, which ties them back to mental health and its critical role in the quality of life and health of society. Deaths of despair and income inequality are highly correlated. Inequality can undermine a person's sense of self-worth, and this, in turn, can lead to behaviour such as domestic violence. Inequality can also create fertile ground for a toxic environment, which can poison the way people think about themselves and their future.

---

303 Case, A & Deaton, A (2020). *Deaths of Despair and the Future of Capitalism*. Princeton University Press, p3.

304 Ibid., pp49-61.

They see a world where they have no control over their destiny and family.

Much of the data on the links between education and deaths of despair is based on US research. Still, Case and Deaton ask if other apparently wealthy nations are at risk of following the path of the US. The answer is that as inequality grows, as more jobs risk being automated through applications such as AI, as house prices increasingly rise out of the reach of many, as drug use and other addictions increase, as mental health continues to deteriorate, as communities continue to fragment as divorce rates continue to increase, as domestic violence becomes an ever-growing stain on society, that risk cannot be dismissed.

A 2024 report highlighted the relevance of the US data to Australia. It showed that as of 2023, one in five Australian students drop out of school before year 12, a ten-year high. At the same time, students' attendance rates in years 7 to 10 have declined dramatically. The figures are more encouraging in the private sector, but in state schools, fewer than one in four students who start year 10 go on to complete year 12.[305]

The disparities between private and public schools, as discussed in Chapter 3, were also highlighted in the Gonski report in 2011. David Gonski highlighted that the current system over-funds private schools and under-funds public schools, and that more resources were needed in the public system. Like Adam Smith, David Gonski acutely understood the transformative nature of education and its power to change someone's life. Finally, some 14 years after the Gonski Report,

---

305 Hare, J. 'Study shows why kids drop out of school'. *Financial Review*, 26 March 2024. https://www.afr.com/work-and-careers/education/school-dropouts-don-t-always-lack-ambition-just-fewer-choices-study-20240325-p5ff0j

the Albanese government moved on to implement a key recommendation on the funding of public schools.[306]

As the Case and Deaton study highlights, a lack of meaningful education is also linked to the propensity for depression and the use of psychiatric drugs. Dr Anna Lembke highlighted that one in ten Americans (110 people per 1,000) takes a prescribed antidepressant, the highest rate in the world, followed by Iceland (106/1,000), Australia (89/1,000) and Canada (86/1,000), all the way down to South Korea (13/1,000).[307] The annual rate of growth in the use of antidepressants is a feature of Australian society, as it is in other rich countries – a topic I return to in the next chapter.

While Adam Smith did not discuss the links between health and education in detail, his views imply that both are critical for economic success and societal well-being.

Back to basics

In Australia, the two primary goals of education are, first, that the education system should promote excellence and equity, and second, that all young Australians should become confident and creative individuals, successful lifelong learners, and active and informed community members.[308] Missing from these goals is a specific emphasis on the fundamentals of education covering core subjects such as English, science and

306 Duffy, C. 'A landmark school funding deal to finally end the war over public versus private is here. It's a big deal'. *ABC News*. 25 March 2025. https://www.abc.net.au/news/2025-03-25/david-gonski-on-public-school-funding-deal/105090326

307 Lembke, A (2021).

308 Quay, J. 'Blind faith in Australia's education "system" is failing our kids', *Pursuit*, 17 January 2024. https://pursuit.unimelb.edu.au/articles/blind-faith-in-australia-s-education-system-is-failing-our-kids

maths. There has been an increase in faddish and woke thinking in education in many rich countries, which has deemphasised the fundamentals. A survey in *The Economist* on education highlighted that even allowing for the negative impact of the COVID-19 pandemic, education standards in most developed countries have either stagnated or been in decline for over two decades according to the Programme for International Student Assessment (PISA), which applies a standard test of education attainment amongst 15-year-olds across the OECD.[309]

The story of the Scottish education system is a cautionary tale of what could happen in Australia. Scotland, a country with a rich tradition in broad-based education, provides an example of how government policy moved away from emphasising the fundamentals to a more popular, less rigorous, student-friendly and loosely defined curriculum. Professor Lindsay Paterson at the University of Edinburgh said, 'No other government in Europe has reformed its curriculum as radically as Scotland has'. The result has seen a gradual and marked deterioration in PISA scores: today, Scotland scores around 20 points below England – which has retained an emphasis on the fundamentals – having been at least ten points ahead of England before the reforms were implemented.[310] In an Australian context, *The Economist* cautioned that 'for some years Australian curriculums have offered teachers only limited detail on what content should be taught, and in what order'. Scotland's example should serve as a warning against any policy that wants to weaken the fundamental rigours of education in pursuit of faddish, woke or fashionable ideas about what

309 Johnson, M. 'Must try harder'. *The Economist*, 13 July 2024. https://www.economist.com/special-report/2024-07-13
310 Ibid.

education should stand for, such as social-emotional learning (SEL), or gamification, where game-like elements are used to enhance engagement but are not grounded in pedagogical practices.

As mentioned earlier, it's alarming that one in three students performed below literacy and numeracy benchmarks in the latest NAPLAN results, and the problems are persistent.[311] These findings encouraged experts to call out the need for urgent action to reform classrooms; otherwise, 'a significant part of a generation looks set to miss out on crucial foundational learning'.[312] The gap between the wealthier private schools and state-controlled public schools was also highlighted, and long-standing educational disadvantage remains deeply entrenched in Australia.[313] The NAPLAN report also highlighted that those students of parents who held a bachelor's degree or higher tended to score better than their classmates whose parents' highest level of education was year 11 or lower. The Federal Education Minister, Jason Clare, in 2024 commented, 'Your chances in life shouldn't depend on your parents' pay packet or the colour of your skin, but these results again show that's still the case.'[314]

A consistent body of research shows that developing an education system based on the foundation of the fundamentals is the most reliable and lasting way to promote economic growth. Professor Ludger Woessmann and economist Eric

---

311 Hunter, J & Parkinson, N (2024).

312 Young, E. 'NAPLAN results reveal one in three students not meeting basic literacy and numeracy expectations'. *ABC News*, 14 August 2024. https://www.abc.net.au/news/2024-08-14/naplan-results-2024-revealed/104205514

313 Hare, J. 'NAPLAN is a measure of wealth, not student ability'. *Financial Review*, 14 August 2024.

314 Ibid.

Hanushek at Stanford University modelled the benefits of improved maths and science skills in the employment market that might flow from a 25-point increase in maths and science results on the PISA chart, and found that this could increase GDP growth in rich countries by half a percentage point. They argued that if a country made a serious commitment to improve maths and science education, particularly with those more able students in the year 2030, then by the end of the century the economy could be about 30 per cent larger than it otherwise would be.[315]

University integrity

The relevance of policy-set educational goals was highlighted in the *Australian Universities Accord* report published by the Albanese government in early 2024, which argued for a dramatic increase in access to higher education, particularly for disadvantaged Australians, and that the financial burden of higher education be eased.[316] The report argued that 80 per cent of the workforce would need vocational education and training (VET) or university qualifications by 2050, with a particular target to increase the participation of people from underprivileged backgrounds. The report highlighted that Australians from low socio-economic status (SES) backgrounds make up 25 per cent of the population but only 17 per cent of undergraduate enrolment. Parallels were drawn to the reforms under the Bob Hawke and Paul Keating Labor government

315 Hanushek, EA & Woessmann, L (2007). *Education Quality and Economic Growth*. The World Bank.

316 O'Kane, M (2023). *Australian Universities Accord: final report*. Australian Government. https://www.education.gov.au/australian-universities-accord/resources/final-report

of the 1980s, which saw the number of Australian teenagers finishing high school jump from 40 per cent to 80 per cent, and the impact this has had on Australia ever since.

There is, however, much criticism of the quality of education in Australian universities (although this problem is not unique to Australia).[317] Critics have highlighted that international students who cannot speak 'basic English' – even though an entrance requirement is that a student completes a mandatory English language test from an approved provider – are leaving leading Australian universities with prestigious degrees. Leading academics have said that the universities' financial reliance on foreign students over many years has 'hollowed out academic integrity and threatened the international credibility of the sector'.[318]

An equally concerning abuse of the system is the reported widespread use of AI, including ChatGPT, which sees a significant number of students submitting assignments that teachers have a strong sense that they did not write – some with perfectly written English from students with poor spoken English. Additionally, despite the use of plagiarism detection tool Turnitin, which searches for signs of copy-pasting from other sources, the use of ghostwriters and the recycling of previous essays, students suspected of these activities still manage to be awarded degrees. One teacher is reported to have said, 'We need to pass students. As a tutor, you don't have the authority to fail students… Departments don't

---

317 Cassidy, C. 'Australian universities accused of awarding degrees to students with no grasp of "basic" English. *The Guardian*, 30 July 2024. https://www.theguardian.com/australia-news/article/2024/jul/30/australian-universities-accused-of-awarding-degrees-to-students-with-no-grasp-of-basic-english

318 Ibid.

want fails because they want money, and if you fail someone, you're cutting off the money stream, and there's so many lines of appeal.'[319]

A different path for everyone

Smith believed that over time, productivity growth would come from the division of labour and specialisation and the development of human capital – knowledge and skills. While formal education plays a fundamental role in this regard, so does learning through vocational training, particularly in developing crafts and practical skills. As I argue in this chapter, there is much evidence that we now live in a world where the main distributor of status, income and wealth is individual educational achievement. A university degree can be seen as a passport to better personal outcomes and is an essential requirement for many jobs. As a generalisation, those who don't achieve a university degree may find themselves in society's slow lane, and this can result in a sense of learned helplessness, a sense of failure, and with that, all the mental health and societal problems that are so often associated with low self-esteem. Naturally, there are many exceptions to this general rule, as discussed later in this chapter.

Despite the compelling evidence that those without a university degree are disadvantaged in today's employment market, if alive today Smith would likely argue that our emphasis on cognitive education credentials at the expense of other forms of training has led to distortions with wider societal implications. The declining status of so much non-graduate employment

319 Cassidy, C, '"Nobody is blind to it": mass cheating through AI puts integrity of Australian universities at risk, academics claim'. *The Guardian*, 31 July 2024.

would concern Smith. This is a view held by Peter Thiel, a high-profile Silicon Valley technology entrepreneur who is a Stanford University graduate with degrees in philosophy and law. Through his foundation, Thiel, an early investor in Facebook and a founder of PayPal, offers grants of up to US$100,000 for qualifying candidates to skip or drop out of university and start companies or nonprofits.[320] He wisely argues that there is a different path for everyone and references Plato, who wrote, 'Knowledge that is acquired under compulsion obtains no hold on the mind'.[321]

That there is a different path for everyone is a vital topic critically explored in David Goodhart's book *Head, Hand, Heart: The struggle for dignity and status in the 21st century.* Goodhart argues that in the modern knowledge economy, there has been an overemphasis on what he describes as 'head' skills and capabilities, which are associated with formal education achievements – the passport to success of a university degree in terms of societal ascribed values and economic outcomes through salary and status – at the expense of 'hand' work such as building or fixing things, or 'heart' careers such as teaching, nursing, early child care and aged care.[322]

We have become, in essence, a society that places more worth on passing exams or getting high marks in IQ-type tests than on social intelligence and imagination. Most large businesses use psychometric testing as part of their IQ assessment; as a result, many talented, innovative, entrepreneurial candidates fail to get to the next stage. As a society, we place more esteem and offer higher rewards to office jobs – many of which now

---

320 Thiel Fellowship™, https://thielfellowship.org

321 Ibid.

322 Goodhart, D (2020).

require a degree, even though the work offers little scope for personal discretion – than more traditional and critical roles, such as bus drivers. In many cases, the requirement for a degree is no more than a signalling effect of an individual's capabilities, a screening method prone to significant error and bias. As Goodhart argues, we are undervaluing critical jobs because they lack cognitive complexity, and this undervaluing of hand and heart skills has unbalanced societies and alienated millions of people. And yet, in a world where AI is likely to change the nature of many jobs and organisations, it is easier to imagine how AI will replace a mid-level accountant, bank officer or lawyer than a garbage collector or nurse. I come back to this critical theme later in this chapter.

One reason for the decline in the standing of hand and heart roles has been the gradual decline of our VET system, which traditionally worked closely with industry, but has suffered from inadequate funding and low-quality service providers. Professor Ross Garnaut AC summed up the problem:

> *This has resulted from inadequate regulation and poor market design. The VET system needs more investment and a greater focus on quality assurance and improvement.*[323]

Adam Smith understood that human capital development, both upskilling and reskilling, included apprenticeships across various sectors, largely the domain of technology colleges and universities. While the development of crafts associated with the apprenticeship model is for the industry to determine, encouragement and often support from the government should be a consideration.

---

323 Garnaut, R (2024). Let's Tax Carbon: And other ideas for a better Australia. La Trobe University Press, p120.

Anywheres and somewheres

Another important factor linked to education is social mobility. In his book *The Road to Somewhere*, David Goodhart described how the 'anywheres', who make up 25 to 30 per cent of the British population, tend to be well educated (at least to undergraduate degree level), often live away from their place of early childhood and their parents, and are more comfortable with change and social fluidity. The larger group, comprising more than half the population, which he calls the 'somewheres', tend to be less well educated and value security and familiarity over social mobility. They place much more emphasis on community attachment than the 'anywheres' and are less comfortable with change. This very simple and incomplete distinction helps highlight the flexibility or optionality that education can provide for those who value it (although Goodhart acknowledges that many highly educated people exhibit the values of the 'somewheres').[324]

As education standards have declined across the population, so has physical mobility. Again, data from the US brings this to life. In his book *The New Class War*, Michael Lind says that 57 per cent of Americans have never lived outside their home state, and 37 per cent have never lived outside their hometown, even when the economic conditions in their environment have deteriorated.[325]

324 Goodhart, D (2017). The Road to Somewhere: The new tribes shaping British politics. Penguin Press.

325 Lind, M (2021). The New Class War: Saving democracy from the metropolitan elite. Atlantic PBS.

Education and democracy

It's not just a healthier population that education can influence but a healthier democracy. In an era of mass populism, propaganda and fake news, the more educated people are, and the more fine-tuned their critical thinking skills, the more likely they are to question and challenge the information fed to them by the corporatised media channels, with their political and other biases. Corporate owners of long-established news institutions have not hesitated in giving editorial direction on what their newspaper can write, such as the example of Amazon founder Jeff Bezos explicitly instructing the *Washington Post* only to publish opinion pieces that support 'personal liberties' and 'free markets'.[326] Numerous examples exist of the media actively promoting a one-sided agenda and implicitly hiding the truth. Trusted institutions like the ABC in Australia and the BBC in the UK increasingly fail to speak for the whole country and balance the propaganda that pollutes many media channels and represents a threat to democracy. A common, trusted national media voice in the US no longer exists.[327] The nature of the media 'truth' crisis was captured in the words of a senior global media executive who described the profit-before-truth dilemma: 'There is an inescapable conclusion that we must reach if we are to have a better society. The only reliable, durable and perpetual guarantor of independence is profit.'[328]

The role of education in democracy was highlighted in the Brexit vote in the UK. About 75 per cent of people with

---

326 *Financial Times*. 'Jeff Bezos focuses Washington Post's opinion pages on "personal liberties" and "free markets"'. 27 February 2025. https://www.ft.com/content/bb816e89-74de-4ba1-a8d8-bd335f3a42f3

327 Goodhart, D (2020), p27.

328 O'Brien, J (2024). How They Broke Britain. WH Allen, p55.

minimal educational qualifications voted for Brexit, and about the same proportion with university degrees voted to remain.[329] A similar divide was reflected in those who voted for Donald Trump in the 2016 and 2024 US presidential elections. David Goodhart argues that both the Brexit and Trump votes represented a protest in part due to the profound status shift occurring over the past 50 years devaluing hand and heart occupations.[330]

*

In Smith's view, a major contribution to modern society was that we are all ultimately a product of our environment. As I explore in this book, many problems people face can be understood as much by their environment and their access to, and level of, education, particularly in formative years, which form learned behaviours and beliefs. Many of the mental health problems that plague society today are viewed as crises. The origins of these problems can partly be understood in how modern society has evolved and ignored the wisdom of Smith. This is just one reason why we must rediscover Adam Smith. The next chapter presents far more.

329 Swales, K (2016). *Understanding the Leave vote*, NatCen. https://www.whatukthinks.org/eu/analysis/understanding-the-leave-vote/

330 Goodhart, D (2020), p28.

6

Why We Must Rediscover Adam Smith

Undoubtedly, the economic consensus in Australia (and some other major economies) has progressively shifted away from liberal values of competitive markets, free trade, individual liberty and freedom, and limits to state intervention. So-called neoliberalism, as Nobel prize winner Joseph Stiglitz unfairly characterises these values, is on the nose.[331] Yet, these trends should not obscure the incredible global advancements that resulted from these liberal values. For example, since Deng Xiaoping 'opened up' the Chinese economy in the late 1970s to embrace market-based principles, over 600 million people came out of poverty. The incredible advancements in China have undoubtedly benefited the Australian economy; some would argue that China has underwritten our economic

331 Stiglitz, JE (2024), p215.

prosperity for much of the past three decades by importing a large volume of our resources.

Concerningly, there is so much evident in the current climate of expansionism that reflects a fundamental misunderstanding of economic history. The lessons of the economic consequences of nationalism, populism and protectionism that caused the great economic depression in the 1930s may seem distant and forgotten, but dismissing the potential for the economic costs of such policies to re-emerge would be foolish. The extensive literature on the economic consequences of a growing state is quite compelling, and two highly regarded economists, Carmen Reinhart and Kenneth Rogoff, remind us that the four most dangerous words in economics are 'this time is different'.[332]

Despite the disappointing regression on some things central to Adam Smith's philosophy, the compelling reason he matters today is partly because his beliefs cut across the unhelpful political labels of left and right and help reconcile ideologies many believe cannot be reconciled. Smith forces us to appreciate that real-world politics and the community's needs will always be too complex for any ideology to address satisfactorily. Society is increasingly unimpressed with the shallowness and sometimes corrupting nature of political manoeuvring favouring 'big business' or powerful trade unions.

Given the challenges that society faces today, together with the dwindling public confidence in the many institutions that have defined democracy, there is a need now, more than ever, to better understand the true meaning of what Adam Smith

332 Reinhart, CM & Rogoff, KS (2011). *This Time Is Different: Eight centuries of financial folly*. Princeton University Press.

had to say and how his philosophy can be shaped to address the numerous and future defining societal issues we face. Sticking our heads in the sand or plodding on as we have been for decades is a complete failure in leadership, and it could see us drift or sleepwalk into a society that resembles many of the characteristics we see as failing with the US. Professors Anne Case and Sir Angus Deaton graphically describe some of those failings in their book *Deaths of Despair*, which I discussed in Chapter 5.

Adam Smith reminds us that conventional ways of quantifying economic growth are incomplete measures of success and can, ironically, damage a healthy society. Smith believed strongly that you cannot separate the success of the economy from that of society, and that social factors affect the way people feel about themselves, which today we partly understand by the crisis many rich countries face with addictions such as substance abuse, gambling, domestic violence and family breakdowns. Throwing billions of dollars at important issues such as domestic violence[333] without addressing the root, underlying cause is arguably another waste of taxpayer money. Politics has become a game of 'quick fix' remedies without properly understanding cause and effect. All of this is at the expense of the taxpayer and those needing a more thoughtful and sustainable approach.

So, if Adam Smith were to visit modern Australia, what would he think? We can confidently predict that he would not be impressed with the growing role of government in our economy, the stifling nature of regulation, our complex and

---

333 Evans, J. 'National cabinet promises $4.7 billion plan for frontline family violence services'. *ABC News*. 6 September 2024. https://www.abc.net.au/news/2024-09-06/national-cabinet-billions-family-domestic-violence/104318912

inequitable tax system, the threats to global trade, the weak nature of competition in the way many of our key industries operate, and how a small number of large businesses generate eye-watering economic rents, often based on privileges granted or protected by the government at the expense of consumers. He would be dismayed at the state of moral and ethical standards in too many businesses, the flawed nature of corporate governance and how it has frequently allowed poor and sometimes damaging corporate behaviour. He would be bewildered at the excessive CEO remuneration without regard for societal views and often poorly aligned with real performance.

Smith would be mortified by the way in which powerful lobby groups, such as those in the gambling industry, are allowed to exert influence on policy in the face of overwhelming evidence of substantial societal harm, and the way that certain sporting codes at the heart of many communities defend and promote this damaging influence given the financial benefits they gain. The pervasive nature of cronyism and corruption would also cause disappointment. He would be concerned by government policies that directly influence industry outcomes, believing there to be a market failure. He would see this as a waste of taxpayer resources. He would certainly not be impressed with the state of education and the growing inequality.[334] He would be concerned that elements that once drove success in the Australian economy are breaking down. He would be gravely concerned about the potential pandemic of mental health problems plaguing the workplace and society. Although mental health concerns were not documented in the

334 Oslington, P & Hart, DM (2023).

18th century, Smith would understand it as a by-product of the issues he wrote about in *The Theory of Moral Sentiments.*

Not all these problems can readily be solved, but several primary issues are worth prioritising and exploring, given their corrosive nature. These issues need bold policy responses in Australia, where tinkering at the edges has defined political leadership.

Big government

As discussed in Chapter 1, Smith saw the role of government to be largely limited to three functions:

1. to ensure a nation's capacity and capabilities to defend itself
2. to establish and enforce the rule of law by protecting citizens from injustice or oppression from others and ensure an effective structure of institutions for the administration of justice
3. to establish and maintain public institutions and public works to ensure the orderly operation of civil society.

Adam Smith was acutely aware of the natural tendency of the 'man of system' to want to grow the size of government in the economy, and he captured this ageless concern when he wrote:

> *It is of the highest impertinence and presumption, therefore, in kings and ministers, to pretend to watch over the economy of private people and to restrain their expense, either by sumptuary laws or by prohibiting the importation of foreign luxuries. They are themselves always, and without exception, the greatest spendthrifts in society. Let them look well after their own expense, and they may safely*

> *trust private people with theirs. If their own extravagance does not ruin the state, that of their subjects never will.*[335]

The growing and pervasive nature of government intervention would cause Smith to warn us against the creeping dangers of the 'man of system' with a vision that they want to impose on the rest of us, and how that can and will erode our personal freedom. Politicians are prone to self-deception and can quickly convince themselves of their own genius. Political history is littered with numerous examples of this, whereas often, the best way for policymakers to make the world a better place is to set the 'rules of the game' and then leave things alone. The battle for small government, leaving more room for private-sector innovation, personal freedom and entrepreneurialism, is largely lost for the foreseeable future. Fast-tracked by events such as the GFC and the pandemic, government spending continues to grow as a share of the economy in all major economies. In the rich world, government spending averaged 30 per cent of GDP in 1960, whereas in 2024, it was above 40 per cent.[336] In the US, the self-proclaimed bastion of capitalism, government spending has risen eightfold over the last century, from under 4 per cent in 1930 to 24 per cent of GDP in 2023 – and 36 per cent when including state and local governments.[337] In Australia, total government spending (federal and state) was 38 per cent of GDP in 2022, up from 11 per cent in 1960 when data was first measured. Federal government spending alone in 2024 reached 26.5 per cent of GDP, the highest level since

335 Smith, A (1776). *The Wealth of Nations*, B.II, ch.3, II.3.36.

336 *The Economist*. 'Governments are bigger than ever. They are also more useless'. 23 September 2024. https://www.economist.com/finance-and-economics/2024/09/23/governments-are-bigger-than-ever-they-are-also-more-useless

337 Sharma, R. 'What went wrong with capitalism?'. *Financial Times*, 25 May 2024.

the 1980s.[338] The welfare state, particularly given the reality of the ageing population, an underfunded health system and the growing demand for greater defence spending, is now a fixed reality, as is the high level of public-sector debt. Yet, as Adam Smith reminds us, excess public debt impedes wealth creation, and countries risk being 'gradually enfeebled' by such debt.[339]

In an era of big government, the broad vision for the industrial future of the Australian economy, espoused by the government in 2024, would certainly be a cause for deep concern to Smith. Prime Minister Albanese pointed out that major advanced economies were pouring trillions of dollars into their industrial bases, manufacturing capability and economic sovereignty, and Australia must do the same. The Prime Minister said, 'We must recognise there is a new and widespread willingness to make economic interventions based on national interest and national sovereignty. And – critically – none of this is being left solely to market forces or trusted to the invisible hand.'[340] This mantra, of course, has a long and underwhelming history. It is a profoundly flawed and expensive policy for which future taxpayers will pick up the tab.

Given the current trajectory of a growing state, an obvious question is whether there is a contemporary equivalent of the 'Third Way' centrist politics popularised by US President Bill Clinton and British Prime Minister Tony Blair in the 1990s. The Third Way philosophy was championed by the British political

---

338 Kehoe, J. 'Government spending addiction adds to RBA recession risk.' *Financial Review*, 14 August 2024. https://www.afr.com/policy/economy/to-avoid-recession-governments-must-help-the-rba-by-cutting-spending-20240813-p5k262

339 Smith, A (1776). *The Wealth of Nations*, B.V, ch.3, V.3, V.3.58.

340 Hutchens, G. 'Do we want Australia's economy to become more self-sufficient?' *ABC News*, 14 April 2024. https://www.abc.net.au/news/2024-04-14/do-we-want-australias-economy-to-become-more-self-sufficient/103704436

commentator Anthony Giddens in his book *The Third Way: The renewal of social democracy* (1998) and was the theoretical framework for what Tony Blair declared in 2009 as the 'new capitalism'.[341] The Third Way has been defined as 'in favour of growth, entrepreneurship, enterprise and wealth creation but it is also in favour of greater social justice, and it sees the state playing a major role in bringing this about'.[342]

The espoused philosophy of the Third Way is arguably closer to Adam Smith than the alternatives of the increasingly redundant right- and left-wing ideologues that still shape much of contemporary political discourse. A variation on the Third Way theme is directionally consistent with the advocacy for a 'strategic approach' of government promoted by Professor Mariana Mazzucato, who heads the Institute for Innovation and Public Purpose at University College London. Professor Mazzucato has influenced how the Albanese government has thought about the state's role. Still, in doing so, she has run the risk of undermining some interesting ideas with a sense, implied in her work, that the state should play a more dominant intervention role.[343]

Professor Mazzucato, in her book *The Big Con*, highlights many problems with the current way many governments work, and in particular, she is critical of the dependence that governments have created on management consultants, a direct result of the hollowing-out of capability within the civil services

---

341 Blair, T, speech at the New World, New Capitalism' conference. https://www.astrid-online.it/static/upload/protected/Tony/Tony-Blair_new-world-new-capitalism_08_01_09.pdf

342 Giddens, A (2000). *The Third Way and its Critics*. Polity Press, p35.

343 van Leeuwen, H. 'Meet Mariana Mazzucato, the economist influencing the treasurer'. *Financial Review*, 28 July 2023. https://www.afr.com/policy/economy/meet-mariana-mazzucato-the-economist-influencing-the-treasurer-20230722-p5dqdp

and the creation of what became a 'shadow public service' in the form of expensive consultants, who through their conduct can create a sense that they are more motivated by growing their fees at the expense of the taxpayer than thinking about the public good.[344] The Australian Department of Defence, for example, reportedly spent more on hiring consultants in 2022–23 than on feeding all military personnel and could have run the entire submarine fleet for a year on the same money.[345] As another example, a 2023 audit revealed that the Morrison government spent $20.8 billion on consultants in its final year – the equivalent of 54,000 full-time staff, or 37 per cent of the actual 144,300 people employed in public service.[346]

Mazzucato argues that the state must build capability within, and reduce the unhealthy and sometimes conflicted dependency on consultants. I agree with this, and the well-publicised ethical conduct of some of the major accounting and consulting firms should not be seen as a one-off but a reflection of a consultancy 'profession' that, in the words of Professor Mazzucato, has become 'a big con' at the expense of the taxpayer.[347] The consulting profession has captured the state

---

344 Mazzucato, M & Collington, R (2023). *The Big Con: How the consulting industry weakens our businesses, infantilizes our governments, and warps our economies.* Penguin Press.

345 Mizen, R. 'What Defence spent on consultants could run submarine fleet for a year'. *Financial Review*, 8 December 2024. https://www.afr.com/politics/federal/what-defence-spent-on-consultants-could-run-submarine-fleet-for-a-year-20241207-p5kwmq

346 Convery, S. 'Morrison government spent $20.8bn on consultants and outsourcing public service in final year, audit finds'. *The Guardian*, 6 May 2023. https://www.theguardian.com/australia-news/2023/may/05/morrison-government-spent-208bn-on-consultants-and-outsourcing-public-service-in-final-year-audit-finds

347 Trinca, H. 'PwC scandal shines light on clout of professional services'. *The Australian*, 23 June 2023. https://www.theaustralian.com.au/business/pwc-scandal-shines-light-on-clout-of-professional-services/news-story/317603b709ba1d725ba728e48ab86603

in many ways. However, the problem is primarily with the government rather than the consultants. There has been a period of hollowing out within the public sector, which Professor Ross Garnaut AC also summed up when he highlighted how governments in the era of major reform relied on a properly resourced professional civil service, and the cuts to the number of public servants since 2013 (particularly under the Abbott government) saw a progression towards substituting public servants with external consultants.[348]

While there is some merit in the views of Professor Mazzucato, history would tell us that there is a need to constrain 'big government'. Smith is clear that when it comes to business, private individuals are constrained in their judgement and behaviour because of the risks of mistakes, whereas politicians largely avoid the consequences: 'Bankruptcy is perhaps the greatest and most humiliating calamity which can befall an innocent man. Therefore, the greater part of men are sufficiently careful to avoid it.'[349] But politicians who bankrupt a city or nation, or leave a crippling burden of indebtedness, do not face the same consequences. Smith concluded, 'Great nations are never impoverished by private, though they are sometimes by public prodigality and misconduct'.[350] The GFC may challenge this conclusion, but perhaps that major event can be explained by state capture in the form of weak regulation championed by the Greenspan Doctrine, as discussed in Chapter 2.

The warning signs are clear: governments in most developed countries are on a mission to play an even bigger part in all our lives. We are living in an over-governed society. As the public

---

348 Garnaut, R (2024), p276.
349 Smith, A (1776). *The Wealth of Nations.*
350 Ibid.

sector grows, the private sector is being crowded out. Personal freedoms are shrinking. Just-in-time laws and regulations are being introduced, often at the behest of noisy minority voices. The original Keynesian idea that the government should save during periods of growth to spend heavily in times of recession has now seen high spending become a permanent feature of how governments operate, which only increases the burden on taxpayers and consequently reduces personal freedom. A direct economic cost of this reality is the role that a large state, and its propensity for 'unproductive hands' and stifling bureaucracy, plays as a drag on productivity.

A taxation system in need of urgent repair

Few reasonable people would disagree with the principles of a just taxation system – fair, proportional, efficient and not discouraging productive effort – as outlined by Adam Smith and summarised in Chapter 1. Yet, the Australian taxation system has drifted away from anything that could reasonably be seen as a 'fair' system, and there are good grounds to say that our tax system is 'broken'!

Many wealthy people would most likely vote for higher taxes on wealth if everyone contributed and taxpayer money was well spent. Most wealthy people would likely support a tax system that addresses current inequalities and improves labour productivity. However, this is a very different world, where wealthy taxpayers try to minimise their taxes using a whole range of schemes only practically available to the rich, with negative gearing at the top of the list.

Negative gearing is an easy target, and people should not be criticised for operating within the 'rules of the game'. The rules, however, need to be reassessed, given the inevitable reality of limits on fiscal prudence and the distorted nature of our current tax system. Equally, as I discuss later in this chapter, negative gearing reform would not be enough; the entire tax system badly needs reform, with the absence of an inheritance tax, for example, a controversial area for review.

First introduced into the tax system in 1936 but only widely used in the property market since the 1980s, negative gearing relates to using debt to support investment in property and other assets so that the cost of debt (and other costs) can be claimed as a tax deduction. In deducting interest costs on growth assets, investors gain a short-term cash-flow benefit ahead of any future capital gains tax (CGT) on selling the invested asset. In its nature, negative gearing encourages speculative investment and is more frequently used by wealthier people to reduce their overall current-year tax liability.

Negative gearing is both a 'negative' on the tax system and a cause of growing societal inequality, particularly in the housing market, where it supports house prices at higher levels. The current estimate of the federal budget for tax deduction on a rental property is $50 billion per year,[351] and based on estimates from the Parliamentary Budget Office (PBO), the net cost to the federal budget of negative gearing and CGT discounts will be about $165.6 billion in the decade

351 Karvelas, P. 'In 2019, Australia wasn't ready to talk about tax and housing. Is now finally the time to talk about negative gearing?' *ABC News*, 9 September 2024. https://www.abc.net.au/news/2024-09-09/housing-negative-gearing-mood-for-change/104325444

to 2033–34.[352] The CGT discounts highlight how the problems with negative gearing have been greatly magnified since they were introduced by then PM John Howard and Treasurer Peter Costello in 1999. The Howard and Costello 50 per cent CGT changes converted negative gearing from a strategy that had been about *deferring* tax liabilities into one that was about *both deferring and permanently reducing* tax liabilities (by, in effect, converting wage and salary income taxable at full marginal rates in the year in which it is earned into capital gains taxable at half marginal rates at a time of the taxpayer's own choosing).

The negative gearing regime is heavily weighted towards high-income earners, who, according to *The Guardian*, account for 5 per cent of taxpayers. According to ATO data, people earning more than $180,000 per annum could lower their collective tax bill by $1.3 billion in 2021–22 through negative gearing. Australians earning $1 million or more recorded the largest negative gearing tax reduction losses. The ATO analysis showed that people in the higher tax brackets were more than three times as likely to claim negative gearing tax losses.[353] In the tax year 2021–22, for example, over a hundred millionaires in Australia, earning on average $3.8 million each, paid no tax, according to the ATO. This cohort of millionaires claimed $279 million worth of different deductions (negative gearing among them) to reduce their tax bill to $0, including claiming

352 Basford Canales, S. 'Negative gearing and capital gains tax discounts to cost Australian budget $165bn over 10 years, analysis reveals'. *The Guardian*, 1 July 2024. https://www.theguardian.com/australia-news/article/2024/jul/01/negative-gearing-and-capital-gains-tax-discounts-to-cost-australian-budget-165bn-over-10-years-analysis-reveals

353 Kelly, C & Nicholas, J. 'How the most affluent Australians disproportionately benefit from negative gearing'. *The Guardian*, 28 September 2024. https://www.theguardian.com/australia-news/2024/sep/27/how-the-most-affluent-australians-disproportionately-benefit-from-negative-gearing

a deduction of $201,000 on average to accountants to manage their tax affairs. Exploiting tax concessions and tax loopholes remains a privilege open to the wealthy, and it plays a role in underwriting the inequality that plagues modern Australia.[354]

In the US, President Donald Trump, a billionaire, was proud that he didn't pay taxes.[355] This insensitive boast by Trump is one that over 1,200 large companies in Australia could also make. The ATO reported that of 3,985 larger business entities that lodged tax returns in 2022–23, 31 per cent did not pay tax. While many had legitimate reasons, such as loss-making and tax offsets, others used loopholes to avoid tax, such as profit shifting to lower tax jurisdictions using complex structures designed by international accounting.[356] Kerry Packer reminded all Australians that their goal should be to minimise their tax (for those who can afford it).[357]

Australia is not the only country with a negative gearing feature in its tax system. Canada, Germany and Japan are among a small group of wealthy nations adopting a similar system. New Zealand did have negative gearing in its tax system, but this has been progressively phased out due to its impact on housing prices and the inherent bias towards wealthier taxpayers.

---

354 Khadem, N. '102 millionaires paid no tax, and the richest and poorest postcodes and occupations revealed'. *ABC News*, 17 June 2024. https://www.abc.net.au/news/2024-06-17/millionaires-paid-no-tax-and-richest-and-poorest-postcodes-ato/103987158

355 Stiglitz, JE (2024), p119.

356 Khadem, N. 'More than 1,200 large companies paid no tax, ATO reveals, as it vows to fight profit shifting'. *ABC News*, 1 November 2024. https://www.abc.net.au/news/2024-11-01/companies-that-paid-no-tax-in-2022-23-revealed-profit-shifting/104545520

357 Peatling, S. 'Corporate tax inquiry: Kerry Packer's infamous committee appearance serves as a cautionary tale'. *The Sydney Morning Herald*, 9 April 2015. https://www.smh.com.au/politics/federal/corporate-tax-inquiry-kerry-packers-infamous-committee-appearance-serves-as-a-cautionary-tale-20150408-1mgfaq.html

ATO taxation statistics for 2021–22 show that 47.2 per cent of the taxable income reported by people in the top tax bracket is in forms other than wages and salaries (forms that are taxed much less heavily than wages and salaries are), as opposed to just 14.6 per cent of the taxable income reported by people who aren't in the top tax bracket.

The absence of inheritance tax is another controversial area of tax policy ripe for mature review. Since abolishing the inheritance tax in 1979, Australia has been one of the few major economies that doesn't impose a tax on inherited wealth – 24 of the 38 OECD countries have an inheritance or estate tax. Research from Griffith University in 2024 estimated that Australians will inherit $3.5 trillion over the next 20 years.[358] Regardless of the accuracy of this estimate, there is little dispute that much has changed since 1979, and many Australians are living in a period of unprecedented riches. They live in conditions that earlier generations would have considered luxurious, even with our high levels of household debt, which I discuss later in this chapter.

In 2020, inheritance or estate taxes accounted for approximately 1.5 per cent of GDP in France and 0.7 per cent in Germany. Of course, there are different thresholds to which such a tax could be applied, such as estates valued over $5 million. The UK applies a 40 per cent inheritance tax above a £325,000 ($640,000) threshold. Critics of inheritance tax argue that it is tantamount to double taxation, as assets have often already been subject to income tax or CGT. Proponents of some

358 Wedesweiler, M. '"Pay their fair share": should Australia tax its $3.5 trillion inheritance wave?'. *SBS News*, 14 February 2025. https://www.sbs.com.au/news/article/why-there-are-calls-to-tax-australias-3-5-trillion-inheritance-wave/yhuvpn495

form of inheritance tax point to the huge wealth accumulation by the 'baby boomers' and the fact that those fortunate enough to inherit that wealth do so without often having had to work for it, further entrenching inequality and the pressure on wage earners to meet the burden of taxation.[359]

As I discuss in Chapter 7, there is also a legitimate case for exploring higher taxation of economic rents as a means, among other things, of reducing the incentive to create market power and to claw back some of the excess profits earned at a cost to consumers. Equally, the low level of taxes paid by multinationals in Australia is another matter needing urgent attention.[360] Income tax exemptions for major sporting codes is another area for review, given that some codes, such as the AFL, are substantial businesses turning over close to $1 billion and run on commercial grounds despite their not-for-profit status, and handsomely reward their executives accordingly, with some salaries reportedly close to or above $1 million per year.[361]

There is also a legitimate argument that the fiscal problem should be partly solved by looking at the goods and services tax (GST), which is less of a drag on the incentive to work hard and arguably a more efficient tax as it gives personal freedom to people on how and what they spend their money on – the exemption list and GST rates can be reviewed and varied to minimise unintended consequences. Nordic countries, for example, used their equivalent of GST to better manage big

359 Leigh, A (2024), p116.
360 Gottliebsen, R. 'Australia must fix its tax crisis before it gets much worse'. *The Australian*, 16 September 2024. https://www.theaustralian.com.au/business/australia-must-fix-its-tax-crisis-before-it-gets-much-worse/news-story/5d78ee84a43ee5846e5f79a17b1ffcce
361 Warner, M (2021). *The Boys Club: Power, politics and the AFL*. Hachette Australia.

government spending by imposing levy rates of 24 per cent.[362] The GST rate in Australia is 10 per cent, compared to 15 per cent in New Zealand and 20 per cent in the UK (the UK's equivalent of GST is VAT).

The Economist argued that while consumption taxes are regressive because poor consumers use more of their income than rich consumers, there is an argument that the less well-off can benefit more from public spending on critical services, and that rich retirees, for example, would also contribute more to tax given their higher marginal propensity to spend.[363] There are, of course, other negatives to increasing GST, particularly the risk of higher inflation given higher prices.

Any debate on broadening the tax base and raising the GST rate must include evaluating the methodology and logic of the current formula for carving up the GST revenue among the states. The current formula, influenced by the political sway of the Western Australian government, is widely seen as inequitable. One of Australia's leading economists, Saul Eslake, describes the current arrangement as 'the worst public policy decision of the 21st century so far'.[364] The GST distribution between states results in Western Australia, Australia's richest state and the only one running persistent budget surpluses, being gifted $54 billion over 11 years out of the federal budget.[365]

---

362 *The Economist*. 'If you must raise taxes, raise VAT'. 26 September 2024. https://www.economist.com/leaders/2024/09/26/if-you-must-raise-taxes-raise-vat

363 Ibid.

364 Coorey, P & McIlroy, T. '"Beyond comprehension": WA's GST deal to blow out to $50b'. *Financial Review*, 12 February 2024. https://www.afr.com/politics/federal/beyond-comprehension-wa-s-gst-deal-to-blow-out-to-50b-20240212-p5f49h

365 Karp, P. 'Meet the men behind "the worst policy decision of the 21st century"'. *Financial Review*, 24 February 2025. https://www.afr.com/politics/how-a-small-group-of-businessmen-helped-wa-win-a-54b-tax-deal-20250205-p5l9qh

The burden of personal income tax is an obvious review area, as the current system is a drag on hard work, productivity and personal freedom, and there is no indexation of tax brackets, which means that tax bracket creep further erodes hard-earned income, particularly at times of sustained inflation. Close to 50 per cent of OECD countries have tax bracket indexation to protect workers. Many hardworking high achievers in Australia pay nearly half their income on PAYE tax (including the Medicare levy). Such individuals effectively work for the state from Monday morning to Wednesday lunchtime every week. In 2023, personal income tax reached the highest share of all taxes in the 25 years since GST was introduced in 2000.[366] John Kehoe, the respected *Financial Review* journalist, wrote:

> *The lack of respect in Canberra for hard-working taxpayers is a disgrace. Tax bracket creep is aiding and abetting this scam … Rather than forcing politicians to explicitly raise revenue more transparently from other tax bases, bracket creep is their hidden get-out-of-jail free card to suck money from workers silently.*[367]

If alive today, Smith would be perplexed by the complexity and inequality of the Australian taxation system and how it violates many of the principles that he suggested should govern taxation policy.

The tax system of modern Australia is badly broken and needs urgent attention. Adam Smith would feel our political

---

366 Kehoe, J & Read, M. 'Income tax hits 25-year high in Chalmers' surplus'. *Financial Review*, 30 September 2024. https://www.afr.com/policy/economy/income-tax-hits-25-year-high-in-chalmers-surplus-20240930-p5keiw

367 Kehoe, J. 'Treasury is addicted to income tax to fund spending', *Financial Review*, 5 June 2024. https://www.afr.com/policy/economy/treasury-is-addicted-to-income-tax-to-fund-spending-20240604-p5jj4w

leadership has failed to steward such an important government responsibility.

The last political leader to show courage and seriously address the taxation issue, particularly negative gearing, was Bill Shorten in the lead-up to the 2019 election. The electorate then had limited appetite for the bold changes the then Labor leader proposed.[368]

The scourge of rentier capitalism

Adam Smith understood the dangers of businesses having a dominant market position. He wrote:

> *The constant view of such companies is always to raise the rate of their own profit as high as they can; to keep the market, both for the goods they export, and for those they import, as much understocked as they can: which can be done only by restraining the competition, or by discouraging new adventures from entering the trade.*[369]

He was even more specific when it came to monopolists and other industry structures of limited competition:

> *A monopoly granted either to an individual or to a trading company has the same effect as a secret in trade or manufacturing. The monopolist, by keeping the market constantly under-stocked, by never fully supplying the effectual demand, sell their commodities much above the natural price, and raise their emoluments whether they consist in wages or profit, greatly above the natural rate.*[370]

368 Ibid.
369 Smith, A (1776). *The Wealth of Nations*, B.V.ch. V.1.99.
370 Smith, A (1776). *The Wealth of Nations*, B.I.ch. 7, I.7.26.

Given how key industries with weak competition dominate the Australian economy, what is most perplexing is the posture of Australian governments in their unwillingness to address the overwhelming evidence of what Professor Ross Garnaut AC describes as the denial of the increasing oligopoly in the economy and the extraction of economic rents at the expense of the wider society.[371] The powerful position Qantas enjoys in the airline industry is an obvious example. As outlined in Chapter 3, this is a widespread scourge evident also in the banking industry, but it goes beyond the banking and aviation sectors to the food retail, telecom, insurance and energy sectors. Taking the banking sector as an example, Professor Garnaut comments, 'Increased concentration of banking business is a large problem. Four big banks put up their interest rates or put them down on adjacent days by the same amount. No effective competition. They know how to work together'.[372]

The former federal treasurer Peter Costello summed things up well:

> *Our banks are absolutely immune from market discipline, living in a highly profitable cocoon; they think all these high returns are from their own brilliance, but what they haven't understood is they have a unique and privileged regulatory system which has delivered this to them.*[373]

---

371 Garnaut, R (2024).

372 Hutchens, G, 'Australia would be raising $70 billion a year from carbon price if it wasn't dismantled, Ross Garnaut says'. *ABC News*, 17 September 2023. https://www.abc.net.au/news/2023-09-17/ross-garnaut-70-billion-from-carbon-price-economic-rent/102850464

373 Creighton, A, 'Peter Costello's blast at the banks: bring in some competition.' *The Australian*, 19 August 2017. https://www.theaustralian.com.au/business/financial-services/peter-costellos-blast-at-the-banks-bring-in-some-competition/news-story/97956f0848cff1dfd218b1a272ebe6e7

The oligopoly banking system's cosy nature is clear in that over 80 per cent of total banking system assets are captured by the Big Four, up from close to 70 per cent in 2000. Ironically, with the acquisition of Bankwest by CBA, St.George Bank by Westpac and Suncorp Bank by ANZ, all under Australian Labor governments, these governments have been the most supportive and accommodating of increasing the power of big banks.[374]

Cameron Murray and Paul Frijters examined in their book *Rigged: How networks of powerful mates rip off everyday Australians* the question of economic rent generation in Australia from sectors such as banking, mining, media, infrastructure and property development. While not providing an accurate figure, they estimate that the number could easily be more than $200 billion per annum. They conclude that the net economic costs to the nation are material, and rent-seeking worsens inequality.[375]

The dangers of growing inequality

While equality is an elusive concept, Adam Smith knew that variations in income and wealth were inherent in a market economy and a function of everyone's varying degrees of motivation, appetite for risk, skills and education. As discussed in Chapter 2, he also saw the social and moral dangers of significant and growing disparities in income and wealth.

Smith would agree with Ruchir Sharma's views in his book *What Went Wrong with Capitalism* (2024). Sharma argues that inequality poisons the politics of capitalist democracies, just as it distorts their economies; through a US lens, Sharma argues

374 Healy, J (2019).
375 Murray, CK & Frijters, P (2022), pp211-218.

that capitalist societies must watch the balance of distributions to avoid a gradual erosion in social cohesion.[376] Where material imbalances build up gradually between those who have prospered from the system and the majority who have not shared in the same way, the conditions are ripe for the poisons to enter the bloodstream, and societal cancers start to grow.

Inequality in the US mirrors other aspects of what many see as a dysfunctional society. Income inequality data reveals that 20 per cent of US national income goes to the richest 1 per cent, double the level from 1990. Close to 67 per cent of total wealth in the US was owned by the top 10 per cent of earners in 2023.[377]

While inequality is much more than the difference in income or wealth, a traditional and universal measure of inequality known as the Gini coefficient, a statistical measure of economic inequality in a population named after the Italian statistician Corrado Gini, measures inequality on a scale from zero to one: zero represents perfect equality, and one represents perfect inequality, where one person receives all the income. Australia's Gini coefficient was estimated at 0.324 in 2019–20 and is forecast to increase to 0.34 in 2024. (It averaged 0.313 between 1995 and 2020.)[378] The equivalent US measure was 0.47 in 2022, up from 0.43 in 1990.[379] Research shows that inequality in Australia has continued to increase over the past 20 years, and

376 Sharma, R (2024), p212.

377 Tierney, A. 'Wealth distribution in the United States in the second quarter of 2024'. *Statista*, 29 October 2024. https://www.statista.com/statistics/203961/wealth-distribution

378 'Australia Social: Gini Coefficient: Annual', CEIC. https://www.ceicdata.com/en/australia/social-gini-coefficient-annual

379 Tierney, A. 'Household income distribution according to the Gini Index of income inequality in the United States from 1990 to 2023'. *Statista*, 16 September 2024. https://www.statista.com/statistics/219643/gini-coefficient-for-us-individuals-families-and-households/

that Australia has the 14th highest level of inequality of the 28 OECD countries surveyed. A separate wealth Gini coefficient shows the Australia data at 0.61 for 2019–20.[380] More granular analysis – averages can hide a lot – shows that the richest 200 people in Australia have seen their wealth triple from 8.4 per cent of Australia's GDP to 23.7 per cent in the 20 years to 2024, adding evidence of a clear trend of greater inequality.[381]

As I discussed in Chapter 3, Thomas Piketty's bestselling book *Capital in the Twenty-First Century* highlighted how, over the past 40 years, there has been a conspicuous imbalance in economic returns accruing to capital (and shared with senior executives) compared to those earned by labour or workers. This reality has been an essential factor in the causes of growing inequality. (Piketty followed up his first book with another bestseller, *Capital and Ideology*, which further explored the ideology and policies that reinforce inequality as a societal norm.) As income inequality grows, society becomes even more fragmented. Nobel Prize–winning economist Joseph Stiglitz observed that economic segregation is growing, with the poorest viewing the world as not working for them while the wealthiest continue to prosper, often in ways that take advantage of a system stacked in their favour.[382]

Smith always saw that when left to its own devices, a laissez-faire approach to economic policy, such as that unfairly and inaccurately attributed to Milton Friedman but implemented by

---

380 Australian Bureau of Statistics. 'Income and wealth inequality'. https://www.abs.gov.au/statistics/measuring-what-matters/measuring-what-matters-themes-and-indicators/prosperous/income-and-wealth-inequality

381 Convery, S. 'The rich are getting richer: Australia's wealth divide continues to widen'. *The Guardian*, 13 August 2024. https://www.theguardian.com/australia-news/article/2024/aug/13/the-rich-are-getting-richer-australias-wealth-divide-continues-to-widen

382 Stiglitz, JE (2024), p281.

Margaret Thatcher and Ronald Reagan, cannot be relied upon to achieve desirable societal outcomes. Echoing the concerns of Joseph Stiglitz,[383] this reality was understood by Professor Sir Angus Deaton, whose work on poverty and inequality shows how widening inequality, partly caused by poor education, has led to widening health and life expectancy gaps. In a US context, Deaton argues that part of the reason is that powerful companies and lobby groups have used their influence to shape government policy, laws and regulations to the detriment of society and the public interest. The gambling industry in Australia provides one of many examples closer to home.

If alive today, Smith will likely ask two obvious public policy questions: why have we come to accept such inequality as a natural outcome, and do we understand the likely long-term consequences of continuing along the current trajectory? Also, do we understand that in a democracy that purports to defend freedom and support meritocracy, people with poor education and on low incomes have little personal freedom, and social division is becoming a new form of social apartheid where certain segments of the community, almost by virtue of birth, are consigned to a life of inferior education, health care and life prospects?

Sleepwalking into a damaged society

Adam Smith reminded us of the importance of moral conduct – the standards of good or bad behaviour, fairness, honesty, prudence, and so on – when he concluded that without reverence for the rules of moral conduct, 'society would

383 Ibid., p176.

crumble into nothing'.[384] He also helped us understand that happiness and fulfilment in life were not a product of financial riches when he wrote, 'What can be added to the happiness of the man who is in health, who is out of debt and has a clear conscience?'[385]

University of Oxford Professors John Kay and Paul Collier wrote that today we live in societies saturated in selfishness, in a world of 'extreme elite individualism – the rise of the self at the expense of the community'.[386] In *The Theory of Moral Sentiments*, Smith writes about a world defined by the people closest to us that define our community – family, friends and neighbours. As discussed in Chapter 2, the reality of the world we live in is that family and community have been allowed to weaken as essential foundations of a healthy society. Today, too many people we interact with are remote and impersonal, a situation made worse by the inflexible working-from-home (WFH) movement – WFH quickly moved from a commitment to flexible working arrangements, which is a good thing, to an inflexible cultural movement that insists on always WFH on certain days of the week. We live in a world defined mainly by impersonal exchange, yet we crave human connections as individuals. Many would quickly agree that the lack of interpersonal interaction is a significant loss. Yet, so many business models are defining what we do and need to drive us towards digital, remote, impersonal interactions. It is rare to find a parent who is not concerned about how much time

---

384 Smith, A (1759). *The Theory of Moral Sentiments*, Ch. IV.

385 Ibid.

386 Collier, P and Kay, J (2020). *Greed Is Dead: Politics after individualism*. Allen Lane.

their children spend on digital devices at the expense of human interaction, sport, cultural activities and community.

Many people see the demise of faith in Western culture as a form of nihilism, which has seen traditional religions replaced with a new 'religion' of consumerism and wokeism, which is equally intolerant of alternative views. There is little argument with the view that we have seen a diminishment in spirituality in our communities. Spirituality is more than being religious; it can mean finding a sense of meaning and purpose in our lives. This reality of shallowness and spiritual void was captured by the then CEO of the AFL, Andrew Demetriou, when he said to a group of Melbourne businesspeople that because of the demise of the Catholic Church, 'Australians are now looking up to the AFL for guidance'.[387]

Adam Smith would agree with his fellow Kirkcaldy native, former British PM Gordon Brown, who observed, 'I don't think we should underestimate the motivational power that religion and ethics provided to people.'[388] This sentiment was echoed by former UK Chief Rabbi Jonathan Sacks, who complained that without God, we have increasingly adopted a utilitarian and economic definition of human worth, and questions of meaning and value have been relegated to the private sphere.[389]

Smith, reflecting in his 'be lovely and be loved' philosophy, would be concerned about the way Australia has become a 'dopamine nation' and how a culture of individualism has dominated the community. Consequently, sympathy and care

387 Warner, M (2021), p94.
388 'Gordon Brown: "I really didn't think we could go as far backwards as we've gone"'. *Financial Times*, 14 April 2024. https://www.ft.com/content/7c0fb9cf-737c-4e43-99c2-4ccae461bc63
389 Goodhart, D (2020), p19.

are weakened in the pursuit of self-interest. The practice of putting ourselves in the shoes of others and imagining how they might feel because of our actions is not, unfortunately, a feature associated with modern society. Our ability to see ourselves as others might see us is not what it once was and not as Adam Smith saw how people should view their actions. It is not the love of humankind that makes the 'man of humanity' willing to make sacrifice, but because he sees himself through the eyes of the impartial spectator. In an individualistic society – the one that defines Australia and much of the West – this is sadly less of a consideration.

Smith also highlights the dangers of allowing the quest for material wealth to dominate and corrode our moral values. The search for more dopamine and the risk of anhedonia is evident in Australia's alarmingly high levels of household debt, which only adds to the stress on household budgets, particularly in times of rising living costs more generally. In the 20 years to 2023, household debt increased from half to twice the average disposable income, and from 40 per cent of GDP to 120 per cent. The average house price in Australia in 2023 was 7.5 times the average income, up from 3.5 times 20 years earlier, the space of one generation.[390] Alan Kohler, in his essay on housing, observed that the houses we live in have become speculative financial assets rather than simply family homes. The amount of wealth Australians have concentrated in their homes has created a national psyche obsessed by property prices – and for many, with excessive levels of debt used to buy their home, a terrible burden which views the likely next interest rate move

390 Kohler, A. 'The great divide: Australia's housing mess and how to fix it.' *Quarterly Essay*, issue 92, 2023. https://www.quarterlyessay.com.au/essay/2023/11/the-great-divide/extract

by the Reserve Bank of Australia (RBA) as national news of the highest importance.[391]

The incentives caused by negative gearing are one cause of this high-risk profile, and so is the banking system's insatiable appetite for lending on housing – in my view, a huge misallocation of capital because of the low-risk profits it generates. These factors should not negate the accountability of poor government policy and individual responsibility. If people choose to take on high levels of debt, and banks, lending prudently, think that is a sensible thing to do, then people must accept the consequences of their decisions in the very same way that a driver of a car under the influence of alcohol must accept responsibility for his or her decision. Yet today, nearly one in four households faces mortgage stress or the so-called mortgage cliff,[392] and the likely date of the next move in interest rates has become a national obsession.

Through APRA and the RBA, the government must be mindful of the risk to the economy of the build-up of speculative lending in the housing market and remember the wisdom of Smith on the risk to the economy of excessive bank lending. This is a risk that builds slowly and hits suddenly. As John Maynard Keynes observed in 1931, the banks can be prone to 'herding' behaviour. They can fall into the trap that then Citibank CEO Chuck Prince did in 2007 when he said, 'As long as the music is playing, you've got to dance. We are still dancing.'[393] This unfortunate quote is reflective of how banks

391 Ibid.

392 Ibid.

393 Nakamoto, M & Wighton, D. 'Citigroup chief stays bullish on buy-outs'. *Financial Times*, 9 July 2007. https://www.ft.com/content/80e2987a-2e50-11dc-821c-0000779fd2ac

think. Citibank was close to becoming insolvent during the GFC, absent government support (which was true also of some other banks in both the US and Britain). Smith understood this risk, as did Keynes, who famously said in 1931, 'A sound banker, alas, is not one who foresees danger and avoids it, but one who, when he is ruined, is ruined in a conventional way along with his fellows so that no one can really blame him.'[394]

High debt levels and a crisis in housing supply are just two of the stressful challenges facing many households. Dr Anna Lembke asks a pertinent question relevant to Australia: 'Why, in a time of unprecedented wealth, freedom, technological progress, and medical advancement, do we appear to be unhappier and in more pain than ever?'[395]

The alarming rise in heroin-linked deaths in Australia is another cause for concern and evidence of a society with the potential for future severe problems. *The Guardian* reports, based on findings from the public health research organisation the Penington Institute, that 'Australia is seeing an alarming and devastating rise in the number of drug-induced deaths, with many of them preventable and being driven by opioids, including a 40 per cent surge in heroin-linked fatalities.'[396]

The growth in drug abuse has seen the deadly opioid fentanyl come to Australia. That drug, together with nitazenes – a group of opioid drugs 50 times stronger than fentanyl and 100 times more potent than heroin – has now created an epidemic in the US, killing over 100,000 people a year, a figure that has doubled

---

394 Healy, J (2019), p30.
395 Lembke, A (2021), p46.
396 Thou, S, '"Alarming" rise in drug overdoses in Australia as heroin-linked deaths surge 40%'. *The Guardian*, 10 May 2024. https://www.theguardian.com/australia-news/article/2024/may/10/alarming-rise-in-drug-overdoses-in-australia-as-heroin-linked-deaths-surge-40

in three years to 2023. The rate of fatalities, mainly the young and impoverished, in 2023 alone was double the combined number of American soldiers killed in combat in Vietnam, Afghanistan and Iraq. Fentanyl, 50 times more potent than heroin, is cheap to manufacture and is highly profitable even when sold for less than 50 cents a pill.[397] (I lost my 24-year-old son George in 2021, while he was at university in the US, to a 'party drug' which an autopsy found was laced with fentanyl.)

It would be a mistake to assume that fentanyl and other opioids are just a US problem, though its natural distribution channel has been from China to Mexico and then into the US. Poverty and societal decline can create fertile ground for this problem to spread into other markets, such as Australia. The fentanyl problem has already taken root in Canada, Britain and Europe, and there is a growing concern that this could also happen in Australia. Some health experts have warned that nitazenes are increasingly present in Australia,[398] with experts warning that it has the potential to be Australia's version of a 'fentanyl crisis'.[399, 400]

---

397 *The Economist*, 'America's ten-year-old fentanyl epidemic is still getting worse', 29 February 2024. https://www.economist.com/briefing/2024/02/29/americas-ten-year-old-fentanyl-epidemic-is-still-getting-worse

398 *Daily Telegraph*, '"Zombie drug" more powerful than heroin hits Sydney streets.' 2 March 2025. https://www.dailytelegraph.com.au/news/nsw/zombie-drug-nitazene-now-a-big-threat-to-australia-abf-boss-gavan-reynolds/news-story/7075fd046e904bb32a4e369fe6114b32

399 Gwynn, L. 'Synthetic opioid nitazene linked to rise in overdose deaths is emerging in Australia'. *ABC News*, 25 June 2024. https://www.abc.net.au/news/2024-06-25/nitazines-synthetic-opioid-warning-australia-overdose-deaths/104013774

400 Gwynn, L. 'The faceless killer'. *ABC News*, 15 September 2024. https://www.abc.net.au/news/2024-09-15/nitazene-detections-australia-overdose-deaths-broadmeadows/104327798

Costs and consequences of poor mental health

While Adam Smith did not explicitly discuss mental health in *The Theory of Moral Sentiments*, it is implied in his writings. If alive today, he would view the crisis in our mental health system as a direct consequence of society's failings and the disconnect between economic growth and societal well-being.

According to a 2020 Productivity Commission report, mental-ill-health-related conditions were conservatively costing Australia about $200 to 220 billion per year.[401] It is hard to think of a more critical issue facing our society than the skyrocketing demand for mental health help and a mental health system of care that is badly broken.

In Australia's population of 27 million people, approximately 8.5 million will experience a mental illness at some point in their lifetime. Many more may go undiagnosed. According to the 2020–2022 *National Study of Mental Health and Wellbeing* conducted by the Australian Bureau of Statistics (ABS), an estimated 43 per cent of the population has experienced mental illness, and 21.5 per cent of the population had had symptoms of a mental illness in the 12 months leading up to the ABS survey. The same survey highlighted that since 2013, there has been a consistent upward trend in the proportion of Australians experiencing psychological distress, and in 2021, 22.9 per cent of females and 22.7 per cent of males were in distress. An estimated 19 per cent of Australians reported being diagnosed with depression, anxiety or any other serious mental illness at some time in their life, an increase from 11 per cent in 2009.[402]

---

401 Productivity Commission (2020), p18.

402 Australian Bureau of Statistics, 'National study of mental health and wellbeing', 5 October 2023. https://www.abs.gov.au/statistics/health/mental-health/national-study-mental-health-and-wellbeing/latest-release

The root causes of this concerning and deteriorating situation are many, with much evidence that societal issues are correlated to the rise in mental health problems, substance addictions, marriage breakdowns and domestic violence, to name just a small number of problems. Mental health illnesses can take many forms, with some of the most common being anxiety-related disorders, depression, post-traumatic stress disorder (PTSD), bipolar disorder, schizophrenia, autism and attention deficit hyperactivity disorder (ADHD). Often, these conditions can be comorbid – that is, more than one disorder can occur at the same time – and in some cases, substance abuse such as alcohol or illicit drugs may also feature.

These problems have ironically been a boost for the pharmaceutical industry, which has seen the propensity for medical practitioners to prescribe medication as a way of solving sometimes poorly diagnosed underlying mental health problems. This often results in the prescription of medications such as antidepressant drugs, which can provide short-term improvements but can, in some cases, have lasting side effects. There are many highly credentialled critics of this 'medication first' approach and some excellent books that document the many problems with over-medicating poorly diagnosed problems. One such book is Richard Bentall's *Doctoring the Mind: Why Psychiatric Treatments Fail* (2009).[403] Several studies have shown a high correlation between overmedicating mental health and socioeconomic status, whereby the lower the economic well-being of a community, the higher the propensity for medication, with opioids too readily and disproportionately

---

403 Bentall, RP (2009). *Doctoring the Mind: Why psychiatric treatments fail.* Allen Lane.

prescribed to the poor.[404] This was a strategy the Sackler family adopted with Purdue Pharma and their deadly drug, OxyContin. Concerningly, studies have also shown a link between antidepressant medication and the increased risk of suicide and violence.[405]

On youth mental health, the social psychologist Jonathan Haidt, in his book *The Anxious Generation*, links the rise of adolescent mental health problems to the increased use of smartphones among young people. The highly acclaimed psychiatrist Bessel van der Kolk describes Haidt's book as raising a huge red flag, but one that society seems ill-equipped to do anything about.[406] Haidt argues that continued access to social media, online video games and other internet-based activities creates four foundational harms in the degradation of youth: social deprivation, sleep deprivation, attention fragmentation and addiction. He writes: 'This great rewiring of childhood is the single largest reason for a tidal wave of adolescent mental illness that began in early 2010'.[407] It is a credit to the Albanese government that it has taken steps and shown real intent to protect Australian youth under 16 from the dangers of online risks.

These findings on the impact of social media on youth mental health are consistent with research in Australia. For example, Dr Andrew Leigh and Dr Stephen Robson found that there has been a substantial worsening in the mental well-being of young Australians (aged 15 to 24), with smartphones and

---

404 Lembke, A (2021), p124.

405 Adshead, G. 'Antidepressants and murder: case not closed'. *British Medical Journal*, vol. 358, 2 August 2017.

406 *Financial Times*, 'Psychiatrist Bessel van der Kolk: when trauma becomes your identity, that's a dangerous thing'. 28 June 2024. https://www.ft.com/content/9ab76454-f2d5-44b7-9a7a-0b342cd4ae93

407 Haidt, J (2025). *The Anxious Generation: How the great rewiring of childhood is causing an epidemic of mental illness*. Penguin Press.

social media playing a major role.[408] The research highlighted a 35 per cent increase in the decade to 2022 in the rate of self-harm hospitalisation of young people and a 34 per cent increase in the suicide rate in the same period. In separate research, Professors Bobby Duffy and Patrick McGorry AO point to the risks associated with the increased use of social media ahead of concerns about drugs, alcohol, bullying and climate change.[409] McGorry, a professor at the University of Melbourne, is a world-leading authority on youth mental health and was Australian of the Year in 2010.

Another wake-up call for Australia came in *The Mental State of the World* 2023 report,[410] a publication by the Global Mind Project, which looks at mental well-being across 71 countries with data from 500,000 survey participants using an online mental health quotient (MHQ) that captures perceptions of 47 aspects of mental capability. Using a range of indicators aimed at measuring the human ability to navigate the normal stresses of life and function productively, the report highlights that mental well-being negatively correlates with measures of economic prosperity such as GDP per capita, and that younger age of first smartphone ownership and higher quantity of ultra-processed food consumption are two measures impacting mental well-being. In the 71 surveyed countries, on average 65 per cent of people are 'managing' and 27 per cent are 'distressed or struggling'. In Australia, 54 per cent are 'managing', ranking

---

408 Leigh, A & Robson, S (2024). *The rise of social media and the fall in mental well-being among young Australians.* Institute of Labor Economics.

409 Duffy, B & McGorry, P (2024). *Youth mental health in crisis? Public and generational attitudes in the UK and Australia.* Orygen and The Policy Institute.

410 Thiagarajan, T & Newson, J (2024). *The mental state of the world in 2023: a perspective on internet-enabled populations.* Sapien Labs. https://mentalstateoftheworld.report/

66th, five from the bottom (above Tajikistan, Brazil, South Africa, the UK and Uzbekistan), and 33 per cent are 'distressed or struggling', ranking 67th, above only Brazil, South Africa, the UK and Uzbekistan.

The unavoidable truth is that we are in the midst of a mental health crisis in Australia, which is symptomatic of wider issues discussed in this book. This crisis places a significant burden on quality of life for many and on the productivity of our economy. Yet, it is a low priority in the eyes of our political leaders, who are more likely to fund a new football stadium than a new mental health facility.[411]

More focus on strong education fundamentals and understanding the productivity drag

On the importance of education to the economy, Adam Smith was very clear:

> *The acquisition of such talents, by the maintenance of the acquired during his education, study, or apprenticeship, always costs a real expense, which is capital fixed and realized, as it were, in person. Those talents, as they make a part of his fortune, so do they likewise of that of the society to which he belongs. The improved dexterity of a workman may be considered in the same light as a machine or instrument of trade which facilitates and abridges labour, and which, although it costs a certain expense, repays that expense with a profit.*[412]

411 Cross, M (2024).
412 Smith, A (1776). *The Wealth of Nations*, B.II, ch.I, II.1.17.

It is indisputably true that educational, career and financial success are strongly correlated to a privileged background, and that those from a poorer socioeconomic background are more likely to be left behind, a reality highlighted in Chapter 5 in the context of persistently poor NAPLAN results. The education system in Australia, when it comes to the fundamentals of education, is broken, which comes at a significant cost to society and the economy. The education system also heavily advantages the rich over the less well-off, thus entrenching a disadvantage that can be life-defining and perpetuating the inequality that is a stain on our society.[413] US historian and Harvard Professor Stephen Jay Gould powerfully captured this cost to society when he wrote, 'I am, somehow, less interested in the weight and convolutions of Einstein's brain than in the near certainty that people of equal talent have lived and died in cotton fields and sweatshops'.[414]

As James Bloodworth argues in his book *The Myth of Meritocracy*,[415] 'environmental mechanisms exist that can turn a dull child into an average one and an average child into a successful one'. To express this as an equation:

> *average cognitive ability + privilege = better chance of a high-paying, high-status job.*[416]

So much has gone wrong with our education theory, which is concerning given how it is central to so much that defines a

---

413 Hare, J. 'NAPLAN is a measure of wealth, not student ability'. *Financial Review*, 14 August 2024.

414 Gould, SJ (1980). *The Panda's Thumb: More reflections in natural history*. W.W. Norton & Company.

415 Bloodworth, J (2016). *The Myth of Meritocracy*. Biteback Publishing, p102.

416 Goodhart, D (2020), p67.

healthy society. As I discuss in Chapter 5, there are arguably diminishing productivity returns for the heavy bias towards a university degree; we have placed too much weighting on the university system and cognitive capabilities ('head' skills) to the detriment of 'hand' and 'heart' skills. Our policy environment and schooling system should be more accepting of the fact that university is not the right or best choice for everyone, and that equally motivating success can be achieved through acquiring other skills essential to a vibrant economy. University should not always be seen as the best post-school education option or superior to other choices, and the mass production of university degrees should be reassessed in terms of the value it brings. The 'graduatisation' of the employment market, particularly for those entering the labour market for the first time, needs review and a coordinated government and business policy.

Education is central to individual freedom as it enhances personal agency and autonomy. There can be little argument that education is critical for personal development and economic and societal prosperity. However, as economist Alison Wolf describes, there is some idealistic thinking around the benefits of university education for economic growth and social mobility. She compares it to the emphasis that the Soviet Union (and China) placed on capital goods as the secret to economic prosperity.[417]

417 Wolf, A. 'Falling productivity and slowing growth: do our post-2008 problems have anything to do with universities?', The King's Lectures 2019, Kings College, London, 25 March 2019.

Cronyism, lobbying and media – dangers highlighted by the US

Adam Smith would view the close working relationship between industry lobby groups and the political system as one that can work against the public interest and force resistance to major reforms. He would have been aghast at the lack of moral values in business culture apparent in the scandals discussed earlier in this book, and would ask how many other businesses would fail the moral values test 'if the whole circumstances of our conduct were known'.[418] This was the 'impartial spectator' test Smith emphasised in *The Theory of Moral Sentiments*. It shouldn't be confused with the test some business leaders might apply when asking, 'What would this look like if reported on the front page of the *Financial Review*?', a test that can imply a 'don't get caught' criteria rather than one of genuine moral and ethical values.

Smith might also be worried that if left unchecked, the Australian political and business culture would follow in the trajectory of the US. In the US, lobbying and political donations can corrupt the democratic process, including extensive donations from lobby groups sometimes representing the interest of foreign nations or promoting an industry which can cause much harm, such as pharmaceuticals. As noted earlier in this book, Smith would be horrified at the influence of these lobby groups. One such example in the US is the powerful National Rifle Association (NRA), which is an advocacy group for the right to own guns despite the endless stories of harm due to gun-related crimes, including frequent high-profile occurrences of school mass shootings. The NRA's response to these shocking

418 Norman, J (2018). *Adam Smith: Father of economics*, p297.

events is that schools should have armed security guards; some US states have installed metal detectors at schools, forcing children to pass through them to enter school.[419]

I have already discussed the gambling industry and its allies in major sports, which can influence government policy and prevent regulation against the damaging impact of gambling on society, particularly on the most vulnerable. It is common for politicians to accept hospitality from the gaming industry to events such as the Melbourne Cup, the Australian Open, and AFL and cricket matches. Tim Costello, the Alliance for Gambling Reform's chief advocate, described the acceptance of such hospitality as 'an undemocratic opportunity to lobby against critical gambling reform ... how our political system can be exploited by the rich and powerful to lobby in secret against popular changes such as the proposed gambling advertising ban to the detriment of the Australian community'.[420]

The gaming industry also donates lavishly to big political parties and some independent politicians. This practice prompted independent MP Andrew Wilkie to argue that such practice 'corrupts governance and is no different from a bribe'.

The deteriorating nature of much media reporting has been a factor in undermining public confidence in institutions, government and democracy. So much of the media today, including social media – think of Elon Musk at X (formerly Twitter), Bezos at *The Washington Post* and Mark Zuckerberg at Facebook – is controlled by a small number of private

419 Stiglitz, JE (2024).
420 Butler, J. 'Gambling companies gifted hospitality to 19 Australian politicians for major sports events'. *The Guardian*, 1 October 2024. https://www.theguardian.com/australia-news/2024/oct/01/gambling-companies-gifted-hospitality-to-19-australian-politicians-for-major-sports-events-ntwnfb

actors who have a huge influence in shaping how many people are informed and think about the world, and resembles the propaganda offered up by state-controlled regimes in authoritarian states.

Eric Beecher outlined the dangers of this reality in his book *The Men Who Killed the News* (2024). He points to data that illustrates just how the media has lost the trust and respect of society: 'Globally, 42 per cent believe the media is a source of false and misleading information. Only 13 per cent of Britons and 18 per cent of Australians say they have a "great deal" or "quite a lot" of confidence in the press.'[421] It is an indictment of our system of freedom of speech and access to information, which are at the heart of a vibrant democracy: that we live in a world of 'fake news' and the corrupting effects of disinformation in politics and the reporting of world events. Equally, public policy in many Western countries, influenced by the media, has seen laws passed that directly attack free speech and personal liberty, often justified as 'national interest' violations or the very loosely defined 'hate speech'. The creeping nature of such erosion in freedom must be guarded against as it happens slowly and then quickly – a classic 'boiled frog' risk.

The danger of sleepwalking into a US-style society

As I have alluded to already, the US is a case study for Australia in the dangers of doing nothing about social trends such as growing inequality, a deteriorating education system, over-medicating mental ill-health, the concentration of power in

421 Beecher, E (2024). *The Men Who Killed the News.* Sydney: Scribner Australia, p312.

small self-interest lobby groups, and a concentrated, corporatised media increasingly lacking a moral compass, as eloquently argued by Eric Beecher.[422] The socialist-leaning former Greek finance minister, academic economist, humanitarian and author Yanis Varoufakis somewhat controversially described the US political system thus: 'The tragedy of the US is that it is not a democracy; it is an oligarchy, with a one-party system with two variants, who oscillate in power like Tweedledumb and Tweedledee. The US is essentially a "deep state", a one-party state.'[423] The social problems that define so much of what the US has become suggest it is a society in crisis. A mid-2022 survey reported that 50 per cent of Americans agreed that 'in the next several years, there will be civil war in the United States'.[424] Ruchir Sharma summed the problem up well when he argued that the growing inequality in income and wealth, and the way that the system is perceived to be stacked in favour of the wealthy, can give rise to popular anger and unrest.[425]

Mental ill-health is another window into the state of US society, with clear warning signs. In a 2020 study, 10 per cent of American children were rated on a scale of attention-deficit hyperactivity disorder (ADHD), compared to 3.5 per cent in other Western countries, including Australia. Part of this outcome is the constant advertising of medical prescriptions on media channels, which is allowed in the US (as it is in New Zealand) and the fact schools have an incentive to get ADHD diagnoses for underperforming children to exclude them from

422 Ibid., p324.

423 Varoufakis, Y (2016). *And the Weak Suffer What They Must? Europe, austerity and the threat to global stability*. Vintage.

424 Sharma, R (2024), p212.

425 Ibid.

test result comparisons with other schools. In Louisiana and Mississippi, two of the poorer states, one in six children has been diagnosed with ADHD and put on medication. A paediatrician or family doctor in the US makes a typical ADHD diagnosis from a consultation that can last no more than 15 minutes.[426]

Australia is not the US, but we must guard against the creeping erosion of political corruption and restrictions on personal liberty, in which the media plays an unfortunate role, often acting as a de facto agent for the government and powerful foreign actors promoting misinformation. In an age of digital information gathering and monitoring individual behaviours, big government should be seen as a potential threat to individual agency, liberty, privacy and autonomy when so much personal liberty is threatened in the name of 'national security'. In extremis, we should not underestimate the risk of sleepwalking into a world of coercion, compliance and control straight out of George Orwell's *1984*. The immortal words of the great Australian legal scholar Sir Zelman Cowen should never be forgotten: 'A man without privacy is a man without dignity; the fear that Big Brother is watching and listening threatens the freedom of the individual no less than the prison bars.'[427]

Adam Smith capitalism – a power for good

Smith believed passionately in the good of capitalism, but not in the behaviour of many capitalists and the conduct of many in damaging the reputation of capitalism. He would also agree with the conclusion of Joseph Stiglitz, Ruchir Sharma, Colin

426 *The Economist*. 'Why so many children in America have ADHD'. 20 February 2025. https://www.economist.com/united-states/2025/02/20/why-so-many-children-in-america-have-adhd

427 Cowen, Z (1969). 'The private man'. Boyer Lectures, ABC.

Mayer and others that capitalism didn't fail per se; it has been ruined. The oversized role of governments in the economy and their willingness to step in and rescue failing or failed capitalism, as was evident in the GFC, has resulted in what Sharma describes as 'socialism for the rich'.[428] Capitalism has been badly distorted by government inaction in promoting competitive markets, creating a bailout safety net for large, reckless firms, and a never-ending regulation culture. Like Adam Smith, Milton Friedman emphasised 'competitive capitalism … where the consumer is protected from coercion by the seller because of the presence of other sellers with whom he can deal'.[429]

Friedman emphasised an important point, a glaring failing in government when it came to competition policy, when he argued that 'government is essential both as a forum for determining the "rules of the game" and as an umpire to enforce the rules decided on'.[430] Governments have failed miserably in this regard, and this public policy failure has deflected much of the blame for its consequences onto the capitalist system, which has proven time and time again to be unable to act responsibly, morally and ethically. Smith was acutely aware of the problems associated with industry structures that limited competition. He wrote in *The Wealth of Nations*:

> *The interest of the dealers, however, in any particular branch of trade or manufactures, is always in some respect different from, and even opposite to, that of the publick. To widen the market and to narrow the competition, is always the interest of the dealers. To widen the market*

428 Sharma, R (2024).
429 Friedman, M (2002), p14.
430 Ibid.

> *may frequently be agreeable enough to the interests if the publick; but to narrow the competition must always be against it, and can serve only to enable the dealers, by raising their profits above what they naturally would be, to levy, for their own benefit, an absurd tax upon their fellow-citizens. The proposal of any new law or regulation of commerce which comes from this order, ought always to be listened to with great precaution, and ought never to be adopted till after having been long and carefully examined, not only with the most scrupulous, but with the most suspicious attention. It comes from an order of men whose interest is never exactly the same with that of the publick, who have generally an interest to deceive and even to oppress the publick, and who accordingly have, upon many occasions, both deceived and oppressed it.*[431]

Despite his scepticism of capitalists (distinct from capitalism), Smith saw the power of self-interest as essential to wealth creation in competitive markets. Smith's thinking was based on morality, justice and doing good. Smith regarded benevolence as admirable and a great virtue. He saw competitive markets as creating efficiency through the profit motive that met societal needs.

It is essential not to view Smith narrowly as the 'founder of economics' but to view his work as creating a much broader foundation for understanding how civil society should operate. He observed that 'society … cannot subsist among those who are always ready to hurt and injure one another'.[432] Few people go out explicitly intending to injure others, yet the incentives

431 Smith, A (1776). *The Wealth of Nations*, xi 10 p267.
432 Coase, RH (1994).

and moral values that define much of how behaviour is influenced do just that. The care factor is very low in our capitalist system. Adam Smith also reminded us that without reverence for the rules of moral conduct, 'society would crumble into nothing'.[433]

Adam Smith was not hostage to the competing ideologies that fragment and have devalued so much of our political discourse and policy agenda. Smith was a classic liberal in the term's original meaning, believing in personal liberty and small government, but he would distinguish between small and weak governments. Smith would argue that government should be 'strong' in areas where government involvement is justified, such as national defence, protecting the rule of law, providing health and education, providing essential infrastructure, protecting and promoting competition, and driving much-needed change that may upset some powerful constituents but is in the best interests of society. Smith cared deeply about human dignity and freedom; his wisdom and philosophy, when properly understood, are more relevant today than ever.

In the final chapter, I outline a reform agenda in some key policy areas based on Adam Smith's principles.

433 Smith, A (1759). *The Theory of Moral Sentiments*, Ch.IV.

7

A Smithian Vision for Australia

This book highlights the real risk of Australia falling into the 'boiled frog' syndrome, where gradual societal temperature changes go unnoticed until it is too late. The 'boiled frog' analogy conveys the simple truth that we often don't notice big societal changes if they happen gradually, so we allow these changes to occur in plain sight.

In Australia, as in other rich countries, there is much evidence that our society has become disconnected from its economic success. The danger is great that future generations will ask in aghast, 'How could our leaders have allowed this to happen? How could they have allowed things to drift so damagingly?'

A new Smithian narrative

To address this danger, a new Smithian narrative is needed. Such a narrative should be rooted in the lessons of *The Wealth of Nations* and *The Theory of Moral Sentiments*, and framed by the most vigorous intellectual and practical rigour, to create a policy framework that balances economic dynamism with social well-being.

Bold new ideas are needed in our system of government, where they have been absent for generations. For several decades, since the era of Paul Keating and Bob Hawke, we have had a system of government largely based on managing the status quo with incremental changes (the introduction of GST by the Howard government in 2000 being a rare exception), rather than transformative leadership in the strategic direction of our economy and society. We need a better framework and language beyond GDP to measure economic well-being; we need a framework that places significant weight on social renewal and well-being.

Social renewal starts with understanding the severe limitations inherent in economic measures that fail to examine society's declining health – evident in part by the growing rate of mental health problems and the concerning trend in inequality, a flawed education system, a tax system that is broken and entrenches inequality, the erosion of ethical and moral values, cronyism, the dominance of rent-seeking actors in key industries, and weak corporate governance.

In the true spirit of Adam Smith, a good society, argues Joseph Stiglitz, allows individuals to flourish and live up to their potential.[434] Greater equality goes to the heart of freedom;

434 Stiglitz, JE (2024), p282.

someone with little education and little disposable income or personal wealth, such as their own home, has minimal freedom to choose. They are, in so many ways, trapped in a system that offers little prospect of escape. A good society would not accept this and would take policy steps to address it. A good society would not accept the condescending notion of 'trickle-down' economics, where if the economic pie increases, eventually everyone gets more. Today's truth is that as the economic pie increases, it tends to result in bigger slices for those who already have more than enough.

A tyranny of the status quo

In a world of enormous inertia – a tyranny of the status quo – in business and government arrangements, conventional wisdom is that it takes a crisis to motivate real change, and change accelerates only in a crisis. That crisis will likely come from disillusionment with the ability of the political process to address the issues outlined in this book. There is already a crisis of democracy, as with capitalism, evident in the rise of populism – the re-election of Trump, the potential re-election of Boris Johnson, Brexit and the shift to the 'far right' in a number of European countries are examples of this – and the low esteem in which many of our institutions and media channels are held.

The challenge for public policy is where to start and what to prioritise. This is not about re-creating the past, it is about shaping a better future, and the philosophies of Adam Smith can guide us in that journey and provide the context in which this can be done. In addressing the failings of our capitalist system, getting the diagnosis right is so important. Greater government intervention, for example, reflects a flawed diagnosis, focusing on the symptoms rather than the causes.

If the government had the fortitude to develop a reform strategy addressing the failings outlined in this book (together with others, such as climate change and the integrity of the media), it would be comparable to other periods of major economic reform in Australia: the full employment framework introduced by the Labor governments of John Curtin and Ben Chifley, the removal of trade restrictions, and the currency floating driven through by Paul Keating and Bob Hawke in the late 1980s and early 1990s.[435] However, such a reform agenda cannot be tackled piecemeal, as it is easy for critics to attack and defeat individual proposals, such as the Minerals Resources Rent Tax introduced by the Rudd government in 2010, which failed. Meaningful reform must be crafted as part of a broad suite of changes aimed at transformational change.

Given natural constraints and the need to be realistic, what should be the priorities in creating a vibrant, growing economy with social well-being, and addressing, among other things, the concerning levels of inequality? In creating a new vision for Australia based on the core philosophies of Adam Smith, I highlight five priority areas:

1. The role of government and regulation
2. Taxation reform
3. Competition policy
4. Corporate governance
5. Mental health.

---

435 Ibid.

The role of government and regulation

There is a credible argument to be made that one of the most fundamental challenges facing the Australian economy in the decade ahead is addressing the creeping scale and scope of government. The size of government relative to the economy has been increasing since the GFC, and the trend suggests that this will continue. In 2024, one in three jobs created in Australia was in the public sector, while three in four new jobs were in government-funded industries such as health and education, which are traditionally sectors resistant to productivity improvements.[436] In a low-unemployment economy, one effect of this is a crowding-out of private-sector growth capacity. This is combined with the reality that growth in public-sector employment contributes to a further drag on productivity, with many jobs becoming 'unproductive hands', as Adam Smith warned.

A path-dependent course would suggest that there are locked-in structural reasons why the size of government in the economy is likely to increase. These reasons include:

- the increased expectation of a higher level of defence spending in a world of growing geopolitical uncertainty and risk
- the impact of an aging and, thankfully, longer-living population on the welfare system, with the reality that the proportion of the working population (people aged 16 to 65) in society will continue to shrink
- the current underfunded state of the education system

436 Read, M. 'Three in four new jobs in 2024 were underwritten by governments'. *Financial Review*, 7 March 2025. https://www.afr.com/policy/economy/three-in-four-new-jobs-in-2024-were-underwritten-by-governments-20250307-p5lhot

- essential infrastructure and public services spending
- the concerning under-investment in the health care system, on health care generally and mental health in particular.

These five reasons align with what Adam Smith called the three core government functions, as discussed in Chapter 1, and represent a significant demand on the taxpayer. Smith warned us about 'man of system' ambitions, and the great economist Friedrich Hayek warned us that government planners would pave the road to serfdom, guided by 'the progressive belief that all we need is the political will to write bigger checks.'[437] The real problem is that the scope of government continues to increase beyond these core functions at an increased cost to consumers, innovation, enterprise and personal freedom. The sharp growth in government spending as a percentage of GDP is illustrated in Figure 1.

Rather than sleepwalking toward an even bigger government, concrete measures should be implemented that put constitutional constraints on its size and scope. Budget-control legislation would be a good starting point, including public sector debt limits – such as those in European Union states – expenditure limits and specific limits of the scope and nature of government spending. This is a blunt-tool approach as, absent statutory checks, governments left to their own devices will continue to grow, and the tax burden will continue to increase. Even the great economist John Maynard Keynes, often cited as the intellectual authority in support of big government, argued that the state should never consume more than 25 per cent of GDP.[438]

---

437 Sharma, R (2024), p275-276.

438 Tanzi, V (2011). *Government Versus Markets: The changing economic role of the state*, Cambridge University Press, p126.

Figure 1: Government spending as a percentage of GDP

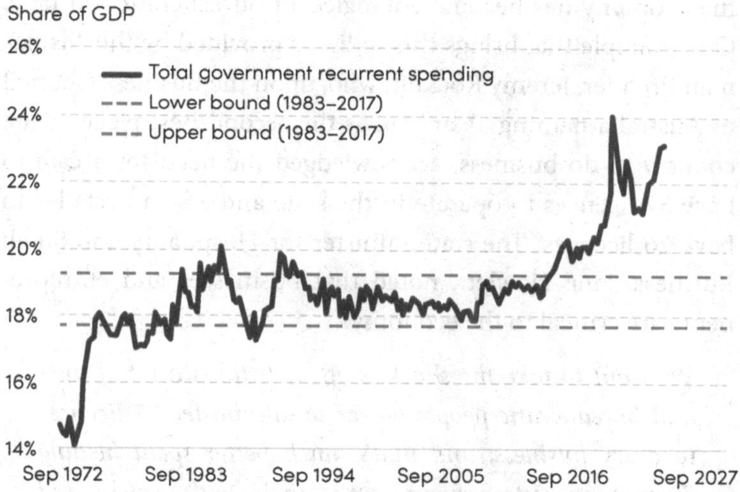

Source: Warren Hogan based on Government Income Account, Australia Bureau of Statistics. Data to December 2024

As discussed in Chapter 6, Professor Mazzucato argues that a 'strategic approach' from the government is not about romanticising the state but about putting pressure on it to be strategic and mission-oriented, and getting all sectors of the economy to work together rather than handing out our money, subsidies, guarantees and favours.

One way in which the government can make a meaningful strategic approach is to tackle the growing burden of regulation in the form of red tape imposed by both federal and state governments. There are aspects of a civilised society and a well-functioning economy where 'good' regulation plays an important role: think of food safety, product safety, workplace safety, bank conduct, competition and road safety (and, arguably, the dissemination of false and misleading information by media channels). However, as discussed in Chapter 2, much of the economy has become entangled in bureaucratic red tape. One example that brings this to life is provided by the Tasmanian Premier, Jeremy Rockliff, who, upon the Business Council of Australia naming Tasmania as the second-best place in the country to do business, acknowledged the need for a café to have 37 licences to operate in the state and a small retailer to have 26 licences. The state minister for Hospitality and Small Business, Jane Howlett, noted that businesses and entrepreneurs are critical to the economy:

> *We want to take the shackles off ... It takes a lot of time and bureaucratic people power to administer 37 licences to every business, and that's much better spent helping Tasmanian entrepreneurs forge their path, safely and properly.*[439]

The Economist noted that excessive rules have choked house building, investment – particularly harmful to small and medium-sized businesses – and innovation for years.[440] Well-intended regulation is often crafted to serve the interests of certain groups in society but at a cost to the broader community.

Ironically, our education system may play an unintended role; there is a downside to an excessive emphasis on cognitive skills that may partly explain our productivity challenge. The American economist Robert Gordon, in his book *The Rise and Fall of American Growth*[441] pointed to the drag on

---

439 Howlett, J. 'Slashing business licence requirements', Premier of Tasmania, 6 March 2025. https://www.premier.tas.gov.au/latest-news/2025/march/slashing-business-licence-requirements

440 *The Economist*. 'The revolt against regulation'. 1 February, 2025.

441 Gordon, RJ (2017). *The Rise and Fall of American Growth: The U.S. standard of living since the Civil War*. Princeton University Press.

productivity of graduate-dominated bureaucratic roles in both the public and private sectors, referring to this as 'professional bureaucratisation'. The growth in legal regulations across the economy, fed by graduate employment, is an example of how bureaucracy is a substantial drag on productivity, often adopting a 'Luddite' philosophy to enforcing regulations. They represent what Adam Smith called 'unproductive hands'. The growing red tape and bureaucracy that defines so much of life is akin to death by meetings, form filling, and online compliance courses, and is a significant drag on productivity.

Corporate bureaucracy is largely a product of regulation, causing the demand for more human resource analysts, diversity officers, compliance executives and other functions to ensure compliance with the demand for greater and growing state intervention. Ruchir Sharma summed this up nicely:

> *Workers in advanced capitalist countries now spend as much as 16 per cent of their time dealing with reviews, training, attestations and other red tape. Academic surveys estimate that at least half that time has no productivity value.*[442]

A good example is the comparison between the *Glass–Steagall Act* of 1933 in the US, which prevented commercial banks from undertaking risky activities associated with investment banks, and the *Dodd–Frank Act* of 2010, which aimed to do the same thing following the GFC. *Glass–Steagall* was 37 pages long and written in relatively comprehensible English; *Dodd-Frank* was 848 pages, supplemented with 398 pieces of rulemaking running to over 30,000 pages.[443] The issue was not that the

---

442 Sharma, R (2024), p239-240.
443 Goodhart, D (2020), p262.

abbreviated *Glass–Steagall Act* was inadequate; it was more that the legislation was relaxed and then repealed during a period when the Greenspan Doctrine was the dominant philosophy, despite the foresight and advice centuries earlier from Adam Smith on the risks and consequences of reckless behaviour by banks.

A helpful analogy is to think of regulation as you would think about cholesterol in your body. There is 'good' and 'bad' cholesterol. The problem is that the arteries of the Australian economy are clogged with 'bad' cholesterol in the form of mindless red tape and regulations. Staying with the medical analogy, just as a doctor would advise lifestyle changes to help address dangerous cholesterol levels, the government must take radical steps to reduce 'bad' regulation without compromising on 'good' and necessary regulation.

On competition policy, which I discuss later in this chapter, excessive and complex regulation entrenches incumbents in industries, making it difficult for new entrants to enter a market and provide competition. The cost of compliance with regulations can often deter new businesses from starting up or discourage existing businesses from expanding. The burden of regulation on small to medium enterprises (SMEs) is a particular concern.

Estimating the macroeconomic costs of regulation and compliance is complex. Various estimates, such as the OECD, suggest a range of 3 to 4 per cent of GDP.[444] In the US, the federal government estimates that regulation costs American businesses an estimated $300 billion annually, only $53 billion less than what the same businesses spend on corporate income

444 Ibid.

taxes.[445] A precise estimate of the cost of regulation in Australia is not the issue and would be difficult to determine, but a reasonable estimate would suggest a cost of tens of billions annually. All these cost estimates fail to consider the opportunity cost of productivity if much of those funds were invested in productive use or innovation, and new businesses were encouraged and able to flourish.

Following the lead of governments in Argentina, Greece, the US and New Zealand, there is much to be gained from declaring a 'war on regulation' and encouraging more entrepreneurialism, innovation and investment without compromising on 'good' regulation aimed at legitimate consumer protection. Professor John Cochrane of Stanford University describes this 'war on regulations' as 'potentially bigger than the Reagan–Thatcher revolution' of the 1980s.[446] This is exciting but needs bold political leadership. The time is ripe for our government to declare a 'war on regulation' as part of a broader agenda for reducing the scope of government in our society. Acknowledging the practical difficulties in removing existing regulation, John Micklethwait and Adrian Wooldridge suggest in their book *The Fourth Revolution* introducing legislation that places a ten-year sunset clause on regulation. The clause causes the regulation to expire on the ten-year anniversary of its introduction, and any renewal is subject to full justification.[447]

---

445 Hoguet, T. 'Estimating the impact of regulation on businesses'. *The Regulatory Review*, 28 February 2024. https://www.theregreview.org/2024/02/28/hoguet-estimating-the-impact-of-regulation-on-business/

446 *The Economist*. 'The revolt against regulation'. 1 February, 2025.

447 Micklethwait, J & Wooldridge, A (2015), p266.

Taxation reform

As discussed in Chapter 6, our current taxation system is broken and entrenches income and wealth inequality. It badly needs reform. Such reform should be aimed at achieving four key goals:

1. broadening the tax base
2. creating a more equitable tax system
3. reducing reliance on personal income tax
4. helping address income *and* wealth inequality.

Consistent with these four goals, the agenda for tax reform should:

- phase out negative gearing on speculative investments, including housing
- assess the scope for the introduction of wealth taxes, such as an inheritance tax above an agreed threshold of, say, $3 million (which could be done in step changes with lower tax rates between $3 million and $5 million and progressively higher rates based on the capital gain)
- review the scope for introducing CGT on the primary residence where the capital gain exceeds a threshold of, say, $3 million (which, again, could be done progressively)
- consider the scope for increasing GST, which is currently at 10 per cent and is low by international standards
- explore the scope for a new special tax category on economic rents earned by businesses operating in sectors with weak competition, akin to the major bank levy, which is set at a far-too-low level of 0.06 per cent per annum given the nature of the 'too big to fail' taxpayer insurance

provided (the UK bank levy is set at 0.1 per cent, which is also too low given the contingent liability on the taxpayer; it currently raises about $1.7 billion a year,[448] and given the economic benefit of the guarantee to the banks, raising it to double its current rate would still represent a good outcome for the banks); an alternative approach for non-bank businesses – which I explore in a moment, citing the work of Craig Emerson, Reuben Finighan, Stephen Anthony and Ross Garnaut AC – is to replace corporate income tax with a cash flow tax, which would encourage investment and likely result in a higher effective tax rate for businesses in rent-heavy sectors[449]

- reduce the personal tax rate for most people, focusing on those earning below $100,000 per annum, which includes abolishing income tax on salaries below $50,000; this population segment has a higher marginal propensity to spend extra income
- consider introducing a higher marginal tax rate of 65 per cent on income above $1 million per annum; this segment of the economy has a lower marginal propensity to spend extra income or reduce spending at higher tax rates
- legislate to stop income tax bracket creep and, like nearly 50 per cent of other OECD nations, introduce indexation of income tax brackets – indexing income tax thresholds to the RBA annual inflation target of 2.5 per cent would

448 Commins, P. 'Fixing a flawed levy on the banks could leave Australia's budget billions of dollars better off'. *The Guardian*, 23 March 2025. https://www.theguardian.com/australia-news/2025/mar/23/how-fixing-one-flawed-tax-on-the-banks-could-leave-australias-budget-billions-of-dollars-better-off

449 Garnaut, R (2024), pp164-165.

cost the budget $4 billion per annum in lost income, rising to $10 billion a year over a decade, assuming an annual inflation rate of 2.5 per cent.[450]

Some of these proposals are directionally consistent with the reform ideas in the Henry Tax Review ('Australia's Future Tax System'; 2010), chaired by then Secretary to the Treasury Dr Ken Henry AC.[451] Some would be considered controversial and difficult to win broad support for, but without a willingness to address these 'difficult' areas, little meaningful progress can be made in tackling the income and wealth inequality that is a feature of our society.

Two of the above proposals – a CGT on gains on the sale of the primary residence where that gain exceeds a threshold of, say, $3 million; and the introduction of an inheritance tax where the inheritance gain exceeds a threshold of, say, $3 million – may be seen as particularly controversial and unpopular, yet they go to the core of the wealth inequality codified in our current tax system. They also reflect that according to the ABS, individuals over 60 hold around 50 per cent of household wealth in Australia, a statistic consistent with other rich countries but highlighting the intergenerational wealth problem.

The bias in these reforms towards wealth reflects that wealthier people have prospered disproportionately since the GFC. The *Financial Review*, in its 2024 'Rich List', highlighted how the top 200 richest people in Australia had seen their

450 Kehoe, J. 'Dutton's "aspiration" to end tax bracket creep is too little, too late'. *Financial Review*, 17 April 2025. https://www.afr.com/policy/economy/dutton-s-aspiration-to-end-tax-bracket-creep-is-too-little-too-late-20250417-p5lse6

451 Henry, K (2010). *Australia's future tax system review final report*. The Treasury, Australian Government. https://treasury.gov.au/review/the-australias-future-tax-system-review/final-report

wealth grow by 11 per cent in the year at a time when real wages saw no growth – real wages have barely moved in over a decade – and the economy's growth rate was 1.4 per cent.[452]

The surge in wealth over recent decades has spotlighted inheritance in many countries. *The Economist* reported that people in rich countries stand to inherit US$6 trillion in 2025 – equivalent to 10 per cent of their GDP, up from 5 per cent over 50 years ago.[453] In Australia, researchers at Griffith University estimate that figure at $3.5 trillion over the next 20 years.[454] In many rich countries, a young person's ability to buy a house is determined not by their hard work but by their inheritance, and inherited wealth is far more unequally distributed than income. *The Economist* argues:

> *This shift has alarming economic and social consequences because it imperils not just the meritocratic ideal but capitalism itself … More worryingly, an underclass of non-beneficiaries is becoming increasingly left behind – and disaffected.*[455]

The current system encourages people to buy the most expensive house they can afford to live in and develop it to the greatest extent possible, knowing that when they sell, their gain is tax-free regardless of its size. This benefits those

---

452 Redrup and Bailey (2024). 'Australia's wealthiest 200 now control $625bn.' *Australian Financial Review*. https://www.afr.com/rich-list/australia-s-10-richest-people-revealed=20240521-p5jfe4

453 *The Economist*. 'Inheriting is becoming nearly as important as working'. 27 February 2025. https://www.economist.com/leaders/2025/02/27/inheriting-is-becoming-nearly-as-important-as-working

454 Insights, 'Australia's millionaire population grows as property values surge', Prime Capital, July 2024. https://www.primecapital.com/insights/australias-millionaire-population-grows-as-property-values-surge/

455 *The Economist*. 'Inheriting is becoming nearly as important as working'. 27 February 2025.

in the sought-after neighbourhoods of major cities but is not a gift available to those in rural or regional Australia, or those who cannot afford a house; these people cannot participate in this generous form of tax-free capital gain. In other words, a minority can gain materially, and the majority are excluded. Is that the society we want?

Introducing a corporate tax rate based on cash flow distinct from accounting profits is a worthwhile concept developed by Garnaut and others in a December 2020 paper published in the *Australian Economic Review* and summarised in Garnaut's book *Let's Tax Carbon*.[456] A tax rate based on cash flow would address some problems with businesses generating economic rents. Such a tax would:

- allow businesses to deduct 100 per cent of capital expenditure immediately
- provide a cash tax credit at the tax rate for businesses experiencing negative cash flows
- exclude any deductions for interest or any other payments for financing, such as lease payments.

Professor Garnaut's book and 2020 paper provide greater detail on an imaginative concept that, in addition to encouraging businesses to invest, provides short-term cash support for struggling businesses and would result in an economically efficient higher tax rate for those businesses enjoying economic rents.

Criticism of the ineffectiveness of the current tax system in Australia is well documented by Garnaut, Dr Ken Henry AC and others. Henry has been a leader in highlighting the detrimental nature of the current tax system and the 'social impact' that it

---

456 Garnaut, R (2024), pp164-165.

has created, which will add to the intergenerational unfairness, the impact on housing and the state of climate policy. These policies entrench a 'poverty trap' for people on low incomes. Garnaut has been equally outspoken in his view that major tax reform is necessary. He argued that had the government retained the carbon emissions trading scheme – which, after a life of only two years, was ended by the Abbott Coalition government in 2014 – there would be $70 billion a year in additional tax revenue. Vested interest from the mining industry managed to defeat any progress on this, even though, according to Garnaut, this would create capacity for significant tax reforms and 'cut every personal tax rate by 30 per cent from the highest to the lowest'.[457] Powerful industry lobby groups once again frustrate reform that would have had widespread societal benefits.

In keeping with Adam Smith's philosophy, Garnaut went on to add:

> *If you added up all the opportunities for economic reform to reduce economic rents or to tax them efficiently and equitably, you'd have a transformational economic reform program to increase productivity and equity. Such a reform project would be historically significant.*[458]

There is no getting away from a reality that our current taxation system is broken and damaging to long-term social cohesion. It requires bold political leadership to fix. Few things are more

---

457 Gareth Hutchens, *ABC News*, Australia would be raising $70 billion a year from the carbon price if it wasn't dismantled, Ross Garnaut says. September 17, 2023

458 Read, M. 'Break up firms that abuse market power, says former competition tsar'. *Financial Review*, 9 July 2023. https://www.afr.com/policy/economy/break-up-firms-that-abuse-market-power-says-former-competition-tsar-20230709-p5dmtq

important, and few policy areas could have the same impact in terms of big-picture, transformational reform.

Competition policy

Consistent with a 'war on regulation' to help address Australia's poor productivity problem, an important priority for the government is to address the chronic state of competition in many key industries. The time is right for a comprehensive review of competition policy and the crafting of a new policy framework aimed not just at addressing the glaring problems with our current 'policy', which have been documented in this book, but also at setting Australian industry up for the future.

Competition drives innovation and productivity, forcing incumbents to wake up and invest for growth rather than focusing on protecting existing privileges and profitability. Despite the benefits of economies of scale, concentrated industry structures damage the economy and society, and can be coercive in nature. Competition creates greater freedom of choice for consumers, rather than holding them hostage to the rent-seeking behaviour of powerful business groups.

Meaningful competition must exist for the market system to work as Adam Smith (and Milton Friedman) intended. In many key sectors of the Australian economy, competition is weak, and government policy in this important area has been, at best, inept.[459] Despite the efforts of the ACCC – in essence, a regulator of current policy rather than an agent of new policy – the policy on mergers requires urgent attention at a fundamental level.[460] As discussed in Chapter 3, five key

459 Durie, J. 'Price battle in the shopping aisles'. *The Australian*, 27 January 2024.
460 Garnaut, R (2023).

sectors highlight this issue: air travel, food retail, electricity, telecommunications and commercial banking. One could readily add media, health insurance and petrol retail. The best form of regulation is competition, but in the case of banking, we have four major banks with close to 80 per cent of the market, and in food retail, the two big supermarkets, Coles and Woolworths, control over 65 per cent of the market.

In his ACTU-sponsored inquiry into competition in key sectors and evidence of price gouging, Professor Allan Fels argued that both Coles and Woolworths were using their market power to increase profits through higher food prices, and by squeezing farmers and other suppliers of products to the supermarkets. A consistent finding was reported in a 441-page 2024 ACCC inquiry, which found that the two major retailers increased prices during a cost-of-living crisis to boost profits, which were already at a level that made them among the most profitable supermarkets in the world.[461] The two dominant firms, despite earning a return on equity in the high 20s to mid-30s – comfortably double if not triple their cost of equity, and clear evidence of economic rents – defended their position by arguing the old line of needing to balance the needs of customers, suppliers, their large workforce and investors. While pointing to inflationary pressures, there was evidence that they were using inflation as a convenient cover for higher price increases aimed at improving profitability.[462] In electricity,

461 Barrett, J & McLeod, C. 'ACCC urges reform as Coles and Woolworths named among "most profitable" supermarkets in world'. *The Guardian*, 21 March 2025. https://www.theguardian.com/australia-news/2025/mar/21/accc-report-supermarkets-coles-woolworths-aldi

462 Barrett, J. 'ACCC should scrutinise Coles and Woolworths' market power, former watchdog chair says'. *The Guardian*, 23 January 2024. https://www.theguardian.com/australia-news/2024/jan/23/accc-supermarket-price-gouging-inquiry-grocery-prices-woolworths-coles

a sector that Professor Fels called 'highly concentrated' with three firms – AGL, Energy Australia and Origin – dominating, price rises have been a common challenge for households. Professor Fels pointed out that energy prices had risen 22.3 per cent between March 2021 and September 2023 in a system that was 'clearly not fit for purpose', with the three dominant firms price gouging.[463]

These are just some examples, and there are others throughout this book. The message is clear: the lack of meaningful competition in many key sectors of the economy is the root cause of many of the problems we face today. It is a significant reason why capitalism has been damaged in the eyes of society and why people are angry. Weak competition is also – together with other factors outlined in this book – a significant contributor to poor productivity. Over the decade to 2024, productivity in Australia increased by just 0.4 per cent annually, marking the lowest growth rate since the 1950s. While not unique to Australia, this low level of productivity has the potential to distort future economic policy in unhelpful ways.[464]

Professor Fels, who was Chairman of the ACCC from 1995 to 2023, called on the government to consider laws that would break up dominant firms in key sectors and explore a revival of Paul Keating's national competition policy, devised in response to Fred Hilmer's review of competition in 1993. Professor Fels pointed to international examples of governments using laws to break up powerful firms. In the US, for example, this was

463 Fels, A (2024).

464 Read, M 'Growth slump could fuel inflation and spending blowout: central banks'. *Financial Review*, 4 October 2024. https://www.afr.com/policy/economy/growth-slump-could-fuel-inflation-and-spending-blowout-central-banks-20241004-p5kfvi

done in sectors such as oil, tobacco, chemicals and, in recent years, telecommunications with respect to AT&T.[465] The case for separating Jetstar from Qantas is an obvious example of how competition could be invigorated in domestic air travel, benefiting consumers.[466] However, Labor Prime Minister Albanese dismissed such laws to address market abuse when he is reported to have said Australia is 'not the old Soviet Union'.[467] This is true, but is an economic system where consumer abuse goes largely without consequence an acceptable alternative? The government should rethink its commitment to creating a pro-competition environment in all our industries, and as Garnaut outlines, 'Australia needs more sector-specific rules to promote competition and prevent the worst abuses of market power'.[468]

Corporate governance

Just as Adam Smith saw the dangers of weak regulation of banks, he saw that there were always going to be problems when directors and managers manage the affairs of others. On corporate governance, long before Harvard's Michael Jensen popularised the theme in the economic literature, Smith understood with incredible foresight the principal–agent

465 Read, M. 'Break up firms that abuse market power, says former competition tsar'. *Financial Review*, 9 July 2023.

466 McKenzie, B. 'Is it time to force Qantas to break up with Jetstar?' *Financial Review*, 9 September 2024. https://www.afr.com/companies/transport/is-it-time-to-force-qantas-to-break-up-with-jetstar-20240908-p5k8sg

467 Martin, P. 'Worried about price gouging? For banks, there's a simple solution'. *The Conversation*, 27 February 2024. https://theconversation.com/worried-about-price-gouging-for-banks-theres-a-simple-solution-223821

468 Garnaut, R (2024), p180.

problem of separating ownership from the management and governance of a business. In 1776, he prophetically wrote:

> *The directors ... being the managers rather of other people's money than of their own, it cannot well be expected that they should watch over it with the same anxious vigilance with which the partners in a private firm frequently watch over their own. Negligence and profusion, therefore, must always prevail, more or less, in the management of the affairs of such a company.*[469]

Corporate governance in Australia is no better or worse than that in other Anglo-Saxon economies. This is despite our system being characterised by a significant volume of regulations, creating a sense that corporate governance has become more of a compliance checklist. Boards prioritise ensuring compliance with rules at the expense of effective management oversight and their business's strategic evolution. This is not surprising given that lawyers and accountants dominate most boards of ASX-listed companies: research has shown that nearly 50 per cent of the top 300 directors in Australia had a legal, accounting or banking background, and less than 20 per cent had direct industry experience relevant to the company on whose board they sit.[470] These facts help explain the emphasis on compliance and the propensity for weak management oversight. The *Financial Review* summed up the underlying corporate governance problem neatly: 'Australia's boardrooms have a problem. Too many people who sit on them are not up

469 Smith, A (1776). *The Wealth of Nations*, B.IV. ch.9, IV.9.51.
470 Healy, J (2019), pp262-263.

to the job because they are drawn from narrow circles or are more interested in building their own brand than their firm's'.[471]

This emphasis on compliance and weak oversight of management is part of the reason the business community's reputation is damaged in the eyes of the broader community. In the Qantas case study discussed in Chapter 4, the board did not have a compliance problem; it had a management oversight problem. The boards that governed several major financial institutions in the period before the Hayne Royal Commission in 2018 did not fail the compliance test but the management and cultural oversight test.[472] Other high-profile scandals, some of which were discussed earlier, illustrate this. Quentin Beresford's book *Rogue Corporations: Inside Australia's biggest business scandals* provides more analysis of corporate governance problems through several contemporary case studies.

At the heart of the problem with corporate governance is an overly bureaucratic system dominated by a box-ticking compliance culture, which crowds out important consideration of strategy in a world that is subject to technology-driven revolutionary change. Veteran business journalist Tony Boyd wrote:

> *The dismal state of affairs is perpetuated by the dominance of the Australian Institute of Company Directors (AICD), the world's largest membership organisation devoted to teaching compliance-driven governance.*[473]

471 *Financial Review*. 'The question that hangs over boardrooms'. 18 May 2018.
472 Healy, J (2019), pp249-286.
473 Boyd, T. 'The ASX's legal mess reveals deep-rooted problems in boardrooms'. *Financial Review*, 19 August 2024.

An alternative approach is to simplify corporate governance and ASX-listing rules by strengthening directors' fiduciary duty to shareholders. In addition, a public company would legally be required to describe its *culture* and clearly state its *values* and *purpose*, and have directors obligated by law to ensure that the company is managed in accordance with those statements. The values statement should cover matters regarding employees, the environment and how customers are to be treated (that is, to 'do no harm'). In line with recommendations made by Professor Colin Mayer, the corporate purpose statement should carry the weight of legal enforcement (and penalty when violated) and be codified in corporate law.[474] Businesses that produce or sell products that can harm customers or the environment should prominently state these risks in their marketing materials and web pages, and outline why they feel that conducting business in this way is satisfactory.

To address Adam Smith's concerns regarding the power imbalance between employer and employee – issues still evident today – a company's governance architecture should include an employee advisory board, with the chairperson of that board also a company board member. In other words, there should be employee representation on the company's main governance oversight forum. Such a development would give employees a voice in a business's affairs, which is particularly important given the implications of AI could be profound on the future nature of work, potentially impacting 30 per cent of current jobs. Such an inclusive approach would be consistent with models in several European countries, such as Germany, the Netherlands, Spain, France and the Scandinavian countries.

474 Mayer, C (2024), p261.

These proposed changes would considerably streamline corporate governance's legal and regulatory complexity, and provide businesses with an ethical and moral framework. The framework would also rebalance the current culture of profits over purpose and act as a check on activities that could harm consumers and the environment. This would go a long way towards addressing the business community's confidence crisis. The involvement of employee representation on boards would strengthen governance and would represent a more inclusive governance model.

Finally, more should be done on corporate governance to encourage employee participation in trade unions, which is too low at 13 per cent. However, clearer rules and regulations should be designed to ensure that trade unions foster a constructive culture that serves workers' needs and businesses' sustainability. The poor governance culture within the trade union movement has to be addressed. The adversarial culture of the past was damaging and should be guarded against. Employee welfare should be a high priority given the rising impact of work-related mental health problems and the magnitude of change that is likely to impact how we work in the future.

Mental health

The impact of mental ill-health has become a major burden on economic growth and productivity. That burden will likely increase unless prevention strategies and care availability are addressed. The prevalence of mental ill-health cases at a diagnostic level indicating a need for care has risen by an alarming

50 per cent from 2007 to 2021 to 39 per cent of cases, with 75 per cent of mental disorders emerging before the age of 25.[475]

In a 2020 report, the Productivity Commission outlined the scale and scope of these problems. It is estimated that the cost to our economy of mental ill-health and suicide is around $220 billion per annum.

While government and social awareness of this problem has grown in recent years and overall health spending has increased, mental health care remains a poor cousin regarding overall health funding. One of Australia's leaders in the field of mental health, Professor Patrick McGorry AO, captures the reality of the current crisis, writing that despite the perception that there has been greater investment in mental health care, 'Spending on mental health care as a proportion of the health budget has fallen to a new low of 6.8%'.[476]

The fact that 14 per cent of Australians are currently taking antidepressants – one of the highest rates in the world – highlights what Dr Matt Fisher, a senior research fellow with the University of Adelaide's Stretton Institute, describes as 'a failed attempt to medicate away what are, in fact, social problems'. Fisher argues that social problems and chronic stress – for example, being in too much debt, low income, poor working conditions, exposure to discrimination and domestic violence – are root causes of mental ill health.[477]

---

475 McGorry, P. 'The mental health crisis and solutions', in Chang A & Grundy, A (eds.; 2025). *What's the Big Idea?* Australia Institute Press, pp143-149.

476 Ibid.

477 Davey, M. '"A pill for every ill": doctors say Australia overprescribing antidepressants to mask toxic social conditions'. *The Guardian*, 21 December 2024. https://www.theguardian.com/australia-news/2024/dec/21/a-pill-for-every-ill-doctors-say-australia-overprescribing-antidepressants-to-mask-toxic-social-conditions

It is hard to think of a more important issue facing our society today than the skyrocketing demand for mental health care – particularly among young Australians – and the quantitative and qualitative benefits that would flow from meaningful reform into the way we currently provide that care. Adam Smith would see this problem as part of the disconnect between economic success and societal well-being, the growing inequality evident in our communities and the self-centred culture that has come to define our society.

Mental health conditions don't discriminate between the rich and the poor at an individual level, but social circumstances, as highlighted by Dr Fisher, impact the less well-off. This is another example of the scourge of inequality. One study, for example, highlighted how one in four of the poorest Australians experience high levels of psychological distress compared to one in 20 of the wealthiest Australians.[478] Many less well-off Australians are unable to access professional care for treatment, and this may, in part, explain the unacceptably high use of antidepressants.

Concerningly, estimates suggest that only 35 per cent of people with a mental health condition will access professional care, with McGorry pointing out that a 'staggering 1 or 2 million Australians simply cannot access mental health care of appropriate quality and duration in a timely manner and engaging way'.[479] There are several reasons for this, such as a sense of stigma (both societal and self-stigma) and the difficulty

---

478 Isaacs, AN et al., 'Lower income levels in Australia are strongly associated with elevated psychological distress: implications for healthcare and other policy areas', *Frontiers in Psychiatry*, vol. 9, no. 536, 26 October 2018.

479 McGorry, P. 'The mental health crisis and solutions', in Chang A & Grundy, A (eds.; 2025). *What's the Big Idea?* Australia Institute Press, pp143-149.

in accessing care promptly – current waiting times for an appointment with a psychologist can be up to 12 weeks or even more, and securing an appointment with a psychiatrist can take longer. Accessing services can be difficult and confusing. We have a situation today where mental illness is the number-one reason people are visiting their GPs, and suicide is the number-one cause of death among Australians aged 15 to 49.

Everyone involved in the provision of mental health care agrees that the mental health sector needs urgent investment and substantial reform. The policy response should involve a commitment to full-scale reform with a strong focus on prevention, particularly of youth mental ill-health. The commitment to reform should bear in mind McGorry's words:

> *Mental health care must be financed, redesigned, staffed and nurtured to bring it up to the same standard as the rest of our health care system. The contrast between what is offered when someone is diagnosed with cancer or has a stroke, and when someone is experiencing an episode of a major mental illness, is stark.*[480]

The National Mental Health Service Planning Framework predicts that there will be a shortage of nearly 87,000 mental health staff by 2030, and this will be most pronounced in rural and regional areas. When you consider that it takes at least six years of training and education to become a clinical psychologist or psychiatrist, the outlook is not promising, particularly since clinicians are leaving the profession in droves due to burnout. Yet despite this, investment in training and recruitment of

480 Ibid.

professional staff is essential – and here, immigration policy can play an important role.

In looking for role-model nations in providing mental health care, Sweden, Denmark, Norway, Finland (all Scandinavian nations with a strong welfare system) and the Netherlands provide some examples of a strategic approach and best practice.

Finally, on this topic, I would hazard a guess that at least 75 per cent of people reading this will have had first-hand experience of some form of mental ill-health, experienced either by themselves, a member of their extended family, a work colleague or a close friend. This brings home to everyone the need to completely change the way we think about mental health and why it must be added to the list of priorities.

Final words

The reform vision outlined in this chapter is limited to various themes linked to Adam Smith's philosophies. Many important themes relevant to our contemporary society and economy are not covered. These themes include climate change – which Garnaut's book *Let's Tax Carbon* (2024) does an excellent job exploring – immigration policy, housing supply and media reform (given how central media can be to a healthy democracy), to name but four important themes on which, if alive today, Smith would likely have much to say.

Adam Smith believed in the power of capitalism and markets but expressed many important caveats regarding their limitations and dangers. He would not recognise our capitalist system, with its many flaws, as reflecting what he had in mind. He would also argue that despite these flaws, it represents the best system, and that the challenge is ensuring its flaws are fixed and its benefits are more widely shared. He would warn us of the real risk of the 'boiled frog' syndrome already evident in Australia, and would ask that we always maintain that the economy is supposed to serve a vibrant society.

Bibliography

Aspromourgos, T (2008). *The Science of Wealth: Adam Smith and the framing of political economy*. Routledge.

Aston, J (2024). *The Chairman's Lounge: The inside story of how Qantas sold us out*. Scribner Australia.

Beecher, E (2024). *The Men Who Killed the News*. Sydney: Scribner Australia.

Begg, D, Fischer, S and Dornbusch, R (1994). *Economics*. New York: McGraw-Hill.

Bentall, RP (2009). *Doctoring the Mind: Why psychiatric treatments fail*. Allen Lane.

Beresford, Q (2023). *Rogue Corporations: Inside Australia's biggest business scandals*. NewSouth.

Bloodworth, J (2016). *The Myth of Meritocracy*. Biteback Publishing.

Boettke, PJ (2024). 'Why read Adam Smith today?'. *GMU Working Paper in Economics No. 24-15*. https://papers.ssrn.com/sol3/papers.cfm?abstract_id=4741993#.

Boucoyannis, D (2013). 'The equalizing hand: why Adam Smith thought the market should produce wealth without steep inequality'. *Perspectives on Politics*, vol. 11, no. 4, pp1051-1070.

Brown, G (2010). *Beyond the Crash: Overcoming the first crisis of globalisation*. Simon & Schuster.

Brown, G (2018). *My Life, Our Times*. Vintage.

Case, A & Deaton, A (2020). *Deaths of Despair and the Future of Capitalism*. Princeton University Press.

Cassidy, J (2009). *How Markets Fail: The logic of economic calamities*. Picador.

Chang A & Grundy, A (eds.; 2025). *What's the Big Idea?* Australia Institute Press.

Christophers, Brett (2020). *Rentier Capitalism: Who owns the economy and who pays for it?* Verso.

Coase, RH (1994). 'Adam Smith's view of man'. *Essays on Economics and Economists*. University of Chicago Press.

Collier, P and Kay, J (2020). *Greed Is Dead: Politics after individualism*. Allen Lane.

Conlin, J (ed.; 2019). *Great Economic Thinkers: An introduction – from Adam Smith to Amartya Sen*. Reaktion Books.

Cross, M (2024). *Mental State: The insanity of Australia's mental health system – and how to fix it*. ABC Books.

Davies, J (2022). *Sedated: How modern capitalism created our mental health crisis*. Atlantic PBS.

de Soto, H (2003). *The Mystery of Capital: Why capitalism triumphs in the west and fails everywhere else*. Basic Books.

Fleischacker, S (2004). *On Adam Smith's* Wealth of Nations: *A philosophical companion*. Princeton University Press.

Frank, R & Cartwright, E (2010). *Microeconomics and Behaviour.* 3rd edn. McGraw-Hill.

Friedman, M (1962). *Capitalism and Freedom*. University of Chicago Press

Friedman, M (1976). 'Adam Smith's relevance for 1976'. *Selected Papers No.5*. University of Chicago Press.

Friedman, M (2002). *Capitalism and Freedom: Fortieth Anniversary Edition*. University of Chicago Press.

Garnaut, R (2024). *Let's Tax Carbon: And other ideas for a better Australia*. La Trobe University Press.

Giddens, A (1998). *The Third Way: The renewal of social democracy*. Polity Press.

Giddens, A (2000). *The Third Way and Its Critics*. Polity Press.

Goodhart, D (2017). *The Road to Somewhere: The new tribes shaping British politics*. Penguin Press.

Goodhart, D (2020). *Head, Hand, Heart: The struggle for dignity and status in the 21st century*. Allen Lane.

Gordon, RJ (2017). *The Rise and Fall of American Growth: The U.S. standard of living since the Civil War*. Princeton University Press.

Haidt, J (2025). *The Anxious Generation: How the great rewiring of childhood is causing an epidemic of mental illness*. Penguin Press.

Hanley, RP (2009). *Adam Smith and the Character of Virtue*. Cambridge University Press.

Hanley, RP (2017). 'Practicing PPE: the case of Adam Smith in social philosophy and policy'. *Social Philosophy and Policy*, vol. 24, no. 1, pp277-295.

Hanley, RP (2019). *Our Great Purpose: Adam Smith on living a better life*. Princeton University Press.

Hanushek, EA & Woessmann, L (2007). *Education Quality and Economic Growth*. The World Bank.

Hari, J (2018). *Lost Connections: Why you're depressed and how to find hope*. Bloomsbury.

Haskel, J & Westlake, S (2017). *Capitalism Without Capital: The rise of the intangible economy*. Princeton University Press.

Hayek, FA (1948). *Individualism and Economic Order*, University of Chicago Press.

Healy, J (2003). *Corporate Governance & Wealth Creation in New Zealand*. Dunmore Press.

Healy, J (2019). *Breaking the Banks: What went wrong with Australian banking?* Impact Press.

Healy, J & Hornery, D (2023). *Black Belt: A masterclass for start-ups and entrepreneurs*. Major Street Publishing.

Henderson, JP & Davis, JB (1991). 'Adam Smith's influence on Hegel's philosophical writings'. *Journal of the History of Economic Thought*, vol.13, no. 2, pp184-204.

Herman, A (2002). *The Scottish Enlightenment: The Scots' invention of the modern world*, Fourth Estate.

Hill, L. (2016). 'Adam Smith and political theory', in Hanley, RP (ed.). *Adam Smith: His life, thought, and legacy*. Princeton University Press.

Howe, DW (1989). 'Why the Scottish Enlightenment was useful to the framers of the American Constitution'. *Comparative Studies in Society and History*, vol. 31, no. 3, pp572-587.

Hume, D (1978). *A Treatise of Human Nature*. 2nd edn. Oxford University Press.

Kahneman, D (2012). *Thinking, Fast and Slow*. Penguin Press.

Kay, J (2004), *The Truth About Markets: Why some nations are rich but most remain poor*, Penguin Press.

Kohler, A (2023), 'The great divide: Australia's housing mess and how to fix it', *Quarterly Essay*, issue 92.

Leigh, A (2024). *Battlers & Billionaires: The updated story of inequality in Australia*. Black Inc.

Lembke, A (2021). *Dopamine Nation*. Headline Book Publishing.

Lind, M (2021). The New Class War: Saving democracy from the metropolitan elite. Atlantic PBS.

Likierman, A (2025). *Judgement at Work: Making better choices*. Profile Trade.

Liu, GM (2022). *Adam Smith's America: How a Scottish philosopher became an icon of American capitalism*, Princeton University Press.

Locke, J (1690). 'An essay concerning human understanding'. Nidditch, PH (ed.; 1975). Oxford University Press.

Lukianoff, G & Haidt, J (2019). *The Coddling of the American Mind: How good intentions and bad ideas are setting up a generation for failure*. Penguin Press.

Magnusson, M (2001). *Scotland: The story of a nation*. HarperCollins.

Mandel, E (1971). *The Formation of the Economic Thought of Karl Marx.* Pearce, B (trans.). Monthly Review Press.

Marshall, A (1890). *Principles of Economics.* 8th edn. Macmillan.

Marx, K (1932). *Economic and Philosophic Manuscripts of 1844.* Milligan, M (trans.; 1959). Progress Publishers.

Mason, P (2016). *Postcapitalism: A guide to our future,* Penguin Press.

Mavin, D (2022). *Pyramid of Lies: The prime minister, the banker and the billion pound scandal.* Macmillan.

Mayer, C (2024). *Capitalism and Crises: How to fix them.* Oxford University Press.

Mazzucato, M & Collington, R (2023). *The Big Con: How the consulting industry weakens our businesses, infantilizes our governments, and warps our economies.* Penguin Press.

McCloskey, D (2006). *The Bourgeois Virtues: Ethics for an age of commerce,* University of Chicago Press.

Micklethwait, J & Wooldridge, A (2003). *The Company: A short history of a revolutionary idea.* Modern Library.

Micklethwait, J & Wooldridge, A (2015). *The Fourth Revolution: The global race to reinvent the state.* Penguin Press.

Mitter, R (2004). *A Bitter Revolution: China's struggle with the modern world.* Oxford University Press.

Montes, L (2004), *Adam Smith in Context: A critical reassessment of some central components of his thought.* Palgrave-MacMillan.

Mullins, R, Smith, C & Mochrie, R (eds.; 2023). *Adam Smith: The Kirkcaldy papers.* Adam Smith Global Foundation.

Norman, J (2018). *Adam Smith: Father of economics.* Basic Books.

Norman, J (2018). *Adam Smith: What he thought, and why it matters.* Allen Lane.

O'Brien, J (2024). *How They Broke Britain.* WH Allen.

Orwell, G (1945). *Animal Farm: A fairy story.* Secker & Warburg.

Oslington, P & Hart, DM (2023). 'Adam Smith and why he matters today: essays on the relevance of Smith after 300 years'. *Occasional Paper 199.* The Centre for Independent Studies.

Phan PH & Jensen, MC (2002). 'A theory of the firm: governance, residual claims, and organizational forms'. *Administrative Science Quarterly*, vol. 47, no. 2, p387.

Phillips-Fein, K (2023). 'The betrayal of Adam Smith'. *New Republic.* https://newrepublic.com/article/170242/betrayal-adam-smith.

Phillipson, N (2010). *Adam Smith: An enlightened life*, Yale University Press.

Piketty, T (2013). *Capital in the Twenty-First Century.* Belknap Press.

Piketty, T (2020). *Capital and Ideology.* Belknap Press.

Pilcher, S & Hurley, P (2020). *Skills for recovery: the vocational education system we need post-COVID-19.* Mitchell Institute for Education and Health Policy, Victoria University.

Porter, ME (1990). *The Competitive Advantage of Nations.* Free Press.

Rasmussen, DC (2017). *The Infidel and the Professor: David Hume, Adam Smith, and the friendship that shaped modern thought.* Princeton University Press.

Rawls, J (1971). *A Theory of Justice*. Harvard University Press.

Reinhart, CM & Rogoff, KS (2011). *This Time Is Different: Eight centuries of financial folly*. Princeton University Press.

Roberts, R (2015). *How Adam Smith Can Change Your Life: An unexpected guide to human nature and happiness*. Penguin General UK.

Robson, D (2020). *The Intelligence Trap: Why smart people make dumb mistakes*. W.W. Norton & Company.

Rothschild, E (2001). *Economic Sentiments: Adam Smith, Condorcet, and the Enlightenment*. Harvard University Press.

Ross, IS (2010). *The Life of Adam Smith*. 2nd edn. Oxford University Press.

Sagar, P (2018). *The Opinion of Mankind: Sociability and the theory of the state from Hobbes to Smith*. Princeton University Press.

Sagar, P (2022). *Adam Smith Reconsidered: History, liberty and the foundation of modern politics*. Princeton University Press.

Samuelson, PA (1976). *Economics*. McGraw-Hill.

Sanders, B (2023). *It's OK to Be Angry About Capitalism*. Allen Lane.

Sapolsky, R (2023). *Determined: A science of life without free will*. Penguin Press.

Schwarzman, SA (2019). *What It Takes: Lessons in the pursuit of excellence*. Simon & Schuster.

Sharma, R (2024). *What Went Wrong with Capitalism*. Simon & Schuster.

Skidelsky, R (1992). *John Maynard Keynes, Volume 1: Hopes Betrayed, 1883-1920*. Picador.

Smith, A (1759). *The Theory of Moral Sentiments.* Raphael, DD & Macfie, AL (eds.; 1976). Oxford University Press

Smith, A (2000; originally published 1776). *The Wealth of Nations.* Random House.

Stewart, R (2024). *Politics on the Edge.* Vintage.

Stiglitz, JE (2024). *The Road to Freedom: Economics and the good society.* W.W. Norton & Company.

Tanzi, V (2011). *Government Versus Markets: The changing economic role of the state,* Cambridge University Press.

Tavris, C & Aronson, E (2007). *Mistakes Were Made (But Not by Me):Why we justify foolish beliefs, bad decisions, and hurtful acts.* Houghton Mifflin.

Tepper, J & Hearn, D (2018). *The Myth of Capitalism: Monopolies and the death of competition.* Wiley.

Tomasi, J (2012). *Free Market Fairness.* Princeton University Press.

Vance, JD (2016). *Hillbilly Elegy: A memoir of a family and culture in crisis.* HarperCollins.

Varoufakis, Y (2016). *And the Weak Suffer What They Must? Europe, austerity and the threat to global stability.* Vintage.

Ware, B (2012). *The Top Five Regrets of the Dying: A life transformed by the dearly departing.* Hay House.

Warner, M (2021). *The Boys Club: Power, politics and the AFL.* Hachette Australia.

West, EG (1990). *Adam Smith and Modern Economics.* Edward Elgar Publishing.

Whyte, J (2019), *The Morals of the Market: Human rights and the rise of neoliberalism.* Verso Trade.

Wills, G (1978). *Inventing America: Jefferson's Declaration of Independence.* Doubleday.

Wolf, M (2024). *The Crisis of Democratic Capitalism.* Penguin Press.

Yueh, L (2019). *The Great Economists: How their ideas can help us today.* Penguin General UK.

Index

www.ingramcontent.com/pod-product-compliance
Lightning Source LLC
LaVergne TN
LVHW040514210926
848480LV00005BA/1456